STUDIES IN EXISTENTIALISM
AND PHENOMENOLOGY
Editor: R. D. Laing

The Leaves of Spring

The Leaves of Spring

A Study in the Dialectics of Madness

Aaron Esterson

TAVISTOCK PUBLICATIONS

First published in 1970
by Tavistock Publications Limited
11 New Fetter Lane, London, EC4
This book is set in 12 pt Bembo
and was printed in Great Britain
by T. & A. Constable Ltd., Edinburgh

© *Aaron Esterson 1970*

SBN 422 73210 9

To Naomi and Julian

Contents

Acknowledgements

The study presented in this book was originally intended by me for inclusion in the second volume of an earlier work, *Sanity, Madness, and the Family*, by Dr R. D. Laing and myself. But as my research proceeded it seemed more appropriate that it should be embodied in a work by myself alone.

The reader is strongly urged to pay close attention to the definitions of various of the terms I have used. Many of these will be familiar, being currently employed by others, including Dr R. D. Laing, but not necessarily in the sense in which I am using them.

I have reason to be deeply grateful to a number of people for their constructive criticisms of the manuscript. They are Dr D. G. Cooper, Dr John Heaton, Professor Sidney Jourard, Dr R. D. Laing, Mr H. Phillipson, and Dr J. D. Sutherland. I particularly wish to thank Dr Paul Senft for his detailed comments and for my discussions with him.

I deeply appreciate too those many exchanges over the years among Dr Cooper, Dr Laing, Dr Senft, and myself, exchanges out of which, in a sense, this book has come.

I gratefully acknowledge also the research facilities extended to me by the Tavistock Institute of Human Relations, and for their help with the secretarial work.

Introduction

Point of Departure

This is a report on a family and a possible method of studying families. Family and method have been described to some extent in an earlier work.[1] There, the first eleven of a series of families of diagnosed schizophrenics were presented in some detail. The group described here, the Danzigs,[2] is one of the eleven.

In that report a social phenomenological method of study was outlined. The method, a synthesis embodying the Sullivan tradition of participant observation of interpersonal relations and the phenomenological tradition in philosophy – particularly the philosophy of Sartre – allowed the clinical method of approaching 'schizophrenics' to be *depassed*,[3] i.e. dissolved and preserved in a wider synthesis. The theory and practice of communications analysis acted as catalyst so to speak. This work is intended as a contribution to dissolving, reconciling, and depassing in a new synthesis the social phenomenology of the earlier work and the psychoanalytic way of studying experience.

The method described is derived from the philosophic tradition of dialectical investigation, particularly as it is embodied in the work of Hegel, Marx, and Sartre, though it is not a direct application of any of these. It takes as its starting-point the experience, expressed in the British philosophical tradition by Macmurray[4] for instance, that the primary philosophizing position is the person acting in relation to others, not the solitary, detached thinker

[1] Laing, R. D. and Esterson, A., *Sanity, Madness, and the Family.*
[2] See p. xiii for the earlier study of this family.
[3] The term is derived from Sartre, J.-P., *Critique de la Raison Dialectique.* And see Laing, R. D. and Cooper, D., *Reason and Violence.*
[4] Macmurray, J., *The Form of the Personal.*

implied by Descartes's *'cogito ergo sum'*. And it sees the primary sciences to be those of persons and groups of persons.

More specifically, it attempts to apply a principle of reasoning adequate to the complexities of the interaction and interexperience of persons. This means, among other things, considering the nature of the *shared* experience of the group, and leads at times to inferences about the nature and content of this experience similar in certain respects to the interpretations that might be made about the unconscious phantasy relations of the members, using current psychoanalytic theory. Be this as it may, the method is offered as a possible way of examining data and systematically inferring and clarifying the group members' reciprocal experience of one another and of the group as a whole, and testing the inferences made.

The earlier work was concerned to show how the experience and actions of persons whom our society calls 'schizophrenic', make much more social sense than is commonly supposed when they are viewed in the contexts of their families in a certain way. In each family the labelled person was seen to be caught in an interactional web of misunderstanding, characterized by ambiguities and contradictions of a highly mystifying kind. An important aspect of this pattern of contradiction was an unrecognized confusion between praxis and process[1] in the family's experience of the behaviour and experience of the diagnosed person. They saw his acts as if they were the result of process, and not the expression of his intentions. The confusion was most marked when the person tried to act autonomously.

These findings in respect of the diagnosis of schizophrenia now

[1] I am using the terms praxis and process after Sartre. *Praxis* refers to events that are the deeds of doers or groups of doers, or to the intended outcome of such deeds. It refers to the acts of an agent. *Process* refers to events or a pattern of events of which no doer or agent is the author. Thus, praxis expresses the intentions of a person or group of persons, while process does not. Process in a system may be initiated by praxis, e.g. a blow to the head; but the pattern of events that follows the blow, the pattern of trauma or physiological change within the organism, is determined mechanistically. This pattern of change is one of process.

The ordinary medical concept of illness is a concept of process. It refers to events occurring within the person, and affecting his organism according to the laws of natural science.

raise the question of the family praxis itself. And in this study, the focus of inquiry will be switched from the 'schizophrenic' to the family as such, from the question of the social intelligibility of the behaviour and experience of the labelled person and the problem of testing this, to the question of the intelligibility and comprehensibility of the family's mystifying pattern of interaction. Specifically, I wish to see what sense, if any, can be made of the contradictions and ambiguities of the Danzig family praxis, particularly those leading to their daughter Sarah becoming diagnosed as suffering from something 'gone wrong' inside her called an illness of the mind.

At this point I shall remind the reader of the details of that praxis by presenting the earlier study, reprinted from *Sanity, Madness, and the Family*. This was based on a certain way of observing and totalizing family interaction, and recording and organizing the data.

Briefly, family members were seen in hospital, consulting-room, and at home. They were observed singly, in pairs, and in various combinations. The sessions were tape-recorded or written up immediately afterwards. All tape-recordings were transcribed. Based on the observer's totalization of the family interaction, a concordance-index was compiled in which the raw data was organized in a way that related the different viewpoints to one another and to the pattern of interaction. The index revealed that the diagnosis of schizophrenia was socially intelligible. Using the index and its findings, the following description of the family was written.

The Early Study: Family Interaction[1]

CLINICAL PERSPECTIVE

From the clinical psychiatric viewpoint, Sarah Danzig began to develop an illness of insidious onset at the age of seventeen. She

---

[1] Adapted from pp. 95-117 of Laing, R. D. and Esterson, A., *Sanity, Madness, and the Family*, by permission of the publishers.

began to lie in bed all day, getting up only at night, and staying up thinking or brooding or reading the Bible. Gradually she lost interest in everyday affairs and became increasingly pre-occupied with religious issues. Her attendance at commercial college became intermittent, and she failed to complete her studies. During the next four years Sarah failed to make the grade at whatever job or course of study she undertook.

When she was twenty-one her illness took a sudden turn for the worse. She began to express bizarre ideas, for instance that she heard voices over the telephone and saw people on television talking about her. Soon afterwards she started to rage against members of her family. After one outburst against her mother she fled the house and stayed out all night. On her return she was taken to an observation ward where she remained for two weeks. Thereafter, she was listless, apathetic, quiet, withdrawn, and lacking in concentration. Although from time to time she made bizarre statements, for example that she had been raped, on the whole she was able to live quietly at home, and even return to work, this time in her father's office. She continued like this for fifteen months, and then relapsed. Once more she persistently expressed bizarre ideas. She complained that people at the office were talking about her, were in a plot against her, and did not wish her to work with them. She insisted they intercepted and tore up her letters. She also insisted that her letters were being intercepted at home. She complained to her father that his staff were incompetent, and quarrelled with him and his secretary over keeping the books. Eventually she refused to go to work, and took to lying in her bed all day, getting up only at night to brood or to sit reading the Bible. She spoke hardly at all except to make occasional statements about religion or to accuse her family of discussing her, or to complain that the telephone operators were listening in to her calls. She became irritable and aggressive, particularly towards her father, and it was following an outburst against him that she was again brought into hospital.

STRUCTURE OF INVESTIGATION

The family consisted of mother (aged fifty), father (fifty-six), Sarah (twenty-three), John (twenty-one), and Ruth (fifteen). At her parents' request, Ruth was not included in the investigation.

Interviews	Occasions
Daughter	13
Father	1
Mother	1
Mother and father	4
Mother and daughter	1
Father and daughter	1
Son	3
Son and daughter	3
Mother, father, and daughter	8
Mother, father, daughter, and son	4
	39

This represents 32 hours of interviewing time, of which 18 hours were tape-recorded.

THE FAMILY SITUATION

In this case the necessity for a variety of 'sightings' of the family in action is revealed particularly clearly.

We shall first describe certain aspects of the family interviews, with particular reference to what makes intelligible various delusions and psychotic manifestations relating to Sarah's behaviour in hospital. She said that:

1. The Ward Sister was withholding letters from her and failing to pass on telephone messages from her mother. She knew the letters from her mother were being withheld because her mother was writing to her every other day. She knew that her mother was writing to her every other day because she was her mother's child, and her mother loved her.

2. The hospital was maliciously detaining her, while her parents wanted her home at once.

3. She was afraid of being abandoned in hospital and never getting home again. She did not say who would abandon her, but the heart of her fear was that she would be cut off from her mother.

4. She said that her mother had only agreed to her coming into hospital because she had not wanted her to leave home. Her mother did not want to lose her children. She said that she did not blame her mother, and emphasized that she and her mother loved each other.

5. She was angry with her father and was afraid of him. She saw him as the prime agent in her detention in hospital. She said that he was a liar, and would tell lies about her.

Throughout these interviews Sarah, for the most part, passively complied with her parents and her brother.

In the first family session the issue of her fear of being abandoned was raised. Her parents and brother reassured her that they had telephoned every day, and had left messages for her. This was not in fact so. They told her that she was ill, that they only wanted her to stay in hospital for her own good, not because they wanted to abandon her. They loved her and wanted her back home. Sarah made no attempt to argue.

John was soon to remark that she was unusually amiable and acquiescent, whereas 'normally she was highly resistant to suggestion'. The significance of this remark emerged more fully when he warned us in private against being fooled by her. She was just pretending to agree with them. It was an act to get out of hospital. With her, however, he was sympathetic and loving, giving *her* no hint that he thought she was trying to fool him.

It seemed therefore that a mistrustful perception of the hospital was necessary for her if she was to maintain her trust in her family, since greater perceptual and cognitive dissonance would have been experienced by Sarah had she distrusted her family rather than the hospital.

When her family was asked in what way they felt she was ill, they replied that she was lazy, stubborn, sluttish, terribly impudent to her father, obscene, and so on. They seemed to be describing wickedness, not sickness. At least this is how Sarah felt it. She remarked timidly that she had changed her mind about going home.

One of the main features of her illness in the view of her parents was an unreasoned, senseless, persistent hostility to her father, but when seen alone her mother, without any apparent awareness of being inconsistent, also described Sarah's hostility as a meaningful response to various things her father did. Indeed, she said he acted in the same way towards her (mother) and John, making them angry too. In fact it emerged that they were constantly quarrelling. It thus became clear that Sarah's anger against her father, which her family now could not tolerate, was hardly more intense than the enmity her mother and John had directed against him for years. But they objected to Sarah acting similarly. Sarah was finally singled out by her mother, father, and brother as the one person who was *really* expected to comply with her father's wishes. This was not put to her in so many words, but each of the others privately realized that she was put in a special position, although without their being fully aware of its consequences for her. They argued that if Sarah could not get on with her father she must be ill.

But it was not her father who was the promoter of the idea that Sarah 'had to go'. Although he and Sarah fought and screamed at each other more than her mother and John could tolerate, they also got on together in a much more affectionate and intimate way than her mother or John liked to admit.

When interviewed alone, her mother said plainly that if Sarah did not give up her hostility to her father she would remain permanently in hospital. When she was with Sarah, however, she conveyed to her, again without any sense of inconsistency, that it was not she, but her husband and John, who wanted her put away. She told Sarah plainly that John was fed up with her, that he could not stand her at home, and that he was not going to be bothered with her. This was true, but it contrasted with John's frequent reassurances to Sarah to the contrary. John admitted that Sarah was only saying to his father what he had said to her about him. But, like his mother, he thought that Sarah must be ill if she said such things, since it was not her place.

When he was alone with the interviewer, Mr Danzig said that his wife had wanted to get rid of Sarah for some time, had wanted to 'sacrifice' her, but he had refused to agree. He regarded himself as Sarah's ally, but the support he accorded her was more imaginary than real, since he did not support her either when his wife and son were attacking her, or when he was alone with her.

He did, however, remonstrate with them in Sarah's absence, even to threatening to leave home himself if they did not leave her alone.[1] It is ironical that Mrs Danzig insisted that it was for her husband's sake that Sarah had to be 'treated' in hospital for her 'illness'.

Thus, Sarah's construction that her father and the hospital, not her mother and John, wished to keep her locked up was as reasonable as it was unreasonable – in fact, with the evidence available to her, it was possibly the most likely construction.

Sarah was continually mystified in this respect. For instance, when the interviewer introduced the issue of whether Sarah got on everyone's nerves, and not only her father's, Mrs Danzig took this up the wrong way and told Sarah how 'ungrateful' she was for upsetting her father. Sarah tried feebly to defend herself, and then pleaded that she was tired. Her mother sympathized, and then went on to describe Sarah in her usual terms as selfish, ungrateful, inconsiderate, and so on. It was always difficult to get past such attributions to specific items of behaviour. When Sarah listlessly fell in with her, her mother took it as evidence that she was right. She then advised Sarah to follow our advice and to stay in hospital, in the interests of her health. We had not given any such advice.

Another mystifying feature of this family is the marked

[1] His motives for leaving home were more mixed than this and he had never been clear about them (see p. xxvii).

conspiratorial tone and manner they adopt with each other and with us in Sarah's absence. They have then a solidarity otherwise lacking. It is impressive how their conflicts are then forgotten.

On one occasion, when Sarah left the room, her mother, father, and brother began a furtive whispered exchange about her. As Sarah re-entered she said uncertainly that she had the impression that they were talking about her. They denied this and looked at us significantly, as though to say: 'See how suspicious she is.'

After these glimpses of this family in action in the present and recent past, we shall now try to reconstruct some crucial historical facts.

Sarah left school at sixteen to go to secretarial college for fifteen months, then to art school for two years. Recently she had been working in her father's office. She had had a previous 'breakdown' eighteen months earlier.

According to her mother and father, until the age of twelve she had been a most lovable child. She had always tended to lack self-confidence, however, and to be concerned about how she appeared to others, continually relying on her parents and her brother to tell her how people saw her. Nevertheless, according to them, she had been very popular, and had had a number of friends. She had had a sharp wit, a good sense of humour, and she was artistic. She liked paintings, good music, good books, and had an exceptional talent for writing and drawing, showing promise in these respects at school. She had insight into other people's characters and did not like cheap talk. They did not, however, wish her to be an artist.

After fifteen months at secretarial college, she stopped attending. She lay in bed until late in the morning, and stayed awake all night thinking or reading. She began to lose her friends one by one. At this time she began to read the Bible and tried to interpret for herself what she read.

Father, mother, John, and Sarah all agree on the following features of Sarah's behaviour *before* admission to hospital.

1. She had been saying for some months that telephone opera-tors (or someone) had been listening in to her calls.
2. She believed that people in her father's office had been talking about her and did not want her to work there.
3. She believed that someone at the office intercepted and des-troyed her letters, and that some of the staff were incompetent.
4. She believed that her parents and brother were talking about her.
5. She believed that they were keeping letters from her.
6. She was irritable and aggressive towards members of her family, especially her father, towards whom she did not have the right attitude for a daughter. In particular she called him a liar, and said she no longer believed in him or trusted him.
7. She was very shy and self-conscious.
8. She did not mix with other people, but was quiet, withdrawn, miserable, and discontented.
9. She lay in bed all day and sat up into the small hours of the morning.
10. She lacked concentration and had been thinking too much.
11. She had been reading the Bible a great deal.

Twelve months earlier Sarah had gone to work in her father's office. She soon began to feel that she was being discussed dis-paragingly. In her turn she complained to her father that certain employees were incompetent. Finally, she refused to go any more. About this time (it is not clear when it began), she discovered that her salary had been over-stated in the books and told her father. He tried to explain it to her, but she failed to understand either his explanation or that of his son and secretary. 'She wore us all out' (Mother). She insisted that the clerk responsible was incompetent, and when they did not agree accused them of being against her, and began to act provocatively at home, e.g. by smoking in front of her father on the Sabbath, putting lemonade into his tea, and so on. These acts were regarded with a mixture of anger, guilt, shame, and concern by her parents and brother, who eventually resolved their dilemma by treating them as signs of illness.

Her parents regarded Sarah's 'madness' as a calamity visited on the family.

MOTHER: Well I did sort of think all this business of going, you know, thinking unusual things, saying people are not – to me these sort of things – they always happen to other people, they never happen to us. You know the sort of thing, you think it always happens to other people – you know these people flooded out in Exeter, you know, I feel sorry, but you do sort of think 'Oh I'll never be flooded out where I'm living now' – you see? I'm only giving you an example. It's never occurred to me that I'll ever get flooded out where I live now – that's how I look at it.

And:

FATHER: We didn't realize what was happening.
MOTHER: We didn't, as I told you, we thought those things only happened to other people's children. You read in the paper a little girl is murdered, or kidnapped. You feel very sorry for the people, but you don't associate it with your own child. As I say, when – everything terrible happens to other people.
FATHER: When it happens to you –
MOTHER: And then it happens with you unfortunately, then other people say 'Oh, how terrible'.
FATHER: Then it becomes a tragedy.
MOTHER: It *never* occurred to me that she'd ever sort of go sort of mentally like this, to turn out in this sort of way.

What was the calamity comparable to these floods, murder, and kidnap, that had befallen this family? The more we probed, the more elusive it became, but what was obvious was her parents' shame and fear of scandal. In particular, they were worried about Sarah's social *naïveté* and lack of discretion. They regarded her as a 'breaker of the family front'. When she first went to work in

her father's office he had urged her to keep quiet about her breakdown. Unfortunately it leaked out, and his staff began to gossip
behind her back, although to her face they were kind and for-
bearing. She was also resented for being the boss's daughter.
Sarah felt their hostility without being able to get her feeling
confirmed by anyone.

She also discovered certain actual mistakes that had been made
and told her father. She was resented more than ever now, but
she could not be attacked directly. Instead, she was exposed to
more innuendos that no one would confirm explicitly. She became more and more isolated and unhappy. At this time some of
her correspondence was mislaid 'accidentally' by another employee. She perceived the 'unconscious' motive of the other, and
tried to challenge her. The other girl insinuated something about
her sanity, and in an agitated state she went to her father to
complain. Her father, anxious to avoid any open recognition
among his employees that his daughter had been a mental case,
pooh-poohed her complaints, casting doubt on the validity of her
suspicions – 'You are unwell. No one dislikes you. No one is
talking about you. It's imagination', and so on. Without confirmation from her father she became more agitated, and started
calling him a liar, accusing him of being in collusion with the
others. She refused to return to the office.

In addition, while working with him, she had discovered that
her father, while generally a meticulously honest man, engaged
in certain petty dishonesties. We, of course, have no difficulty in
reconciling this paradox, since it is quite characteristic of the
compulsive-obsessive person, but Sarah could not understand this
and became very confused, especially as her father now had to
defend himself desperately, not against his own dissociated impulses, but against her. This involved him, unwittingly, in order
to preserve her trust in him, in destroying her trust in herself,
and as far as he could he enlisted his secretary, wife, and son to
this end.

They said in effect: 'You are imagining that there is a flaw in
your father', *and* 'You are mad or bad if you imagine such a

thing', *and* 'You are mad or bad if you do not believe us when we tell you that you are mad or bad to trust your own perceptions and memory'.

Much of what they called her illness consisted in attempts to discuss forbidden issues, comments on their attempts to keep her in the dark, or to muddle her, and angry responses to such mystifications and mystification over mystifications. She had been put in the position of having to try to sort out secrecy and muddle, in the face of being muddled up over the validity of trying to do so. With some justification, therefore, Sarah began to feel that they were in collusion against her.

We have to explain why this girl is so naïve in the first place. It may be argued that with such a naïve girl the family would want to keep her in ignorance of their secrets, that their mystification of her was a consequence of her *naïveté*. This was partly so. But our evidence shows that her *naïveté* had itself been preceded by a prior mystification. The family was thus caught in a vicious spiral. The more they mystified her the more she remained naïve, and the more she remained naïve the more they felt they had to protect themselves by mystifying her.

Mr Danzig lived a scrupulously correct family life, and needed to be seen as a man of stern and perfect rectitude, and as the head of the family. His wife complied with him in this, but at the same time encouraged John to 'see through' him, but not in public. John helped to maintain his father's public image, but his cooperation at home was intermittent, and he was often supported in these lapses by his mother. Mr Danzig knew of the mother-son alliance, and mother and son knew he knew, and he knew they knew he knew. There was thus complete understanding among the three of them in this respect.

With Sarah, however, it was different. Mother and son often criticized Mr Danzig in front of her, but she was not supposed to do so. They thus presented her with a very difficult task. Mr Danzig's view of his marriage (and, incidentally, something of his style of thinking in general) can be seen in the following passages.

'It may well be that my wife in her moments of forgetfulness speaks to me sharply in the presence of the children. In other words she doesn't show for me the respect that a wife should in the presence of children. And I've told her more than often, "If you've anything to say to me, say it not in front of the children".'

'We differ a lot on that [keeping the house clean – e.g. the children's bedrooms]. One of the excuses is "I haven't got the time, patience", or – "Have no help". All right, I try to alleviate her worries. I chime in sometimes. I help her. Then she comes back – I have no right to interfere. I get erratic. I say, "No, I like – I'm only interfering when I see something which I don't like." '

'I want a certain clean way and it can arise from an attitude – perhaps she may think – indifference on my wife's part. She feels – or – she can't go out very well. I can accept this. She feels she doesn't go out very well. I object to her – I want her to dress very nicely, very neatly and cleanly and smartly. I want to go out watching her. She doesn't care. She's indifferent to this. I don't like that. I say, "Whatever position arises between me and you privately or otherwise, publicly, come out clean. Go out occasionally. It's not nice for the children. It gives an example to the children if you go out occasionally." It may well be perhaps, shall I say – I may even go a bit further than this. It may well be, and I've often thought about it, it may well be that *I* may not have been her ideal in marriage – and I'm going to admit to you that *she* may not be *my* ideal in marriage . . .

'. . . She was an only child. She was quite an intelligent person, well-read, musical, I thought, "We might blend. Possible, possible. I may be a possible to her." You get near enough the possibilities, near the next best. Maybe she felt the same thing. I did have ideals in my mind but – my wife wasn't bad-looking. And so I came to the point. We met and it seemed possible. We didn't dislike one another, not to say – I'm not going to say I was ravingly in love with my wife, and I don't think my wife was with me, but maybe I wasn't experienced enough to understand certain things. Oh I wasn't a bargain – I wasn't a bargain – I was a young man. I hadn't the remotest idea of running around with other people – with other women – picking them up at dance-halls or a ball, when I was single, and I thought, "Well this is a nice set-up – I might be able to work this round" – So we both felt the same thing. We were both of the same mind.'

It was not surprising that Sarah maintained an idealized picture of her father, dissociated from her dissonant perceptions, until she was over twenty-one. She had had squabbles with her father before, about unannounced intrusions into her bedroom when she was undressed, unsolicited insistence on tidying up her bedroom, listening in on her telephone calls, intercepting her letters, and so on, but in none of these was she sure that her father was in the wrong. All such behaviour was either denied by him (e.g. telephone calls), or rationalized as out of love for her. If she found this love annoying, she felt that she was at fault.

As her idealization of her father broke down, she clung all the more desperately to her idealization of her mother, which her mother helped her to maintain. Her mother's behaviour over the issue of Sarah's lying late in bed illustrates this. Both her parents continually reproached her for not getting up early. They shouted at her to mend her ways, saying that now she was grown-up, and should not behave like a baby. Their actions, however, were markedly at variance with this, for her father insisted, for instance, on his right to enter her bedroom whenever he wanted, which her mother did not oppose, and the latter, while complaining bitterly of the inconvenience, continued to cook Sarah's meals whenever she chose to get up. When we asked why she did not lay down fixed times for her daughter's meals, and refuse to let her routine be disorganized, she replied that if she did that she would feel guilty and a bad mother. Sarah's father replied indignantly that if that happened he would carry food up to his daughter himself, and Sarah felt that her mother would be mean if she did not give her meals whenever she felt like eating.

The more her parents did things for her, the more they wanted her gratitude and the more ungrateful she became. Searching for gratitude, they did even more for her. Thus, while expecting her to grow up they treated her as a child, and she, while wanting to be considered as an adult, behaved more and more as a baby. Her parents then reproached her for being spoilt by them, and she reproached them for not treating her as an adult.

When Sarah said she was afraid of her father her parents not only could not understand this, they refused to believe it. After all he had never abused her or shouted at her or hit her. Apart from insisting that she obey certain religious rules such as not smoking on the Sabbath, he had made no demands on her. In their opinion the trouble was that he had not been firm enough and had over-indulged her. Nor could Sarah gain any support from John. His position was very equivocal. He was, as noted above, privately supported by his mother against his father, and he obtained her open support when he defied him to his face. He was also encouraged by both parents to see Sarah as the favoured and indulged child. For a short time in his teens he had supported his sister, but had broken with her. He then engaged in an alliance with his mother. We have evidence that she was jealous of the closeness between him and his sister. To what extent was she responsible for stimulating John's jealousy of his father's 'indulgence' of Sarah as an aid to bringing him to her side? To what extent did she stimulate his defiance of his father, and win him by supporting him in it? What is the evidence that Sarah was indulged more than him?

According to them all, Mr Danzig was 'firmer' with John than with Sarah and Ruth, because John was a boy. But John reproached his father for not being firm enough with him. He said that his father should have hit him to make him work better at school. He was not afraid of his father as a child, and he thought he should have been. All children should be afraid of their fathers. He thought his father had bad children, although there had been worse boys than himself. He tried to comply, but did not always succeed. He did not think his father's demands were unreasonable, but . . .

Mr Danzig felt he had over-indulged his son. He should have 'bullied' him more. He had spoilt both John and Sarah.

'I was patient with him and very happy to say that although I spoilt him – I spoilt Sarah, I spoilt John. . . .'

We may say that John *believes* Sarah was indulged more than himself. His reasons for so believing, as they emerge, are obscure.

This family therefore functioned largely through a series of alliances – mother and father, mother and son, mother, father and son. Sarah was left out. She received, she said, no 'backing' from anyone in the family, and this seems to have been the case. These alliances offered protection against impossible ideals. Sarah, with no ally, was expected to conform with no let-up to the rules that the others all managed to break. For instance, John was not supposed to have a sexual life, but he had one, with his mother's collusion. Mrs Danzig broke Sabbath rules, with John's conniv- ance, unbeknown to her husband, and so on. Mr Danzig was secretly sexually dissatisfied and had often thought of leaving his wife in recent years. Even though regarded as ill, indulged, and spoilt, Sarah alone was expected to govern her thoughts and actions according to Mr Danzig's obsessive-compulsive inter- pretation of a rigorous orthodoxy. Her social *naïveté* has thus to be set within the context of her parents' demand for *total* com- pliance from her alone.

Nor could she compare her parents' praxis with that of other people, since her contacts with the extra-familial world were effectively cut off. Although her parents were concerned because she had no friends, they were even more worried in case she was seduced if she did mix socially.

FATHER: Well one of the reasons why I personally was interested in her social life is not because I was prying into her private affairs; I was mainly interested in watching that she shouldn't be impressed by funny stories, by all sorts of – all and sundry – I realized she was a very sensitive young lady, very highly impressionable, and that she should not be impressed, to get wrong impressions. Because there are so many young men around with glib tongues and fancy themselves and able to get hold of a girl like Sarah and tell her all sorts of funny stories, and can lead to a lot of complications – that was the main reason why I was interested in her social standing and social life. But I wasn't interested to pry into her private affairs.

They did not forbid her to go out with boys, in fact they told her she should, but they watched her every move so closely that she felt she had no privacy at all, and when she objected, if they did not deny what they were doing, they reproached her for being ungrateful for their concern. She thus became muddled over whether or not it was right to want to go out with boys, or even to have any private life in the first place. Her father tried to investigate her boy-friends without her knowledge in various ways. As John explained:

JOHN: But I don't want you to get the impression that Dad hangs over like an eagle and tries to control Sarah's social life. Before she was ill he was always very careful about his intrusions into her private life, because he knew that if he did make an obviously nosey approach she would *flare* up, so therefore we tried to – very very carefully about her social life – the questions, if there were any, were always put by Mum, put in a sleeky way, sometimes or [protest from Father about the word 'sneaky'] – I didn't say 'sneaky' I said 'sleeky' – a silky sort of way [Mother tries to calm Father, explaining John's statement to him]. By sheer – by continuous nagging on Mummy's part – 'give a name' – whether it was the right name or not, she gave a name – that satisfied her.

And while denying that he minded her going out to places where she would meet boys:

FATHER: But I understand, I fully understand a young lady and a young man enjoying themselves – they enjoy flirting or necking what they call it, and young men, I understand that – I'm human – I was once young myself – I'm still young but –

her father implicitly forbade her to enter these places by uttering vague, ominous warnings about their dangers.

FATHER: I didn't say coffee bars generally – there can be certain coffee bars which are very dangerous to visit as well. I'm not particularizing *any* coffee bar, *any* restaurant, *any* dance-hall, or *any* place of amusement – I'm making a general statement how much I am concerned about *both* of you.

Although John could to a large extent see what was going on he failed to back Sarah in this matter as in others. As we have seen, *he* defied his father's prohibitions and demands with his mother's help, but when similar demands were made of Sarah he sided with his father against her.

JOHN: From my point of view when it comes to *Sarah* it's not intrusion – when it comes to me it *is* intrusion.

In the face of this alliance Sarah gave up attempting to meet anyone outside her family.

Sarah at one point had become virtually catatonic, i.e. she would not speak or respond to their approaches, or only compliantly. While she was in hospital this quietness and compliance were very noticeable. As we have noted, her family took this as a trick to deceive the doctor and get him to agree to her leaving. Her dilemma at this point appeared to be that if she talked about what she thought she would have to remain in hospital, and if she remained silent her family would see this as deception, and would demand of the doctor that she be detained and 'treated' until she had the 'right' ideas. If she tried to impose the 'right' ideas on herself, then in a sense she would be killing herself. But even this would not save her from mental hospital, and from being cut off from her family, because then she would be 'dead', 'a shadow of herself', 'personalityless', to use her brother's description, and so would still need 'treatment'.

Sarah, they said, was obsessed with religion. For the past few years she had been continually reading the Bible, quoting from it, and trying to understand it. They did not believe she understood anything about it, however. According to them, it did not really mean much to her. She merely repeated it parrot-fashion. They suggested her interest in it was possibly due to guilt. It was 'a form of atonement by forced hardship', according to John.

There was deep confusion in this family about the nature of religion.

Mrs Danzig's parents came from Eastern Europe. They were Orthodox Jews, her father because he believed in Orthodoxy, her mother because she wanted to please him. Mrs Danzig was an only child. She respected her father, and never did anything in front of him that she thought would upset him. Her parents had been strict with her, but not as strict as her husband's parents had been with him. Her father had been a diplomatic man and knew when to turn a blind eye towards minor infringements of Orthodox regulations.

For example, on the Sabbath it was forbidden to carry money, but in the summer, on the Sabbath, she used to go to town. Her father, as she left the house tactfully refrained from asking where she was going, or how she was going to get there without carrying money for fares and meals and so forth. She in her turn acted tactfully towards him, and at home she abided strictly by the ritual regulations. Her father never left the house on the Sabbath except to go to synagogue, while her mother stayed home.

According to Mrs Danzig, her husband was very Orthodox. His father had been a Hebrew scholar. She did not object to his Orthodoxy. She knew about it when she married, and was happy to keep a kosher house 'because that's the way it should be'. It was the way her mother had done it.

'I do agree to a certain extent that if you're Jewish you keep to the Jewish religion. You *go* to synagogue on Saturday. There's no harm in going to the synagogue on Saturday, that's all right. I mean you can't turn away from the fact that you're what you are.'

It is true that she disagreed with many of the Orthodox regulations, because they were inconvenient, but she complied with them to please her husband, as her mother had complied to please her father. For example, she now never went out on the Sabbath, and she never struck a light in front of her husband. Although, unlike her mother, she would do certain things such as striking a light if her husband was not present to see it, she would not upset him by doing it in front of him. It was her duty as a wife to comply in these matters, and show respect for her husband. If he wanted her to appear as an Orthodox Jewess, then she was prepared to appear in this way to him. And besides, it was not worth having a row about. There were, however, certain areas that had nothing to do with a man: for example, the kitchen, where she tolerated no interference.

Mr and Mrs Danzig, although regarding themselves as strictly religious, were, in their opinion, also fairly 'modern', for instance in the matter of sex. Particularly was this so with Mrs Danzig. She liked her daughter to go out with boys. It was the right thing to do. She did not even object to her daughter going out with a boy on the Sabbath, though Sarah herself regularly remained at home on that day, trying to comply with her father and with ritual law.

'If she wants to go out with a fellow on a Saturday, I don't think it's such a terrible thing. She's not doing anything immoral. She's not doing anything very bad by going out with a girl or a fellow asks her to go out on a Saturday.'

In fact, Mrs Danzig used to urge Sarah to go out and meet boys. It was good for her. It would help her to get over her self-consciousness.

'I often used to tell her, I said, "I think you ought to go out and meet boys and meet girls. You should go out more and get dates and get to know people and go somewhere else. You meet them if you already know somebody. If you've seen them before you can approach them. You feel you've seen them once before, you know them and it doesn't make you so shy." '

Of course the relationship must be of the right kind. In other words, it was not only all right to go out with the opposite sex, it was a social obligation for all normal girls; but naturally nothing sexual must enter into the relationship.

'Well, I would have liked her to go out with boys. I think it's very normal for young girls to go out with the opposite sex, and I think it's the right thing that she should go out with the opposite sex, in the right way of course, to go out socially, yes.'

Her parents, however, secretly investigated the boys she went out with, and regarded it as their right to listen in on her telephone calls – without, of course, admitting to her that they did so.

Sarah had got into the habit of reading at night and sleeping in the morning. This was repeatedly referred to as 'laziness' by all members of the family. In fact, she slept rather less than they did, and they were trying to get her to take sleeping tablets to sleep more, and tranquillizers to 'think' less. For it was not only the fact that Sarah lay in bed that upset them, it was also the fact that she was thinking so much. As Mrs Danzig said:

'Sitting up all night thinking and not telling anyone what she thought. Not that we particularly want to know what Sarah's thinking or doing, although it's only natural that a mother should be curious.'

Sarah's 'thinking' worried them all a great deal. Mrs Danzig knew that 'thinking', especially a lot of 'thinking', was liable to make you have peculiar thoughts, because it 'turns the brain'.

'. . . sitting up all night in a blue nightdress in the kitchen – just the lights on, nobody making a sound. She's thinking and thinking – goodness knows what the heck she's thinking about. It's enough to twist anybody's mind.'

According to Mother, Father, and John, Sarah's breakdown

was due to lying in bed 'thinking' instead of getting up and occupying herself and meeting people. No matter how her mother shouted at her, she would not stop 'thinking', and to their greater alarm, she thought inwardly, not out loud. She even pretended to put some beauty preparation on her legs as a pretext for staying up in her room and thinking. Mrs Danzig reproached herself. She should have called in a psychiatrist sooner. They know how to handle such people.

'They could have knocked some sense into her. I should have called in a doctor, at that time, and said, "Look – she's upstairs, you talk to her." If she refused to listen to him – he's a medical man, he might give me another suggestion. It didn't *dawn* on me at the time that it was a psychiatric case, or whatever you call her.'

Her father told us that he came into a room and he saw Sarah just standing looking out of the window. He asked her what she was thinking, and she said, 'I don't need to tell you.'

Sarah and her brother argued in front of us about 'thinking'. Sarah claimed that John 'thinks' also.

JOHN: Yes, but not like you do.
SARAH: Well, just yesterday I came into your bedroom and you were lying on your bed – thinking.
JOHN: No I wasn't.
SARAH: Yes you were.
JOHN: I was listening to the radio.

Reading the Bible was also a very doubtful activity, especially for a girl. Religion was one thing, but reading the Bible was another. The Bible was possibly all right to glance through, and perhaps, even, a religious person *should* do that; but to want to sit down and read it and make a fuss if it was missing from its usual place . . .

MOTHER: Well, she couldn't find the Bible, raised havoc out of the bookcases – 'Where is it? – That one's got it – this one's got it' – I said, 'Who wants to read your Bible?' I said, 'Is it

normal for a girl to sit up all night and read the Bible all night?'
I also think it's nice to read. I read. I might read a magazine
or a book, but I've never read the Bible. I've never heard of it.
If I saw another girl read the Bible, I would come home and
say, 'That girl's got a kink somewhere – Yes, know about it,
look at it for five minutes – just a glance through; but you
never make a study of the Bible. I could never sit down and
read the Bible for two to three solid hours. I don't think she
reads it. I think she just glances at the pages.

INTERVIEWER: I'm a little surprised at this, I had the impression
that this is what your husband would like.

MOTHER: What, to read the Bible all night? – Oh no, Oh no,
Oh no. He likes to get down to things. He thinks every girl
should know, you know have natural accomplishments. I used
to teach her music. She didn't want to practise – all right, we'll
drop that. And now with television, they don't want to. And
she used to play – all right, don't learn. He likes her to go out
with boys. He likes her to mix, to go to socials, you know,
like debates. She used to like to go to debates, they used to have
special film shows, you know, interest – show it to a group of
people – Oh he likes her to have an interest in all these sort of
normal things. We used to go very often, the four of us, not
Ruth, she was too young – go out at night to the cinema or to
a theatre – the four of us, and we'd go out and have dinner.
Oh he's not – I tell you – he's been brought up – his father was
very religious, he was an officer of the synagogue and a great
Hebrew Talmudist. . . .

Sarah's thinking and reading of the Bible evoked a mixture of
alarm, concern, dismay, and disparagement. Her brother scorned
her, her mother told her she was lazy, her father rebuked her.
Yet they all felt that they were judged in some way by her. But it
was not difficult for them not to take seriously the stumbling
efforts of a girl to come to terms with her experience.

The fact that she read the Bible in an effort to throw light on
her present experience was completely incomprehensible to this

family. Accustomed to meet with ridicule and admonitions not to be lazy, selfish, or ungrateful, and so on, she either kept silent or gave out a short statement from time to time that only caused her family to lament the more the calamity that had befallen them.

Sarah had taken seriously what she had been taught, so that when she discovered the double standards of her family she was bewildered. She could not bring herself to accept her brother's openly avowed double standards, which were her father's also, but unavowed by him. Indeed, she *was not allowed to do so*. Her mother and father both felt that this was necessary for John, but they insisted that she adopt their point of view without reservation. But it was impossible to do this without adopting their particular stratagems, and this they forbade her to do.

This presentation embodied only a fragment of the data on the Danzigs. It was given then simply to establish the social intelligibility of the diagnosis of schizophrenia 'in' one of the family members. It showed that Sarah's 'mad' behaviour and experience were a significantly intelligible response to her family's praxis, which was muddled and muddling, and which was not socially intelligible primarily as a response to her. It is this confused and confusing familial pattern of interaction that I now wish to make intelligible.

PART I

The Danzigs

CHAPTER 1

Family harmony and family appearance

The shift of focus from person-in-the-group to the group itself entails detotalizing[1] our current experience of the social situation under study, and retotalizing in such a way that the existing picture is dissolved into and preserved in a new, more comprehensive *gestalt*. We start by recapitulating briefly.

Sarah was originally seen from a clinical point of view, and her behaviour and experience labelled socially unintelligible and sick. The picture was radically altered when the clinical method was superseded by a social phenomenological technique. When studied appropriately in her family context Sarah was found to be suffering more from her family than from something wrong inside her. She was seen to be surrounded by multiple mystifications in which her parents and brother invalidated her attempts to make sense of her experience of herself and others, including them. They conveyed she was mad and bad for acting and experiencing contrary to their requirements.

The particular issues over which she was mystified included the following: seeing her parents as quarrelling, getting angry with her father when he entered her room without knocking, seeing her family to be talking conspiratorially about her, accusing her parents of listening in to her telephone calls, lying in bed late in the morning, staying awake at night thinking or reading, reading the Bible, being rebellious, smoking on the Sabbath, being spoilt and favoured by her father over John, being shy and not mixing with people, particularly boys, being afraid of life, not being grown-up, and not being independent when enjoined

[1] For the meaning of *totalizing*, see the discussion contained in Part II.

3

by her family so to be. The principal mystification was over the question of her responsibility for her acts. They attributed to process, praxes of hers of which they disapproved. They told her she was mad in a way that implied she was bad when she was acting and experiencing most autonomously. But they denied they saw her as bad when she tried to clarify this mystification. Thus, when, empirically speaking, she was being most independent, her parents said she was being least so.

However, the Danzigs were not aware they were so mystifying Sarah. For they were unaware they were so contradictory. In their view, the matter was simple. She was sick. Her behaviour showed it. And her attempts to contradict them simply confirmed it. For she obviously failed to realize the significance of her actions. And she was sick because something was wrong inside her. This caused her to behave as she did, not they, as she sometimes contended. They were only concerned for her welfare. Their praxis was a simple and congruent response to hers, while hers was unintelligible.

This failure by the Danzigs to see the mystification in their praxis is the starting-point of our new inquiry. For they defined their group as harmonious, and, by implication, their praxis as non-paradoxical. Reconciling this definition with the existence of their paradoxical behaviour, which appears to contradict it, should help us define the principle of their praxis. We start by examining a double paradox, the paradox in their acts, and the paradox of their non-perception of the paradoxes of their praxis.

Since their perception of Sarah as sick was an empirically un-justified assumption, we may infer her parents' actions expressed a confusion between praxis and process in their experience of her. However, they were unaware of any such confusion. Since they failed to see the contradictions in their acts, they had no occasion to examine the experience of which these acts were an expression. And so the confusion persisted. Their persistently mystifying behaviour was the expression of a persisting unrecognized confusion between praxis and process in their experience of her.

Now, they maintained their view that their behaviour was

simple even when contradictions were pointed out to them. Not that they failed to see those aspects of their behaviour which were contradictory. They often saw them, but they failed to grasp the contradiction the conflicting aspects constituted. For instance, though sometimes they were aware of their anger at Sarah's sick behaviour, even 'admitting' their anger was 'wrong', they failed to grasp their feelings were mixed. Contradiction as such appeared to have no place in their experience of themselves. When contradictions like ambivalence were pointed out in terms like mixed feelings, feelings of love and anger, like and dislike, affection and exasperation, they were either baffled, or more usually they assumed their praxis was being criticized. They then 'justified' the 'criticized' aspects of their praxis by explaining it was a congruent response to Sarah's behaviour.

But their explanations, too, were contradictory, for they usually assumed what they were trying to explain. For instance, they were sick of Sarah's sick behaviour, because her sick behaviour was sickening. They persistently failed to grasp the presence of any inconsistency in what they did. They seemed to lack all dialectical sense of paradox,[1] and consequently lacked all perspective on themselves.

This partial explanation of their paradoxical behaviour raises certain other questions. What was their experience of Sarah, that they confused praxis and process? What was the pattern of their consciousness, that they failed to realize the confusion through failing to see the contradictory nature of the praxis the confusion expressed?

The Danzigs' confusion between praxis and process was twofold. They said she was mad in a way that implied she was bad. That is, while attributing process to her praxis, they attributed praxis to the process already attributed. Let us start with one end of the tangle. Given their perception of her as sick, how did they explain the attribution of praxis to the perceived process? Or, what was so sickening about her sickness?

Though the Danzigs gave different explanations at different

---

[1] Part II comprises a discussion on dialectical awareness.

times, they appeared to see these as consistent with one another. Sometimes they said they were worried sick about the state of Sarah's health, sometimes they said they were worried sick about her reputation, and sometimes they were angrily worried about their own reputation.

FATHER: It may well be that we er – our concern – we overdo our concern, and that we shouldn't be so concerned as we appear to be.

MOTHER: Look, I have cousins. They have girls – they're much younger than Sarah – and they came round to see me. The first thing they asked me was, 'How's Sarah?' 'She's fine'. 'What does she do? Does she go to work?' What can I say? Can I say she doesn't want to get up to go to school – or go to work? [Slight bitter laugh.]

INTERVIEWER: Yes, that's what I'm saying, that Sarah's behaviour threatens your world and your standard of values – that you're ashamed in front of your relatives.

MOTHER: Yes I am. I'm ashamed in front of my relatives. Yes, I am. You see it's not the type of thing I can approach a stranger with – like my friend or my relations – say 'Now look, what do you suggest I should do, she doesn't want to get out of bed!' What – is there anything they can tell me? Now I can't say that to anybody, can I? It's not a type of thing – if somebody's got a pain somewhere, or an illness you say, 'Now look, what doctor do you think I ought to go to – what hospital?' – but, it's a thing that's – it's so sort of abnormal isn't it? They put it down to bone laziness.

They seemed to experience Sarah's 'sick' behaviour as simultaneously sick and scandalous. And they experienced the scandal as affecting their reputation, and hers, as if they, the parents, shared a joint identity which they also shared with Sarah.

This shared identity was the Danzig family, for it was as members of the family that they invariably referred to themselves. Their family identity appeared to be their most constant form of self-recognition. And it was their reputation as a family they feared Sarah's 'sick' behaviour would affect. This fear was so great that they saw her 'illness' as a calamity visited on the family itself.

MOTHER: We didn't, as I told you, we thought those things only happened to other people's children. You read in the paper a little girl is murdered, or kidnapped. We don't know yet what. You feel very sorry for the people. You can sympathize with the people, with the parents, but you don't associate it with your own child. As I say, when – everything terrible happens to other people.

FATHER: When it happens to you –

MOTHER: And then it happens with you unfortunately, then other people say, 'Oh, how terrible'.

FATHER: Then it becomes a tragedy.

MOTHER: It *never* occurred to me that she'd ever sort of go sort of mentally like this, to turn out in this sort of way.

This sort of way was her behaviour that shamed her family. It was the danger to their family reputation they found so sickening about her 'sickness'.

Now, though by their gestures and tone of voice the Danzigs conveyed they experienced Sarah's behaviour as scandalous, they usually insisted they saw her only as sick. It was other people, public opinion, who saw her as scandalous. Public opinion was ignorant and would not understand she could not help what she said and did. And so, to prevent people getting the wrong impression, they persistently tried to hush her up. Of course they knew they were being illogical, for they knew she could not control herself; but after all her behaviour was sickening.

Since we have no reason to suppose they were lying when they said they saw Sarah simply as sick, we may infer they were unwittingly identified with a critically evaluating entity, which they called 'public opinion'. This entity they experienced to be independent of themselves, outside themselves. And they feared that if this entity received a certain impression because of Sarah's behaviour, their reputation would be sickeningly affected.

What was the impression her behaviour was liable to convey?

7

The Danzigs saw Sarah's behaviour as a break in the front the family presented to the world. This front, one of cooperation and harmony, they also presented to me. They insisted that as a family they were united, with no problems worth discussing, except Sarah. It was true they had their little disagreements, for they tended to be rather highly strung, the parents especially; but there was nothing serious in that. Every family had its problems, and one should never allow things to get out of proportion, nor look for trouble where it did not exist.

Of course, Sarah was a problem, they said. She was a source of disharmony. She caused them to worry, even to quarrel. For they sometimes blamed each other for her sickness.

MOTHER: Well we used to go and we used – my husband used to put the blame on me and I used to put the blame on him, when she never used to get out of bed all day, it used to gall me. That did make me ill, that used to upset me.

But apart from Sarah's sick behaviour there was no disharmony in the family. Everyone else got on well together.

Sarah, however, was not quite so sure. Sometimes she agreed, but sometimes she said her parents had been quarrelling as far back as she could remember, which was as far back as her childhood. Her parents denied this, conveying she was bad and mad for saying so. If quarrelling occurred it was because they were worried by her, or by her rivalry with John. They told her this repeatedly.

Now, Sarah's assertion was true. For her parents told me privately they did quarrel over matters other than Sarah. Her father, for instance, said his wife was 'a neurotic' who had been nagging him bitterly for years, even before Sarah was born, since the start of their marriage in fact. Among other things, she continually bemoaned marrying him, and frequently threatened to commit suicide. However, despite this behaviour he appeared not to think there was anything radically wrong with his marriage. For though he strongly criticized his wife's actions, he did not seem to feel these constituted or indicated the existence of any real problem between them. For instance, he told his wife after one bitter quarrel:

FATHER: What happened in the past, forget it. Let's try and harmonize now, and – now we've got a problem we must try *together*. Let's try – all right, forget about the little bits and pieces about ourselves, we've got problems now.

How do we understand this paradoxical stance?

They said Sarah was the only family problem, because she was the only family member out of harmony with the others. But her parents complained bitterly of each other's lack of harmony. We must therefore ask: In what kind of familial harmony could the members of this disharmonious family be?

Since they presented to the world a front of family unity and harmony, their harmony must have been a harmony in maintaining the public appearance of family harmony. This conclusion is borne out by their view that Sarah's behaviour was a break in the public front of family unity and harmony. Her 'sickness', which was their only problem, was her disharmony with the others in maintaining the front of harmony. This disharmony was seen by her parents as the main effect of her 'illness', and its main sign.

Sarah's behaviour was scandalous, not because of the specific problems of family disharmony it revealed. As her parents said, every family had its problems. It was scandalous, because in revealing them, she revealed publicly that the family as a family was failing to cope privately with the problem of coping privately. They were failing to cope quietly with the problem of keeping quiet about family problems in public. This public failure constituted the danger to the family reputation.

The Danzigs as a group in relation to the world, appeared to operate on the principle of cooperating harmoniously in maintaining the public appearance of group harmony in the interests of the group's reputation. Their reasoning seemed implicitly as follows:

Reputation depended on appearance, and good reputation on the appearance of success. Family repute required the appearance of family success. Now, a family was a group, and a successful group was one that was on-going. An on-going group adapted well to public demands. And one public demand a group was required to fulfil was the demand that the group cope privately with group problems, including coping with the problem of coping privately. To appear on-going, and therefore successful, the parents' family reputation required the group to appear to be successfully meeting this public demand. They had to operate smoothly in relation to the world without, by being seen coping privately with disharmony within, and being seen coping quietly with the problem of teaching the children the importance of quiet coping. The Danzigs' family reputation was their reputation as this paradoxical system. This reputation the parents felt Sarah's behaviour had assassinated. This inference, if correct, should help us totalize the basic group praxis[1] in a way that reconciles all persisting contradictions and, in particular, those that apparently threaten its continued existence as the group it is.

Now, the Danzigs had been worrying for years about the effect of Sarah's behaviour on their family reputation – ever since she started being 'lazy', since she was thirteen. But they had always seen her as bad, not sick. Recently they had changed their view.

The problem had become acute shortly after her twenty-first birthday when, following a quarrel with her mother, Sarah had fled the house and stayed away all night. When she returned next day she said defiantly she had slept the night in an hotel with a boy. It was then her parents decided she was ill, a view that was confirmed clinically.

However, their decision did little to ease their worry. On the contrary, through labelling her ill, a cycle of events was set in motion which simply caused the problem to grow, feeding their ever-increasing anxiety that Sarah would burst out even more uncontrollably, bringing shame on them all. The situation constantly threatened to get out of control. Whatever they tried seemed to make matters worse, and at each new point of crisis they could think of no solution other than to remove the focus of potential

[1] See Chapter 17 for a definition and discussion of this concept.

explosion into one of those places made to receive it. With each removal her parents felt confirmed in their view that Sarah was sick.

How do we understand their decision? We must first examine phenomenologically what family and reputation signified to the Danzigs. For this we shall need two concepts: serial group,[1] and what I term 'alterated identity'.

Serial group refers to a certain type of group praxis. Formally speaking, groups may be active or passive. An active group is centred in and between its members, and the reason for its existence is to be found within the group itself. A passive group is centred in an agent or event outside the group, and there is found its *raison d'être*.

A gang of labourers, or a grouping of employees, is a typical serial group. They are a collection of instruments to be used by another. Hence the term 'employee'. The immediate constituting agent of the gang, for instance, is the foreman. Each labourer offers himself as a unit of embodied labour power, in effect, to be used according to a plan made outside the group, and mediated by the foreman, himself a serial instrument in the design of another. The reason for the group's existence thus lies in the exteriorly conceived plan. The group's centre lies there, and the gang experience themselves controlled by 'them'.

When the plan no longer requires the gang, the gang is dispersed; again by action from the outside. Whatever relationships the labourers form among themselves, they will not prevent the group being dispersed if the plan requires it. Their relations to each other as members of the gang as gang are essentially passive. If they do arrange to meet again on the basis of their gang association, they do so as *former* mates.

Similarly, Former Pupils' Associations, Old Comrades' Associations, and so on, exist to revive memories of *former* relationships made within a serial group, but which did not constitute

---

[1] For an extensive discussion on the serial group, see Sartre, J.-P., *Critique de la Raison Dialectique*. For an exposition of Sartre's statement, see Laing, R. D. and Cooper, D., *Reason and Violence*.

the group, and were therefore destroyed when the exteriorly conceived plan in terms of which the group was formed no longer required it to be. For instance, when the war for which the army was formed has been won, lost, or drawn for the persons or group in whose primary interest it was to form the army in the first place.

This type of group is called a series, because from the viewpoint of the constituting agent, or because of the requirements of the plan, no member of the group differs from any other except as a unit in a series of similar units whose *raison d'être* in the group is to fulfil certain functions in respect of the plan. Each member of the gang is, thus, replaceable by another similar unit of similar embodied labour power. That is, any employee can be replaced by another similar. For the group to function according to the requirements of the constituting agent, the members need have no identity other than their rank order.

A serial group is thus always constituted in terms of a common object experienced as external to the group. This common object is called by Sartre 'the serial object'. The *serial object* may be a shared object of phantasy experience, unrecognized as such, and experienced as embodied by others as others, for instance, Public Opinion, the Blacks, the Whites, the Reds, the Jews, and so on.

The danger to the existence of a serial group is always that of dispersal because the serial object no longer requires it, or because the object has ceased to exist. The plan is fulfilled, for example, or the firm has gone bankrupt.

The term *alterated identity* derives from *alter* (other).

Identity should be distinguished from being. By *being*, I mean all a person is. By *identity*, I mean the pattern of experience and being by which a person is recognized by himself and/or others in his relations with others, i.e. who he is recognized or defined to be.

Persons experience themselves directly and immediately. They also experience themselves through the eyes of others. A person's direct experience of himself is his being-for-himself, or his being-for-self. His experience of himself mediated by the other is his being-for-the-other. A person's definition of himself in relation to others is his identity-for-self. Whom he feels himself to be in the eyes of the other, or whom he is in the eyes of the other, is his identity-for-the-other, or what I term his 'alterated identity'.

A person may be confirmed or disconfirmed by the others in his experience-for-self; for instance, his identity-for-self may be confirmed by his identity-for-other. John, who sees himself as good, feels confirmed when he sees James seeing him as good.

A person may interiorize or identify with the other's view of him. For instance, if John interiorizes the John he sees James seeing, when he sees James seeing him (John) as good, then John has identified with James's view of him. But this is not the same as confirmation, even if John saw himself as good initially. It is what I call *identification with his alterated identity*. And his identity-for-self now comprises an alterated component.

If a person's view of himself is contradicted by the other, and the person later changes his view to one similar to the other's, this does not constitute alteration if he has arrived at the new view of himself through an enterprise of self-discovery. For instance, John sees himself as a warm, friendly man. He sees James seeing him as cool and reserved. If John identifies with James's view of him, his identity-for-self is now significantly alterated. If he realizes through existential self-examination that James's view is more accurate than his, and he sees in what way this is so, his new view of himself is not based on alteration, but on insight facilitated in his relation with the other.

We can now return to the Danzigs and to discovering what family and reputation meant to them. We do so in and through a re-gressive-progressive movement,[1] totalizing the basic group praxis. We start with their history.

---

[1] See Part II for a discussion on the regressive-progressive method.

CHAPTER 2

The marriage

The Danzigs had been quarrelling bitterly for years, practically from the day of their marriage. In the last four or five years the quarrels had been more intense. She said he was more pernickety than ever over cleanliness and tidiness, and more irritable. He said she was becoming more nervous and lacking in self-control. She said he was continually picking on John, expecting a too rigorous compliance with religious ritual regulations. He said she was complaining she had too much to do at home, and continually threatened to do herself in because she was fed up being married to him. Both appeared thoroughly miserable and discontented with each other, yet paradoxically they never seriously considered separating. They remained married, or did they? Had they ever been married? Certainly in the eyes of society they were married, and had been for over twenty-five years, but what did this mean in practice? Simply that they participated in an institutionalized social praxis that allowed them to live in the same house, and share the same domestic economy without fear of scandal. In no other sense than the institutional could they be be said to be married. Neither in anything they said of each other, past or present, nor in any intonation or gesture did either reveal any sign of love, tenderness, or affection for the other. And this appears to have been the case from the start. They had never been erotically attracted to one another. Nor had either been attracted to, or in love with, anyone else.

INTERVIEWER: Have either of you at any time ever been in love?
MOTHER: What do you mean – with somebody else?

INTERVIEWER: With anyone.

MOTHER: At any time? Well I can answer for myself – no, I can't answer for my husband. He may have, he may not. I don't know.

FATHER: I'm in love with life.

MOTHER: Sometimes you get used to people. Some people put it down as love, don't they?

This is not to say they had no respect for each other. They had a certain respect; but it was that of one businessman for another who meticulously fulfils his side of a bargain. Said Mrs Danzig, speaking of her life with her husband:

MOTHER: I didn't sort of *miss* going out. And in the winter when the Sabbath was out round about five[1] and – used to go out by six. It didn't matter that much. In the summer I used to find it rather boring. But still it didn't matter that much. I mean it wasn't that important. I had other things. I had other, well I had Mr Danzig which compensated to that small thing – which I think is small. I think it's small. I think it's small, it's not so material. And when a man has other bad qualities, well then it's something that you have to sort of ponder over, but – it's not a *bad* quality in a man, if you like. I wouldn't call it a *bad* quality. It's not convenient but it's not what you call a bad quality. If he went out gambling *then* it's a different thing or if I thought he was spending money recklessly or playing the horses.

Their marriage, in fact, had *never* been anything but a business contract instigated and arranged by their parents as a match between families, and the Danzigs had acquiesced in the arrangement.

MOTHER: Yes, well, I mean. Well, when I met Mr Danzig he looked a very nice young chap at the time – came from very nice parents. They were very, very nice people, and the two brothers were very nice. They also had very nice houses and

[1] The Sabbath ends at sunset. Traditionally in Judaism a day is reckoned from evening to evening.

had very nice lives and he made a living, not much, but there was something there that could be – hopes for a better future. He wasn't a millionaire, not by any means, not by any means at all.

FATHER: I did have ideals in my mind, but I'd got to that stage when my father wasn't very well. My father wanted me to get married, and he told me that 'I'd like you to meet this girl' – he knew her father very well – 'And she's a nice-looking girl.' My wife wasn't bad-looking. And so I came to the point. We met at the end of Boxing Day nineteen-thirty-three, and it seemed possible. We didn't dislike one another, not to say – I'm not going to say I was ravingly in love with my wife, and I don't think my wife was with me, but maybe I wasn't sufficiently experienced to understand certain things.

The girl he met had undertaken to be a cook-housekeeper, child-producer, and child-trainer. While Mr Danzig had undertaken to keep her in the manner to which she was accustomed.

FATHER: My wife was *never* short of anything. I went short, but she didn't. Never was short. We started off married life with a maid – no children for five years. Wasn't short of anything. I've always worked very hard to build up a business, and you only build a business by one – one method – by certain standards. We're judged by certain standards. There was no question of shortage. I've always worked very hard, day and night.

This contract between a senior and a junior partner, Mrs Danzig had entered into for the sake of what she called security. While Mr Danzig had done so out of filial piety.

Now, Mrs Danzig, if she had had her way, would not have married at all. She would have preferred to have gone into business like her father, and to have remained there; but business had been bad in those days. And so, after she left school she had taught children to play the piano. Not that she had liked teaching the piano. She had loathed it, but she taught because her father had spent money on having her taught, and, according to her, had expected a return. However, she never objected to this expectation of his. It seemed to her reasonable enough. And besides, she said, she was told it was better for her to teach. Her father had said so, and she trusted him. And so, she taught the piano. She had been brought up, she indicated, to honour her father and her mother.

MOTHER: Well I was always brought up at that time – now it's different of course. If your father and mother said anything you had to obey them. That was something that I couldn't with anybody. Whatever Mum and Dad said at the time we used to listen to them.

And some years later when they told her that business was bad, and she ought to get married for her own sake, she again complied. She believed her parents knew best. And anyway, one liked to have security: 'You like to feel you can make a living.'

Besides, she continued, her parents were not pressing her into doing something she did not want to do. They had never done that, over marriage, or anything else. They would never have tried forcing her into marrying someone she disliked. They had allowed her a completely free hand, though naturally they insisted on vetting the boy to ensure he was the right one for her.

MOTHER: And had I chosen a man who wasn't Orthodox[1] and who sort of was – like myself, he [father] would not have objected. Of course, if he'd been a nice, you know what he thought, a really nice, a nice chap, what he called – the right fellow for me.

She had had no objection, and indicated she still had none, to their vetting her prospective husband, because she felt their logic was superior to hers. As she knew from the many occasions when they had reasonably pointed out to her how wrong she was. If she had objected to marrying the man they thought was right for her they would not have forced her. They would simply

---

[1] That is, Orthodox Jewish.

have talked the matter over sensibly with her, and she would have been convinced.

MOTHER: . . . I think they would have pointed out *why* you marry the fellow. They would have pointed out logical reasons and I would have seen the light.

They respected her opinion, she said, even though she was a good girl.

MOTHER: Well I was a good girl at home, but when I had anything to say which I thought was right they used to listen to what I had to say. They used to listen if I said so and so was the case. If I went out with a boy they used to say 'Go out with him again'. I used to say 'No, I don't like him'. They used to try and persuade me. I used to give my opinion about it, but I just don't remember very much made about that.

And because she had had no complaints she had never disobeyed them. Besides they would have been hurt, and, she said, she would never have done that to them. She never had the courage.

MOTHER: Well to defy one's parents needs great courage. At least I didn't have the pluck. I wouldn't have done it to them.

And eventually, when they told her about Mr Danzig, what a nice chap he was, what a nice family he came from, how bad business was, she felt she had to recognize the logic of their argument, and married him.

As for Mr Danzig, he said he too had been brought up to honour his father and his mother. He had strong views on filial piety, on what a parent could expect from a child. He believed a child should respect its parents no matter what the parents were like. Said he:

FATHER: Just by the mere fact that they are parents don't you think they deserve it, that they should get respect, receive the respect?

And though he was prepared to concede there might be parents who did not behave well towards their children, he was by no means convinced of this. And even in such an unlikely event the children should still respect their parents' wishes and do whatever was required of them, as Mr Danzig had done when he married the girl his parents had chosen. And he expected his children to demonstrate their respect for him as clearly as he had demonstrated his for his parents.

Unfortunately, to his great unhappiness they failed to do so, at least to his satisfaction. And for this he blamed his wife, for in his view she failed to show him proper respect, particularly before the children. This caused them to quarrel, he said, or at least to quarrel worse.

FATHER: My wife had a little objection in her mind because I was previously engaged to be married to another girl, and she never had the idea of marrying a boy who was engaged previously. That I got to know from her; but she married me. And she more than once brought this up. She said in front of the children, 'I should have broken my neck when I married you' – in front of the children. Not a very nice thing. And certain other unpleasant remarks in front of the children. And so – I've got a sense of humour sometimes. So I said, 'It must have been a blackout when I came into your house' – nineteen-fourteen war. It doesn't mean anything. If you've got children – it doesn't mean anything. I said it for a joke, but it's the impression children get. That impression says: Here Father and Mother are arguing. So Sarah sometimes says, 'You two keep on arguing. Why don't you divorce?' Sarah says that.

Mr Danzig, who married his wife out of filial respect, now felt his children's respect was undermined by the wife he had so married.

But why was filial respect so important to the Danzigs?

Mr Danzig was a businessman, and he was a family man. As a businessman he was moderately successful, but as a family man things were not going so well. However, even in business he found success was not complete. Success involved an unceasing struggle, and the key to success was not hard work or principle, ethics or integrity, but simply reputation – how one was perceived by others, by 'public opinion'.

FATHER: Well, you've got to break it down in certain categories. Whether you're in business or whether you're engaged in a profession you've got to conform to certain standards. Unfortunately we are judged by certain standards. You very often hear of a doctor with a bad reputation, not a good reputation, or an accountant who hasn't got a good reputation or a solicitor or even a barrister. Lots of things – they're judged by reputation, by conduct.

INTERVIEWER: But you said earlier on that ignorant people seeing the minister taking the car[1] –

FATHER: Might – they could –

INTERVIEWER: So public opinion could be ignorant?

FATHER: Could be, could be. But that could be very dangerous.

INTERVIEWER: It could be very dangerous in terms of one's integrity.

FATHER: But unfortunately I would say the majority of people are inclined to be somewhat ignorant in certain directions.

INTERVIEWER: Then if you're basing your standards of behaviour –

FATHER: – very largely on twofold issues, on the ethics, principle and religion.

INTERVIEWER: And what about the ethic of public opinion?

FATHER: Ah [sighs], it's very difficult. So far I've tried my best to adhere to certain principles. I may not have succeeded and so far I try to attain certain standards. I've built up my business over the years – by reputation, by public opinion, within my own sphere, of course, and by recommendation by other people who have known me for a number of years and felt fit to

---

[1] I.e. on the Sabbath. Forbidden to an Orthodox Jew except under special circumstances, such as the need to preserve health or life. The minister was visiting his daughter, who was seriously ill in hospital.

recommend me for certain things in certain directions. They know I've got three children.

In this struggle his family life was as much part of the battlefield upon which reputations were won and lost as his business. Indeed he looked upon his family much as he looked upon his business. One had to preserve one's reputation if one was going to succeed, and one was entitled to expect one's children to co-operate. He had, for instance, hopes for Sarah to marry the son of some associate, whom he would take into the business. After all:

FATHER: We want to preserve those standards. I mean when you're working at a business or you do other matters in this world, we are judged by certain standards – I want to preserve that.

INTERVIEWER: Yes.

FATHER: That's the fight I have. I'm not saying it – maybe it's an irrational one, but I'm unelastic. I don't expect unreasonable attitudes or unreasonable conduct by my wife or my children or by my son or my daughter. My daughter Sarah, I had plans for her. I'm holding on to a good business. Why? I thought I had perhaps ideas that she might marry the son of some business associate – take him into the business.

Perhaps I'm expecting too much of my children. Sarah – I hoped she might even marry a doctor – because I can do a lot of work with doctors. I do a lot of work with doctors. Or the son of some associate – it's not unreasonable. I told her, 'Don't marry a doctor because I want you to. If you like him, if you might happen to meet a doctor, all right.' I'm giving you the general picture – perhaps I'm grumbling – I don't know whether I'm grumbling or not – I leave that to you to judge.

And his son, was it unreasonable, he asked, to expect him to get experience in the same business as himself? With children it was simply a question of giving a return.

FATHER: There's nothing unreasonable in asking a child to do certain small things to give pleasure. It's a matter of capital investment. Look upon it from a practical point of view, as a businessman. You put money into a business and you expect some interest. Interest – right. If parents sacrifice their life for their children's, it's capital, it's outlay. The interest you get back – little – give and take, give and take.

Of course he loved his children, he said. He felt great love. He felt he loved them more than he felt his wife did, for he believed she loved them only for security, whereas he loved them because he loved them. However it appears he loved them for much the same reason as his wife. Speaking, for instance, of John, he said:

FATHER: Well, I'm not quite sure, I think I'm fond of him, more so than she is. I think she loves him from a point of view of security, and I love him because firstly he's my child, secondly because he's my son. I intend he will carry on the good name. I hope so and I feel I can make a personality of him. On the other hand, my wife may love him because of security, holding on to something.

Neither parent appeared aware of their children as persons. Neither appeared to understand that love could mean helping their children realize their own true possibilities. For instance:

INTERVIEWER: If you had a child who wanted to make his or her life in his or her own way and shows, the child shows that it had become an autonomous human being, an independent person able to make his or her own life in his or her own way, which might be different – utterly different – to *your* way, would you regard that child as a – would you regard that as a good thing?

FATHER: I wouldn't regard the child with any less – any – any worse than she would otherwise, or he and she would other-wise – but I would regard it as a slight to my leadership, to my management and to my self-respect and dignity.

The children were for the most part experienced as the property of the parents, a capital investment from which parents were entitled to expect a profitable return. Said Mr Danzig:

FATHER: It's an investment – if you put money in a business you
expect to get interest. So the marriage – I say children and
marriage is a sort of investment, look upon it from that point
of view. I want to have my little bit of interest, I may not have
my gilt-edged security. Give me two per cent interest on my
capital investment. By that I mean let's have something back
in return for my effort on their behalf, on my wife's behalf.
They say it's my duty, well where does their duty start and
end? Must it always be my duty? You talk about responsibility-
not-responsible, of course I want her to be responsible, but
where does *their* responsibility start and end?

MOTHER: They also have a duty. Why shouldn't they be made to
please us?

What was this return?

As parents, the Danzigs saw themselves responsible for the way
their children behaved, and the return they expected was for the
children to behave in a manner that maintained or increased the
parents' reputation. This was their children's filial duty.

Now, the reputation Mr Danzig desired was of an efficient
paternal businessman and successful leader and organizer who
had everything under control including his family, which he was
expected to train properly.

FATHER: As a matter of fact a certain amount of discipline – why
do you have policemen in the streets? Why do you have
soldiers at points, palaces, clubs? Why do you have generals –
discipline? There must be a certain amount of discipline even
at home. A fact that a father wants certain things done in a
certain way, it's not because he wants to impose his will. It's
not because – it's what he thinks is *right*.

And:

INTERVIEWER: Her [Sarah's] reputation reflects on you. So it
comes back to your reputation again.

FATHER: Yes, and hers as well, because they judge leadership. It's
a question of leadership.

23

INTERVIEWER: Yes, so it gets back to your reputation again.
FATHER: Yes, leadership. If I'm not able to control, if I cannot control or infuse, or inject a spirit of good will and leadership and a way of conduct in my house, I'm lacking in leadership.
INTERVIEWER: And people will judge you?
FATHER: Will judge me accordingly.

If his children behaved badly they would acquire a bad reputation and he would appear incompetent. And since his success depended on the appearance of success, it was plainly the duty of his children not to do anything that would give them a bad reputation. They must not do anything that public opinion would take to indicate that Mr Danzig did not have them properly trained and under control.

As for Mrs Danzig, she wished to be seen as a hard-working mother and housewife who competently did everything on time – in practice, a hard-working cook-housekeeper who had properly trained the children she had produced. She feared being allocated a reputation for laziness and neglect of her housekeeping, child-rearing duties.

INTERVIEWER: But you would feel in some way you had failed as a mother – that somehow or other you're responsible.
MOTHER: Yes, made her lazy. Nobody likes a lazy person.

Like her husband, she expected her children to act in a way that established and maintained the reputation she desired.

The Danzigs believed one index of successful parenthood which public opinion used was the index of filial piety. A properly trained, controlled child was one that respected its parents, and the criterion of respect was that it would do nothing that reflected on its parents' reputation. This was called 'having consideration for others', 'being responsible', 'being grown up', and so on. Thus, in the Danzigs' view, their reputation depended on their children showing respect for the parents' reputation, while the children's reputation also depended on showing respect for the parents' reputation.

The Danzigs had acquired this view in the course of their relationships with their own parents. For instance, Mr Danzig recalled an occasion, before he had met his wife, when he had visited 'a young lady's' house and heard her being 'rude and crude' to her parents.

FATHER: Well – you see – well, I went into a young lady's house before I met my wife, a very nice young lady. I went in three times and I was told – I said, 'I want to meet the parents.' They invited me up. Permission was given to me to go to see the parents and the family. I went in there – so we met, and I was invited into the house. I was there a number of hours, and when I saw the young lady just being rude, when I heard her being rude and crude to her father and mother, it made a very bad impression.

That had been enough for him. He knew she would get a reputation for being disrespectful, and this would give her parents a bad reputation. If he went out with her this would give him a bad reputation. And if he got a bad reputation his parents would get one. Prudence and filial piety both demanded he should promptly stop seeing her, and stop seeing her he did. And later, when the proper time came, it was as a dutiful son paying his respects before public opinion that he agreed to marry the respectful girl his sick father chose for him.

And the Danzigs expected their children to act with similar piety. Respectful compliance with what the children learnt to be their parents' wishes and values, ensured the parents' reputation as conscientiously successful in training them to be conscientiously respectful of their parents' reputation as conscientiously respectful.

And what was Mr Danzig doing being a business family man and a family businessman? Precisely what his wife had been doing when she had married him – seeking 'security'. Filial piety, public reputation, success and security implied one another. Put more colloquially, it meant: 'Do as you are told by your parents, behave respectably and properly and you will be all right.' It was on the basis of this doctrine that he and his wife had entered into their partnership. And indeed he was all right so far as his business was concerned. For he became in time a moderately successful businessman.

Now, an essential feature of respectable or proper behaviour was regular work and routine living. This was the formula that ensured success. And the Danzigs, who had received it from their parents, had never questioned it, far less refused to comply with it. For instance, in contrast to Sarah, they had never failed once to rise early in the morning at the 'right' time. To the Danzigs the formula was self-evidently valid. For had not compliance brought them success? And success obviously justified continued compliance.

However, though they could justify compliance by pointing to success, their compliance appeared at least as much determined by phantasy as by ordinary economic realities. For they acted as if the construction and maintenance of their world was less the expression of socio-economic praxis in the usual sense, than the consequence of each person in the family behaving 'properly'. For instance, Sarah's failure to attend college, although having no effect upon them financially, was experienced as a dire threat.

INTERVIEWER: Yes, but I think you have a sort of anxiety about this which is far wider than anything which could possibly happen in respect of Sarah. I think there's something about Sarah's lying in bed which threatens *your* world, your whole vision of the world.

MOTHER: Exactly – you've summed it up.

They tried to avert the threat by urging her to comply with the formula. We may, therefore, infer from their praxis that the security they sought through the trinity of filial piety, public reputation, and security-success was to a considerable extent security against an event in phantasy, which they did not realize was phantasy.

What was the threat?

The threat was complex, for the Danzigs were in the position of serving two masters. Mrs Danzig was afraid people would see her as lazy if she did not regularly rise early. But she also rose early because she knew the difference between right and wrong. And failure to rise early, she felt, was wrong. While Mr Danzig said his behaviour was determined by public opinion and what he called 'religious ethics', which gave him his sense of right and wrong. This ethical sense he and his wife experienced to be determined by an authority other than themselves. This authority they called 'God'. 'God' and 'public opinion' were their masters.

Now, so long as their masters agreed, things went well; but when contradictory injunctions were received, the Danzigs' position was most unhappy.

These contradictions operated intrapersonally, interpersonally, or both. For instance, Mr Danzig might receive injunctions from 'God' and 'public opinion' which were mutually contradictory, or he might receive mutually compatible injunctions in respect of his wife, which contradicted mutually compatible injunctions she had received from her 'God' and 'public opinion' in respect of him. We shall later explore in more detail how this affected their praxis.

They never dealt properly with this situation for they had never grasped the contradiction of their position. They simply felt life was very complicated at times, and they tried to deal with the complications by applying the formula of regular work and routine living in a stereotyped manner.

And in business it worked. Phantasy and ordinary economic reality coincided closely at this point. For the type of business Mr Danzig had chosen involved work of a routine, regular nature most suited to the formula. His business success was the expression of a self-actualizing phantasy. And because he was successful he had no occasion to question the formula, or the nature of the security he sought.

Now, the Danzigs felt secure when their reputation was good. And their reputation was good when they felt perceived approvingly by public opinion, which allocated reputations.

But though they regarded public opinion with great respect

and trepidation, they did not realize that, empirically speaking, it was an experience in phantasy, a phantasy presence embodied by others as others. For instance, though they said 'people' were ignorant, there appeared to be no question of enlightening 'them'. All one could do was placate 'them' by conforming in 'their' presence. For '*they*' could never be personally reached. Though the Danzigs felt themselves constantly observed and liable to be gossiped about, 'they', the gossipers, were highly elusive. 'They' were everywhere, even at home. Yet though 'they' were everywhere, 'they' were always elsewhere. 'They' were never here. 'They' never resolved into specific persons of their acquaintance, who would refuse to do business with them, or refuse to speak to them. 'They' never became a 'you' to be confronted. 'They', 'the others', remained always other.

As for the danger the Danzigs feared from 'the others', apart from gossip, it never resolved into specific action 'they' were likely to take, economically or otherwise. Thus, though there was no escaping 'them', there was no pinning 'them' down either, and the dreaded event remained vague and fearful.

What was the nature of this danger from 'the others'?

One of the complaints Mr Danzig made against his children was they would not let him be a father. By rejecting his guidance, they were depriving him of his *raison d'être*. As he said when speaking of their resistance to his inquiries about their friends:

FATHER: Is it unreasonable? As a father I wouldn't be justifying my existence at all.

We know, too, that any move by them to live a life by values other than those he tried to inculcate in them, would be felt by him as an affront to his self-respect. Thus the filial piety he expected from his children was for the purpose of maintaining his sense of being, through maintaining his paternal identity.

Now, neither parent had apparently ever attempted to enter into a relationship of direct reciprocity with any person. Not only had they never been in love, but they disapproved of it as something that logical people like themselves never attempted. It was a highly dangerous business that could lead one to defy one's parents, and to ruin one's reputation.

INTERVIEWER: Well, some people might call getting used to people loving them, but other people might say that's not –

MOTHER: Habit, yes. I tell you sometimes you let your head rule your heart, sometimes you let your heart rule your head, it depends on the circumstances. I've known people who've been terribly in love and who are most unhappy people now. That's also another example, you see. That's also likely to go bad. They've even defied their parents.

INTERVIEWER: They've even defied their parents?

MOTHER: Yes. And now they've gone back to their parents. What I mean was – well, being in love, if – well, at the time – well, I'm beyond that stage now. When I was young, I mean, when I was at the age of twenty, nineteen – that you meet somebody – go somewhere, you meet somebody – never mind marrying, never mind anything else. You feel this is the man you'd love to spend the rest of your life with and you throw discretion to the wind – not necessarily an affair, because I didn't like that. You have to have pluck for that sort of thing. When your parents disagree with you, and think it's not the right man, it needs a lot of moral courage for the girl to defy her parents. She has to think of the aftermath should it not come out well.

In a relationship of direct reciprocity each confirms the other in his sense of being through the reciprocal revelation of each to each other. In precluding themselves from such a relationship with anyone, the Danzigs had made themselves dependent for their sense of being on how each as an other appeared to the other. Their relationships, exclusively exterior, were thus based on each being an other-to-the-other. Consequently their identities were almost entirely altered. By this, I mean based on the interiorization of the appearance of each as an other in the eyes of the other as other. And, since each was an other in the world of the other, each was an object. Each 'I' was 'it' before the otherness of the other and related to the other as 'it'.

The particular identity of each depended upon the particular object-other that each felt himself to seem to be in the eyes of the other as object for him. And what he seemed to be was conveyed by the other as other playing the role that complemented it. Thus Mr Danzig knew himself as a husband, because Mrs Danzig played the role of a wife to him.

Now, his appearance in the eyes of the other as other was precisely the issue with which Mr Danzig was so concerned when he spoke of how important it was for his reputation for him to be seen by 'the others' as a father respected by his children. For Mr Danzig his sense of being, his alterated identity, and his reputation were synonymous. Since his security depended on his reputation, it follows it also depended on his alterated identity. But according to him, his *raison d'être* depended on having a particular alterated identity (a father); therefore his *raison d'être* depended on his reputation. He was thus dependent on public opinion for the justification of his being and for his security.

Since the security he sought was to a significant extent a security in phantasy, we may reasonably infer that the nature of this security related to having an identity that allowed the person to feel his being was justified. The feeling of being is the feeling of being a continuous entity in space and time. The form of security related intrinsically to such feeling of being may be termed *ontological security* or *security of being*. It was his security of being that Mr Danzig implicitly felt threatened when his children lacked filial respect. In seeking the approval of public opinion, Mr Danzig was in an alienated way implicitly seeking a form of ontological security. This form, which depends on being one's appearance for the other rather than on actualizing and being confirmed by the other in one's true possibilities, I term *ontic security*.

And similarly with Mrs Danzig, the security she sought through a good reputation was ontic security.

This security they experienced when they and their children

complied 'publicly' with the formula of regular work and routine living. The formula was a recipe for respectable conformity. Since they had been taught it by their parents, the Danzigs as the respectful children of their respectable parents could only conform. For in so doing they publicly demonstrated their parents' parental success, securing their parents' reputation, and their own. Their parents, the original others to whom they had appeared as other, had themselves each been an other for 'the others'. And their parents had embodied and mediated to them 'the others', before whom they, the children, were other. For the sake of their altered identities, their respectful being other-to-the-other, the Danzigs had to recognize their parents were others-to-'the others'. They had internalized themselves as other to the parental other embodying 'the others', and thus internalized 'the others' embodied by the parental other. They each became an other (for-the-other (for 'the others')). They each lived under the eye of a 'public opinion' that could not be reached, and so could not be influenced, and in the presence of the parental other, even when the parental other was physically absent.

For the sake of their ontic security, the Danzigs had to preserve the parental other from 'the others' by being, for this other, the other this other felt 'the others' required them to be.

But in being nothing other than this being for 'the-others', the Danzigs became totally alienated. Negating all possibility of direct reciprocity, each became simply the role he was playing. Each became a negation of a negation, a quasi-thing isolated in his concreteness from all others; one of a series of concrete entities whose unity resided simply in their common being other to every other. Their otherness, the negation of interiority and direct reciprocity, was all they had in common with any other. And what they had in common separated them.

Alienated from themselves and all others, the Danzigs were compelled to play out their roles. Their reputation was now all. They had no alternative to maintaining themselves in their alienation as comfortably and securely as possible. Their marriage was an expression of this project of their existence.

31

We can now see why their children's respect was so important to the Danzigs.

Failure to be shown respect would be seen by 'the others' to be the consequence of failure to train their children to conform to the grandparents' formula. And this would indicate failure by the Danzigs to respect the grandparents' parental reputation. In the business of family, the Danzigs' reputation for success depended on seeming to be the successful product of their own successful parents. And, they, as products, were tested in and through their relationship to their own familial products.

Their continued ontic security depended on continually demonstrating their parents' familial success.

Marrying was such a demonstration. Children should marry, and 'everyone' should see. It went without saying they should marry respectably. And their parents should discreetly advise, so the day of the wedding would be a day of parental pride. Then, before 'the others', their filial products would be seen successfully matched.

Since the Danzigs seemed unable to choose any eligible other for themselves, their parents chose an other for them. And the Danzigs, each as other, respectfully married each other.

Once embarked on their loveless union, the logic of their situation demanded they remain married. Said Mr Danzig:

FATHER: And now the practical side. My wife is very practical and was very practical in the way she embarked upon marriage with me. We're both very practical. We both saw the logic of our union with the hope that the future would bring that cement, or at least bring that love and affection that young couples, who embark upon marriage without rhyme or reason – and we've got to accept it as such.

To divorce or to feel anything less than gratitude would have shamed their loving parents, and therefore themselves. For they discovered 'the others', embodied and mediated by others, had constituted them as a single entity, 'a partnership'. And the scandal of separation would be even greater than the scandal of not marrying in the first place. They had to make the best of it.

Apart from their fear of scandal, there was nothing to hold them. They were united only by their common terror of what would happen if they separated. As the practical persons they wished themselves to appear to be, their only course was to invest in their marriage, and obtain as great and secure a return as possible. Constituted as a partnership in the eyes of public opinion, they protected themselves against their own free possibility of dissolving the partnership by each interiorizing and identifying with the unitary entity, which the partnership was for the others. They cemented their joint being, and secured themselves individually by establishing a relationship mediated by their internalized joint being-for-'the-others'. Such a group praxis directed against the dissolution of the group from within was an affirmation of the group, a *pledge*.[1]

To such an affirmation Mr Danzig implicitly referred when he described marriage and family life as an investment in which one gave and took. Each was to help the other act in a way that allowed the other attain the right reputation with public opinion. Each required the other to complement publicly the familial role each felt obliged to be.

FATHER: Let's show each other a little more respect – I to you, you to me. You try to do things to please me and I will try to do things to please you.

If this was done in a mutually satisfactory way, then the dividends would be high. Each would reap security directly through his individual identity and separate reputation, and indirectly through his joint identity, his reputation as a member of a solidly founded partnership. Their security would then be gilt-edged. However, it did not work out like this.

As a partnership, they had a joint reputation to preserve. This reputation depended on the appearance of permanency of the

[1] See Sartre, J.-P., *Critique de la Raison Dialectique*, for a discussion on the *pledge* as a group praxis.

partnership. And the appearance of permanency depended on their appearing to function smoothly and harmoniously like any other successful firm. Once more, for public opinion, success was the appearance of success. Unfortunately, their joint reputation was threatened from the start. To appear permanently and, therefore, successfully established, they were required to appear publicly to love one another. But it was difficult to achieve this appearance, for not only had they excluded love from their relationship before marriage, but by virtue of their pledge they had made such direct reciprocity impossible after it. For the pledge, in introducing a mediating inertia between them as partners, the partnership-for-'the-others', had separated them as persons.

To give the required appearance they would have to pretend; but this, too, was difficult, for they began to quarrel bitterly, right at the start. Mr Danzig, aware of the danger to their reputation, did his best. By virtue of his role as senior partner and head of the house, it fell to him to guard their joint reputation by ensuring their quarrels did not erupt publicly. He tried to smooth things between them. It was a complicated task.

FATHER: At that time I didn't think much of it because she was inclined to be a bit – temper – she would go off the deep end, but would cool down, but I thought – I had the first clue to her temper when I went to a wedding. We had to go to a wedding and I was held up at the office. In those years, nineteen-thirty-three, 'thirty-four, 'thirty-five, weddings you know, dinner started nine p.m. and went on till two in the morning. I got home late from the office. I went into the bathroom to shave to get ready for the wedding. And when we got to the wedding they hadn't started dinner. So my wife was very upset because she was ready to go and she lost her temper and talked a lot of rubbish and I was shaving and I cut myself in shaving, at that time. That was when I had the first display of temper. But I kept cool and calm and smiling. I said, 'Don't be silly, there's plenty of time. You must look nice at the wedding, otherwise you look – you'll be upset, you'll have an argument. Let people think we love each other. Come to the wedding.' I used to make nothing of it – make light of it. I realized *then*.

He was constantly worried their pretence would fail.

CHAPTER 3

The family

With the birth of children the Danzigs became a family, and the simple partnership had the possibility of some day becoming a company with a board of directors. The Danzigs were a family, because they were now a group in the eyes of 'the others' which the others called 'family'.

Since the life of respectable people revolved round the family, the Danzigs' life, too, had so to revolve. More than ever they had to remain married. As a family for-'the-others' the scandal following separation would be greater than ever. They had to affirm their partnership as the basis of the permanence of the family. Structurally speaking, they constituted a pledged group which they were bound to maintain as a unitary entity in the face of the constant threat to their reputations of their ever-present possibility of opting out.

They dealt with this possibility by each once more interiorizing the-group-for-'the-others'. This ensured their identities, and their relationship now revolved round 'the family'.

But through introducing this inert structure to mediate their relationship, they made direct reciprocity less possible than ever. They continued to quarrel as they had always done. The threat to their reputation from the appearance of disunity remained.

Since the birth of the family was a function of the birth of children, the children were expected to play their part in maintaining the group. In their parents' view this was no more than just. As the Danzigs said, children also had a duty. Why should they not be made to please their parents?

And so, as their parents' property or as capital to be invested, the children were initiated into a pattern of reciprocal rights and obligations aimed at maintaining the group. Their future was mortgaged for them before they had any chance to understand what was happening. They were initiated into the ideology of family respectability and conformity. They were pledged before 'public opinion' to experience and act in a way that maintained the group as solid and respectable, ensuring an adequate return in security of reputation for their investors and owners, the founders and directors of the group.

And this pledge, which had been made on their behalf, they were expected to reaffirm willingly when they came of age. This affirmation was called 'family loyalty' and 'consideration for others in the family'.

Since respectability implied filial respect, they were required by virtue of the pledge to live and experience the standards their parents had inculcated in them, standards that helped maintain their parents' reputation as successful parents, the loyal offspring of their own successful parents. To experience differently, or to choose another way of life, was a radical threat to the parents' self-respect.

And so, the parents sought to cooperate in training their children in the paternalist ideology of filial respect and respectability. They sought to cooperate with one another, even when they disagreed with the content of the lesson the other taught. For the content was less important than the fact of obedience. Filial respect required the pupil to learn the lesson of learning the lesson. The more meaningless the lesson, the more complete the compliance necessary to learn it. And the more complete the compliance, the more certainly the parent felt himself (or herself) perceived as an effective manager or leader in control.

MOTHER: This religious complex with John, honestly it drives me mad. I didn't want to say it in front of Mr Danzig. He drives the boy mad and drives everybody else mad. He wants John to say early morning prayers. Mr Danzig does this. Well, if he wants to do it, I never say 'no'. If he wants to pray every morning, all right. But – um – John doesn't like to do it and he does it under pressure.

And:

MOTHER: But still, praying doesn't make one bad, praying doesn't make one good. It's what you do yourself, but Mr Danzig says, 'No,' he says, 'let him grow up. Let me teach him what to do.' He said, 'When he gets married and has a home of his own then I can't control him, but,' he says, 'while he's here – it's a little thing to please me. Let him do it.' Well I agree with Mr Danzig.

Until the children came of age they were not part of the management. The family was thus not necessarily the same for the children as for the parents. For the parents it was a pledged group, while for the children, at least until they came of age, it was simply a nexus. For the parents, the fear that occasioned the pledge in the first instance was a fear in respect of an object felt to be external to the group. While for the children, their cooperation in the pattern of reciprocal rights and obligations was occasioned by the fear of the violence exercised upon them from within the group by its directors. The parents feared the scandal of seriality, the dissolution of the group into a series of separate units. While the children, until they came of age, feared exclusion, or 'excommunication' as John called it.

Now the parents' fear of the dissolution of the group into separate units was based on their perceiving themselves publicly perceived as having come of age. As formally adult, they could no longer rely on any other being constantly present to allow them to be the persons they were now publicly required to appear to be. As adults, they were expected to appear independent, and they depended on each other for this appearance. For the persons they were now required to appear to be were persons who had come of age, and marriage was a necessary part of this appearance. Marriage was less the expression of maturity than the public show necessary for their reputation. As the obedient children they felt they were publicly required to appear to be, they, for the sake of their parents' reputation and their own, had to appear grown-up and independent. In maintaining their marriage they helped each other maintain appearances, and so maintain their reputation, their parents' reputation, and the security of all.

Their view of marriage as the public show of adulthood, rather than its visible expression, could be seen in their attitude to their own children's marrying. For instance, both parents thought it only right that John should comply in detail with his father's requirements until he was married. His mother, as we shall see, was prepared to tolerate some furtive evasion by him, but that was another story. While he lived under his parents' roof, no matter how old he was, he could not expect to be regarded as fully adult, nor expect to be openly backed in his evasions. And he, for his part, accepted this state of affairs as valid. In his own view, he had not yet fully come of age.

Now, the sign that the children were coming of age was the presence to the children of the fear present to the parents, the fear of dissolution of the group through opting out. This fear could not occur before the children, in order to maintain their feeling of being, had internalized the family as a group-for-'the-others'. Not until their identity was largely a reputation, and their reputation a family identity, could they 'realize' their reputation depended on maintaining that of their parents. And since their parents desired a reputation as successful parents of respectful, loving children, the children, to demonstrate their love and respect, were required to remain with the family. The only way they could leave the group and still preserve their parents' reputation was through a respectable marriage.

Such a marriage was at some stage obligatory as the public sign their parents had successfully produced independent, respectable adults. But it could not occur before the parents were ready. To marry prematurely – prematurely from the parents' point of view – or to marry non-respectably, would be a major blow to the parents' reputation, resulting in retaliatory expulsion of the offender from the group.

FATHER: Even a stranger – I have customers with daughters asking my opinion about their daughters. I've occasionally been invited to their home to help them to decide on a young man – about their own daughter, but my own daughter – am I unreasonable to expect a certain amount of confidence? If they have no confidence in their own father, then –

JOHN: But the point is, Dad, I've never yet come home to you and said, 'I'm getting married tomorrow'. I've never met the girl.

FATHER [laughs]: It's not a question of getting married. It's not the point.

JOHN: When you get serious – when it gets serious –

FATHER: When it gets serious, it'll be too late.

And:

MOTHER: No. If I was very Orthodox, if I was very Orthodox, and they didn't want to follow, I'd think, 'Well, they're old enough to choose their own way of life'. I would certainly be very upset if John wanted to marry a non-Jewish girl. That's something altogether different. Then I should be terribly upset. I'd never let him come into the house again, but that's apart from anything else. That's got nothing to do with religion, you see.

Consequently the Danzigs, while insisting they were tolerant in the matter of their children's friends, saw it as their right to vet their friends closely, even when by empirical standards their children were adult.

Now, though John was not regarded as old enough to think of marriage, he was showing signs of coming of age. He had begun to accept the validity of his father's right to expect him to conform to his beliefs and expectations. Speaking of existential issues in economic terms, he said though he resisted many of his father's injunctions, he believed his father's expectations of him were just. After all, his father was responsible for maintaining the family in being. For John, the family as a group to be maintained was becoming real. He was becoming aware of the danger of serial dissolution, and helpless exposure to gossip by 'them'. He thus felt impelled to preserve the group by demonstrating to his parents and to 'the others', his solidarity with it.

JOHN: Well, I think it's a natural habit, because maybe we're so conscious of differing among ourselves in private, that for the public we put on a united front.

He was becoming aware of how much his father's reputation depended upon his, and vice versa.

JOHN: Never mind how naughty I might feel I am to Dad, and however a disreputable son I appear to him. To his friends, I'm the epitome of a good son and vice versa. Whatever feeling I have about Dad, if I think he's wrong or right when company comes, when my friends come, I show the utmost respect for all his wishes. Because why should I shame him or why should I flout his authority in front of friends?

It was as a boy-for-'the-others', who wanted to be seen as a good boy, that he sought to preserve the reputation of his parents as the competent managers of the group. This even involved presenting himself as bad to preserve his parents' reputation as good.

JOHN: Well I don't think Dad is a bad father [slight laugh]. I think he's got bad children [slight laugh]. I haven't been a good boy.

Consequently John was regarded by his parents with some approval. Despite initial difficulties he was, in their view, now maturing satisfactorily. As his father said:

FATHER: I fought like blazes to get my son on the right road. By my attitude towards him – I wasn't strong enough – bullying him and going for him, hammered it into him. Otherwise he would not have done his O-levels now, late in the day, but he's done it. He's done seven O-levels between June of last year and January of this year and one Advanced-level and I arranged for him to go into a very big firm in the City with a very good salary. By reason of his experience with me, by being with me and around me, he's been able to pick up. He's not a fool, he's quite intelligent. He was able to – er – gain know-how and he makes a good impression. He's quiet. He's very wise. He's grown twenty-one, he's older than twenty-one in my mind. He's matured. I'm pleased with him and I've got – I thought – I've got ideas. I still want to make him, within reason, a more perfect young man and I try to guide him along certain standards. Maybe I'm – perhaps I'm expecting too much for my children. Sarah – I hoped she might –

John was now beginning to embody and guard the family ideology, and the principle of the appearance of family harmony. He was on the way to qualifying as a responsible member, entitled to criticize ideological backsliders like Sarah.

John's initial difficulties, which had worried his parents, had been to do with thinking about himself. This difficulty he was now growing out of. Thinking about oneself was for the Danzigs an indication of immaturity. Coming of age meant giving it up. It meant no longer being concerned with one's relationship to oneself and to others, nor with reflecting upon one's life and how to live it. It meant instead becoming 'objective about oneself', which was equated with being 'normal' or even with being 'natural'. As John, who was now successfully making the change, said:

JOHN: I'm really looking at myself objectively. But if I start to talk about myself *subjectively*, then I'd definitely feel that this was presuming. You made a point of asking me about myself and I'm here to tell you about myself, therefore I don't really feel embarrassed – I feel a bit – it's not normal. It's not quite natural for somebody to just talk about himself constantly. But you've asked me, so I'm telling you. So I don't think it's presumptuous. If you don't ask me and I started going on about myself, this introverted nature, I should think I would be presuming.

And:

JOHN: I think I have no right to be burdening my little petty problems on another person. Because I know – I know from experience – this is the way I looked at it when I was seventeen and I still do – I know from experience that I'm more interested in myself than most people are, and therefore why should I burden this other person who's more interested in *himself*, with me – with *my* problems I mean.

And:

JOHN: I think it's just the normal process of growing up. I mean, I don't think I'm different from many other boys. I'm sure they all went through this sort of phase. Maybe a little less intensive – some more intensive – but when you start meeting older people and you start maturing, you must grow out of these things.

Coming of age required the children to give up trying to be themselves. Such a project was regarded as completely invalid. Such self-being, if revealed, could expect to receive no confirmation from the managing directors.

INTERVIEWER: I see. What about your parents – have you – would you regard it as presumptuous to tell them [about himself]?

JOHN: Not presumptuous. I would regard it as a waste of time. They have no understanding of that sort of thing at all. I'd *never* – I'd *never* come to my parents with that sort of problem.

They were required to be 'objective', objects in the world of the other. Their being was to be a being-for-the-other, their identity entirely altered, specifically an altered group identity in which their feeling of being was dependent upon the reputation of the group with 'the others'.

This metamorphosis to 'objectivity' required them to interiorize the interiorization of the group as an object for-'the-others'-outside-the-group. If they did this, they would no longer be concerned with themselves. For who they were, their identity, would be restructured round the internalized internalization. They would be pure organization men, constituted by the group they were constituting, and constituting the group they were constituted by.

This was the Danzigs' ideal for their children. The family was to be brought to birth *in* the children. The children, respectably aborted in the image of their parents, as 'responsible', 'practical', 'considerate of others', 'socialized and adult', constituted the pabulum that assured the continued existence of the family, in much the same way as their parents in their day had constituted a pabulum to sustain their families of origin.

But, unfortunately for the Danzigs, their last condition was worse than their first. Each new interiorization of their collective being as object in the eyes of 'the others', whether as partnership or as group, made direct reciprocity less and less possible. The interiorization of each group object-for-'the-others' required a restructuring of their identities round the object. With each re-structuring, they each become more and more a role and less and less a person. Constituted by that which they had themselves in the first instance constituted, each embodied the group object-for-'the-others'. And each depended for his reputation on the reputa-tion of the group. The group was now an aspect of themselves, while at the same time experienced as an object other than themselves. Since the reputation of the group depended on how it was seen to function by 'the others', to preserve its reputation they had to act properly for its sake. They had to act to sustain it. And since the family was now experienced as a present other-object by the children-coming-of-age, the children, now em-bodying the group the parents had inside them, expected their parents to serve it in the same way as the parents had expected the children to do. Each member of the family, as other to the familial others, felt called upon to do his duty by each of the others embodying the group. Each as other was overseer to each other.

Now, everywhere, including their home, the place of the family, the parents were expected by 'the family' to continually enact their proper roles. There was virtually no area of privacy for backsliding. Their creation had taken on a quasi-independent existence. Their Golem[1] had become a monster with a kind of life of its own. The family had become a pseudo-organism to which they were now obliged to relate in a pattern of reciprocal rights and obligations.

Through interiorizing the interiorization of the group-for-outside-others, the family as group praxis, as persons in relation, became process, an opaque object with laws and a being of its own. This family object they experienced as other than the praxis of the persons comprising it. Totalization in action was now inert totality, and this totality had to be served and preserved.

The servant in thus becoming master marked a change in the character of the Danzigs' relationship to the family. Public opinion had been an unpredictable tyrant which had ruled by fear, and their problem had been to placate it and forestall its critical attacks. But, though it had been a tyrant, it had allowed them freedom to resent and criticize it.

This was no longer possible under the new tyranny. The child who was to be their saviour was as unholy as the tyrant from which it was to save them, but its tyranny was a tyranny of love. No criticism of the family could even be felt. Before it all members were the same – empty roles serving it for the sake of preserving *its* unholy name. And these roles they had to play without let or relief. Even within the four walls of their house, their constant service was required. Appearances had to be preserved at all times. More than ever the parents pretended to their children, and the children pretended to their parents.

---

[1] A human-like creature made from clay to act as a servant in time of danger.

CHAPTER 4

Love without question, the positive end of experience

We have now totalized the basic group praxis and reconciled[1] with it the parents' constant bitter quarrelling which appeared at first incompatible with the group's continued existence. And, in and through making this reconciliation, we are better able to understand why Sarah's behaviour was seen as both sick and scandalous.

The parents had organized round themselves a family world of familiar objects and received or serial roles. In this world everything was 'as it should be', and everyone behaved 'nicely' as they ought. Here a father acted like a father, a wife like a wife, and a daughter like a daughter. Each knew his proper place, and each did his proper stereotyped duty. Said Mrs Danzig:

MOTHER: It's the *duty* of a wife to look after her husband. Don't you think so? That's what I think. Well I *think* so. Perhaps I'm old-fashioned, I know.

INTERVIEWER: I'm not disagreeing with you, Mrs Danzig.

MOTHER: You get married – you're old enough to get married – then you must assume the same responsibility – a husband doing what – what *she* should do – and the husband doing what he should do.[2]

Everything in their world was ordered and predictable. And they tried to relate to this world of objects and persons playing roles,

---

[1] See Part II for a discusion on dialectical reconciliation.
[2] The sexual confusion implied by this statement will be discussed later.

in a way that maintained the proper order. For on maintaining this proper order depended their reputation as competent managers and respected parents.

But Sarah's behaviour threatened their system, for she failed to fulfil her filial role.

JOHN: It had been going on for months but this was building up to a really big climax, and this was it.
INTERVIEWER: Over a period of months?
JOHN: Mm.
MOTHER: She wasn't like that the whole time, we couldn't have stood it.
JOHN: No, but –
MOTHER: It was little things. Do you know what I mean? Her attitude, you could sort of see. It wasn't a sort of father and daughterly attitude.

In this role she was required to appear as a maturing child who had affirmed the family pledge. She was to be seen to be maintaining her parents' family reputation. And this she was to do by showing they had successfully trained her to be independent. Her parents' mystifying praxis of ordering her to be autonomous, and enjoining her to comply without appearing compliant, was simply the reflection of this familial requirement.

FATHER: I want her – I'm not expecting too much, doctor – from my, from Sarah.
MOTHER [voice raised]: A lot is up to her. She's got to help herself get well.
FATHER: *I want her to be independent* in every way.
MOTHER: But she's got to help herself as well.

And:

FATHER: Well I don't want you to do it, Sarah, because we feel so strong. Don't make a condition of it. You must in your own mind make up your mind whether, er – you should get up early or not.

MOTHER: You must feel it's right, your own self Sarah – not because we tell you to, but –

SARAH: Well yes, it'll be all right to get up.

MOTHER: You think we're right to –? [Father starts to speak]. Just a moment. No, let me get her opinion.

SARAH: Yes, I think so.

FATHER: That's submissive. I don't want a submissive attitude.

Since, despite all admonitions, Sarah persisted in not acting in the way her parents required of her, the Danzigs were in a dilemma. She was acting badly, but to protect their reputation as successful, i.e. loved and competent, they dared not see her as bad.

FATHER: Yes, I don't think you can say bad children. I don't think any child is really very bad, unless they go off altogether. No child is bad and no parents are bad, really bad.

Instead they saw her as not responsible. She was unfilial, but this was an illness.

However their last position was no better than their first. Since they were alienated from the 'public opinion' they were, they could not alter its evaluation of her behaviour. They could only alter their own. And this required them to change their view of 'public opinion'. In altering their evaluation of Sarah, they had to dissociate themselves from 'the others', who were experienced as ignorant and unjust for continuing to see Sarah as scandalous.

Thus, labelling her ill did not save them from anxiety over their reputation. It was still felt to be threatened by 'them', but now unjustly.

Their defence against this object of unrecognized phantasy was to call in the doctor. In confirming their view, he implicitly confirmed them in their reputation as successful parents.

But the more she was treated as sick, the more unfilially Sarah behaved. Either she protested against their perception of her, or she passively and dependently complied. And the more unfilially she behaved, the more they required clinical collusion.

We have now returned to the starting-point of our inquiry. It is not open to everyone to act on their experience and, without sense of contradiction, see another person's praxis as process. What was the pattern of their consciousness that this was possible?

I pointed out earlier that the Danzigs' persisting confusion between praxis and process was not the only unrecognized contradiction in their experience of Sarah. They could not see, for instance, the contradiction involved in ordering her to be independent, even when it was pointed out to them.

FATHER: Independent to herself, to earn her own living, make her own way in the world, with a little help when necessary, whenever she wants it, if we're here.

INTERVIEWER: But you're insisting all the time on her doing what you want her to do.

MOTHER: No, she told – she – that was her own choice to go to school.

FATHER: I haven't said she should go to school.

MOTHER [voice raised]: We left it entirely to her.

Contradiction as such was an experience they could not grasp. Contradiction can only be recognized dialectically, and the Danzigs appeared to have lost completely any capacity for dialectical examination they may once have had.

Such examination requires the investigator to examine his own behaviour and experience of self and other, in a way that allows him to become aware of valid ideas and possibilities that contradict his current notions and mode of being. He then negates his present position, transcending it to form a new totalization that reconciles and preserves the contradictions in a wider experiential synthesis, which becomes the basis of a new mode of being-in-the-world.

Such praxis was for the Danzigs literally unthinkable. Through acting on themselves, the pattern of their consciousnesses was such that they simply could not reflectively experience negation.

Dialectically speaking, negation involves the experience of non-being, the anxiety of the dissolution of what is, prior to a possible new synthesis. And it was precisely the negation of the possibility of experiencing such dissolution which comprised the central project of their lives. The Danzigs, as negations of negation, were only concerned with feeling secure. No experience of conflict was legitimate, no experience of the presence of contradictions, of the simultaneous existence of opposites.

Their consciousnesses were thus almost entirely positivist, and they had achieved this by denying, splitting, projecting, introjecting, re-projecting, and controlling the embodiment of those projected aspects of themselves which caused them discomfort.

In depriving themselves of the experience of conflict, they had deprived themselves of the occasion for negation and reflective self-examination. And without negation and reflective self-examination there was no possibility of experiencing contradiction as such. And without reflectively knowing the contradictions in their experience they could not arrive at being truly themselves. In discarding the dirty water they had cast out the Divine Child. Existentially stunted, they depended for their feeling of being, on being the other the other required them to be.

And since they had no reflective knowledge of themselves, they had no point of view which could be called their own. They lived instead in a world of preconceptions, of received truths or serial ideas, which they adopted not because they had reasoned them, however imperfectly, to be more true than other ideas, but because by adopting them they would produce the right impression in the eyes of the other who mediated the ideas in the name of 'the others'.

These serial truths comprised value judgements such as right and wrong, good and bad, sickness and health, and also perceptions, or rather misperceptions, which were made to fit and validate their preconceptions. For instance, Mrs Danzig lectured Sarah on the impropriety of wearing black stockings during the winter, asserting they were worn by no one except scruffy beatniks. When pressed, she admitted having seen sophisticated women dressed in this way, but even when she admitted it she seemed to have difficulty believing her perceptions. While Mr Danzig, who disapproved of Sarah smoking altogether, lectured her for doing so on an empty stomach because it was dangerous, a preconception as compulsive, unquestioned, and incorrigible as his misperception of her as smoking in this way when she in fact did not.

FATHER: There's only one thing – only one point that I get annoyed with her – a very small point. It's in her own interest. I say, 'Don't smoke on an empty stomach.' She comes down from bed. Before she starts to eat – cigarettes. And smoking on an empty stomach I don't think is any good for you. Am I right, or am I wrong there?

INTERVIEWER: There's no evidence that it does any particular harm.

FATHER: All right, Doctor, I'll take your advice. Right, I'll stop criticizing.

MOTHER: She always starts off with a cup of tea, though.

FATHER: Smoking on an empty stomach – a dry throat – doesn't that affect your inside?

INTERVIEWER: As I say, there's no –

FATHER: No evidence – right –

But he still kept on at her.

Serial truths, once internalized and integrated into their alterated identities, were experienced by the Danzigs as part of their essence. The truths were thus applied in a stereotyped manner without discrimination, and were maintained rigidly and imperviously even in the presence of evidence to the contrary. For instance, a parent not only should not hate a child, but simply could not. And conversely, a child could not hate a parent. If their behaviour gave the impression of hatred, it was merely an impression. And so Sarah, whose experience contradicted this view of the relationship between child and parent, was expected by her parents to modify her perceptions to fit with theirs.

Because they never questioned their ideas, the Danzigs could house the most contradictory notions, including the notion of questioning their notions – 'being tolerant'. Any difficulty they met in applying their ideas was never referred to the ideas or perceptions. For, with the radical failure of their dialectical consciousnesses, they had no idea of the idea of contradiction, no experience of inwardness and none of self-doubt.

Consequently, there could be no occasion for examining themselves, or what they experienced and believed. The problem was instead always externalized, and referred to the event that did not fit the preconception or misperception. Thus failure by Sarah to fit their preconceptions, or adopt their misperceptions, was experienced by them as a fault in her.

No amount of difficulty in applying the idea would bring them to examine it. The idea or perception was simply felt to be right, and this feeling was its validation.

This feeling was a feeling of being, and being a feeling of being they did not feel responsible for the idea. It was simply the way things were. For instance:

FATHER: I want to try to remove something in your mind, which you may perhaps have formed – thinking that, er – by reason of our attitude towards her we expect her to conform to *our* standards of living. We want her – to *try* to impress on her to conform to the standards of living of young ladies.

The opacity of the idea, the certainty with which it was held, and the unthinkableness of changing it, were for them the criteria of its truth. To question it was like questioning the world, the natural order of things. To do so was unintelligible, abnormal, even unnatural.

And in a sense it was questioning the world. In the sense that questioning the idea meant questioning the world of their own being, their alterated identities, which was all they were.

Since they assumed without question there was no justification for feeling in any way insecure, they never questioned any serial idea, experience or praxis, including the system called 'the family'. Consequently, their world was congealed into an unchanging pattern of relationships. A pattern in which they rigidly maintained their preconceptions about the identity of themselves and others.

With no point of view of their own, no experience of themselves or the world that was not mediated by 'the others', they appeared to have no possibility of questioning received ideas. For they seemed to have no experience with which these ideas could be compared, and no possibility of such experience.

The trap was closed. Divine Reason, the handmaiden of experience, was completely dethroned. And the Danzigs, radically alienated, lived in a world under the unmitigated tyranny of 'the others'.

It is now clearer why the Danzigs invalidated any attempt by their children to question their own experience. Reflective self-examination was incompatible with the serial behaviour and role-playing that ensured the parents' ontic security. Such serial behaviour, which required the children to fit predictably into the familial pattern, was an application of the formula of regular work and routine living. While the dialectical project upon which Sarah was engaged when she was thinking required her to devote time to internal work, which had its own rhythm.

This project could only be understood dialectically. To her parents, without such understanding, her behaviour was unintelligible. With no point of view of their own, they were incapable of seeing her point of view, which was that she was trying to develop a point of view. And they were incapable of suspending judgement, because they had no judgement to suspend.

Since she did not fit their familial preconceptions, they could only experience her as someone who was not proper. This someone they called 'selfish', 'childish', 'brooding', and in the last resort, to protect their familial reputation, 'sick'.

Now, since the Danzigs totally misunderstood what Sarah was about, and were ignorant of their ignorance, we may infer the improper someone of their experience was a someone based largely on an experience in phantasy unrecognized as such.

This inference is congruent with what we already know of their perception of Sarah as sick. For, in so far as this perception of her was an empirically unverified assumption, and the clinical diagnosis simply confirmed this prior assumption, we may infer that the 'sick' Sarah, too, was an object of unrecognized phantasy.

With these inferences we have arrived back at another of our original questions: the nature of the Sarah whose praxis they confused with process. The clarification of this experience is crucial to the next stage of our study, which is its main phase, the attempt to make intelligible in detail the mystifying praxis the Danzigs misperceived.

CHAPTER 5

The central shared experience

It will be recalled that the Danzigs saw their sick daughter as the only problem in the family. She was the common object[1] by which they explained their, to us, problematic praxis.

Since Sarah was not sick, but an object of shared unrecognized phantasy, we may infer that this phantasy Sarah was the central shared experience of the family. If this inference is true, then elucidating this phantasy Sarah should enable us to render more intelligible the contradictions in their praxis in relation to the person Sarah.

Sarah was seen by her parents as selfish, self-indulgent, lazy, and irresponsible. They also saw her as ill and not responsible for being lazy and irresponsible. She was thus responsible and not responsible for being not responsible.

FATHER: I – it's not – the – er – responsibility.
INTERVIEWER: Responsibility? Irresponsibility?
FATHER: Irresponsibility – irresponsible attitude.
INTERVIEWER: Toward?
FATHER [angrily]: Towards herself and her life.

And:

MOTHER: I think it's a form of an illness. Perhaps it is an illness, this not being able to get up and not wanting to get up.
INTERVIEWER: Your attitude is so contradictory here because –
MOTHER: Yes, well, if it is an illness, I must view it differently then.

[1] See Chapter 7 for definition and discussion of the concept of the common object of shared experience.

Followed a few minutes later by:

SARAH: Well I think they are – their feelings are very strong on it, you know.

MOTHER: On what Sarah?

SARAH: On getting up.

MOTHER: Do you think I'm wrong or right? Well, let's be candid.

SARAH: Well, on the whole I think you're right.

MOTHER: Well that's all right, if you agree. That's something. We're getting somewhere now. So if you agree – so why don't you try to get up for your own sake? [Father starts to speak, but Mother comes in loudly.] She must try. She tries perhaps to get up, but then she thinks 'Well, the bed's warmer' – then putting her bare feet out for the moment – till she puts her feet down in her slippers.

But they also felt they would be held responsible for her being not responsible. They denied they were responsible. They had done their best. Sarah was responsible.

Examining these contradictions phenomenologically, we must ask ourselves the following questions: In general what object or entity is of such a nature that an observer may well have difficulty in deciding whether its movements or changes are due to process or expressions of praxis? Does the object intend these movements or changes, or are they out of its control? Secondly, if it cannot control the movements or changes, is the object responsible for the lack of control? Thirdly, what kind of entity may it be that another person may be held responsible for its lack of self- control?

The entity that best meets these requirements is an infant, and the general behaviour of Mr and Mrs Danzig towards Sarah is congruent with this inference. For instance, they invariably discussed matters in her presence, including the question of Sarah herself, in a way that excluded her. It was generally the interviewer who brought her into any discussions. When her parents did address her spontaneously they usually did so only to invite her to confirm their point of view. They seemed to assume without question that she had little to say that was valid. Indeed their manner at times implied that she was unable to communicate verbally at all.

This implicit assumption effectively precluded them from inviting her help in distinguishing praxis from process. Or rather, it would have precluded them if they had realized this was an issue; but they did not. They assumed, explicitly at least, that the issue was process gone wrong. They also assumed that they knew better than she what she experienced, even when it was a case of experiencing herself. Any attempts by her to correct them were either ignored or brushed aside or invalidated in some other way. This can be seen in the following exchange:

MOTHER: There is – I'll be quite candid – there is, I shan't deny it. It puts *her* out of gear. You get up late, the day's gone already. Ruth's already home for tea – we're all having tea.

FATHER [interjects]: And then she's up late again.

MOTHER [continuing]: And then again it makes it bad for her at night, to get up so terribly late. If you get up early in the morning, by eleven o'clock you're tired, 'Oh, I shall be glad to get into bed,' you know – have a good night's rest. What happens? She'll be up, doing nothing, sitting, thinking, brooding.

SARAH: But I don't. I always find it quite easy to sleep.

MOTHER: Well, whenever John comes in late – honestly he always goes into Sarah and says, 'Turn out your light Sarah, go to bed' – never shouts. He always says it quietly. 'Come on Sarah, turn the light off, go to bed.' Sometimes he even puts it out for you, doesn't he? Well, that's not wrong on his part, is it?

They thus appeared to be experiencing Sarah as an infant with whom they were unconsciously projectively identified. Or rather, each appeared to be relating in phantasy, without realizing it, to an infant entity they had unconsciously confused with their daughter.

What was this phantasy infant entity? Whatever it was, it must have been of a nature to allow the Danzigs to confuse praxis with process when they experienced its actions and movements. An examination of what her family said about her 'illness' should clarify the issue.

They had many things to say, but the common theme was she had things inside her which she did not let them know about. These things were uncomfortable rubbish. Over a period, when she 'did nothing', these things accumulated and reached a point where they had burst out in an unexpected, uncontrollable destructive flood. The following examples illustrate this theme.[1]

Doing nothing

MOTHER: Well I wouldn't make an issue of it but I think it's the normal thing, that everybody knows that at least fifteen or sixteen or whatever age you leave – either you go to study for a doctor or a lawyer or a barrister – but you study for something. If you don't want to study, then you put your hands to it. You either do shorthand-typing or a saleslady and if you've got initiative you can become a buyer; or if you're in millinery – I know plenty of girls, they've worked their way up, assistant buyer, then buyer – to me that's an interesting life, it's something. But stay at home and sleep all day!

And:

MOTHER: And I still say that when a girl leaves school she must go to work – no matter what you do. Whether you serve in a shop you can still be ambitious. From a small shop you can go to a West End store. If they think you're bright they can make you a buyer. There's always something you can aspire to, don't you agree with me? You go to work in an office, they think you're bright, they can also give you a better position or else you try and better yourself. Or if you don't want to do that, do dress-making, it's artistic, do millinery, sketches, also artistic, useful. People like clothes to wear, people like pretty hats. There's something in it, you create something. If you

[1] And see quotation p. 64.

create a dress or – or interior decorating – there's all kinds of things you can put your hand to if you want to. But to sit at home and do nothing –

And:

MOTHER: I put it down to not going to work, I still –
JOHN: Mind you –
MOTHER: I don't know, I say rich girl, poor girl, it doesn't matter what station in life you are, if you do something all day – if you don't want to earn money then do some form of – good work then, social work – do something.

Thinking and doing nothing

MOTHER: And then again it makes it bad for her at night, to get up so terribly late. If you get up early in the morning, by eleven o'clock you're tired. 'Oh, I shall be glad to get into bed,' you know – have a good night's rest. What happens? She'll be up, doing nothing, sitting, thinking, brooding.[1]

Thinking and keeping it to herself

MOTHER: She wouldn't get up – laying in bed from seven in the morning till nine at night. It's an unnatural thing, isn't it? And sitting up all night in a blue nightdress in the kitchen – just the lights on, nobody making a sound. She's thinking and thinking – goodness knows what the heck she's thinking about. It's enough to twist anybody's mind.

And:

MOTHER: She just used to think and think – 'Sarah, are you with me or are you still in the clouds?'
JOHN: Oh no, when she was thinking, in one of her bouts of serious thinking about herself, you couldn't talk to her, she didn't know you were there.

[1] Quoted earlier in context on p. 57. See also pp. 69-71.

MOTHER: And you'd say, 'Come on Sarah, aren't you coming out?' She says, 'What? What? Tell me again, Mummy.' Thinking – withdrawn into herself – not out aloud, but inwardly.

Doing nothing and accumulation

MOTHER: Well she couldn't concentrate [on doing something]. But she did go the first term.
JOHN AND MOTHER [simultaneously]: Yes and –
MOTHER: Yes, because she wasn't very well. It's an accumulation, and the accumulation gets worse and worse and worse.

Thinking, doing nothing, accumulation, and loss of control

JOHN: She's ultra-sensitive, ultra-intelligent so – so therefore she gets – she can see herself in different lights – so she thinks and then she gets – she's very self-conscious, she thinks about herself too much. Then on top of that she starts – um – she's got no occupation so she's got nothing to do during the day and then she starts leading an abnormal life, she stays up all night and all this has a sort of cumulative effect until finally something snaps.

Thinking and rubbish (unintelligible things)

MOTHER: She used to torment herself staying up all night thinking – what? Rubbish – a lot of nonsense, and then sleeping a few hours during the day.

Thinking unintelligible things and destructive uncontrolled flooding

INTERVIEWER: You were saying before, Mrs Danzig, about nervous illness, that you never thought it would happen in your family, it was always somebody else.
MOTHER: Well I did sort of think all this business of going, you know, thinking unusual things, saying people are not – to

me these sort of things – they always happen to other people, they never happen to us. You know the sort of thing, you think it always happens to other people – you know these people flooded out in Exeter, you know, I feel sorry, but you do sort of think 'Oh I'll never be flooded out where I'm living now' – you see? I'm only giving you an example. It's never occurred to me that I'll ever get flooded out where I live now – that's how I look at it.

Interpreting, we may say that 'Sarah', the unfilial phantasy object, was an infant gut that had retained its contents. These had accumulated until a point was reached when they burst out incontinently. Since they experienced her laziness to be self-indulgence,[1] we may also infer that in phantasy they experienced her retaining her faeces for the sake of the pleasure this gave her. The truth of this inference is strengthened when we consider other aspects of the parents' behaviour towards Sarah. They complained that Sarah would not eat properly, and persisted in pressing food on her as if she were an infant, regarding her angry protests with exasperated bewilderment.

MOTHER: You didn't eat properly. You said, 'I don't care about food. Who wants food?' I used to try to give her Nescafé, Nescafé made with all milk. Any of these sort of milk foods, vegetables and that – chicken or meat – 'Oh, I don't want these.' An especially nice tea – 'Oh who wants food?' she says. 'All you care about is food.'

They had pressed this food on her while she was still living at home, even before the doctor was called in. Its clearly invalid-infant nature indicates that her parents implicitly experienced her problem as an infant-gut problem.

Similarly, their behaviour over her lying in bed points to an infant-gut phantasy. Though Mrs Danzig complained bitterly of the inconvenience, she insisted on running upstairs to Sarah's bedroom to urge her to come down for her meals. And with her

---

[1] Laziness and self-indulgence always implied one another in the family idiolect.

husband's agreement, she continued to cook for her whenever Sarah chose to come down.

Further evidence is to be found in their statements about Sarah's outbursts of anger at members of her family. These outbursts were regarded as an aspect of her 'illness'. They appeared implicitly to experience the outbursts as a phantasy loss of control of excreta.

FATHER: If a person loses control he loses everything.

And:

FATHER: If a girl wants to be rude and crude to her mother and father – control herself – if you haven't any sense of control then she's lost a lot.

Another feature of her 'illness', they said, was her failure to be economically independent. They believed this failure was due to lack of self-control and self-discipline. They said, too, that a child is made economically independent through being disciplined by its parents to comply with their demands. If the disciplining is successful, the child becomes self-controlled and, despite inconvenience to itself, gives the parents a return that gives them pleasure.

FATHER: It's not imposing the will because I want at a certain time the child to do certain things because I want to – but what I think. They're not serious demands. They're not serious impositions, if you call it that way. They're not serious requests. There's nothing unreasonable in asking a child to do certain small things to give pleasure.

And:

FATHER: I do – parents do their best to do something for their children. The little things play and give back a certain return. All right it's inconvenient. It might be inconvenient but – let's modernize it and call it inconvenient.

When asked to clarify the relationship between economic independence, compliance with parental demands, and giving a return, the Danzigs were perplexed. They had never questioned the relationship. It was self-evidently logical and true. They compared the matter to receiving interest on money invested, but they were still unable to explain how their receiving interest related to Sarah becoming economically independent.

The logic that makes their reasoning intelligible is a logic of unrecognized phantasy experience. And once more, the inference that allows us to totalize most simply the elements of their reasoning is one relating their experience to bowel control. Namely, that they unwittingly experienced Sarah as a bowel that failed to excrete in a controlled fashion, and failed to do so in relation to another who expected it to so do in accordance with the training the other had given it.

Finally, the implication that the Danzigs' experience of Sarah as lazy concerned a bowel phantasy is clearly present in Mrs Danzig's associations in the following quotation. In their family and sub-cultural idiolect, 'bathroom' was synonymous with 'lavatory', 'toilet', 'water closet', 'powder room', 'cloakroom', and so on.

MOTHER: No I don't – no I still think she shouldn't laze in bed. I mean to say, there's a limit to sleeping! There's a limit. Besides, it's habit-forming – you lay once in bed, you lay twice in bed, you lay three times in bed, and then it gets habit-forming. And getting up is also habit-forming. I get up every morning at approximately half past seven. Why, I hear movements in the bedroom over there. I hear the bathroom, in and out you know, doors, the tap running, and so I feel it's my time to get up.

If we examine what they said about her 'selfishness',[1] we find a common theme of persistent failure to eat and work according to a regular time schedule in the context of a highly routine pattern of living.

MOTHER: The issue is the need to get a regular life – to get up

[1] Selfishness and laziness always implied each other.

early, reasonably early. Have your breakfast in time. Have your lunch when we're having it, not after we're having it, and have to reheat the whole thing over again. That's what I mean. And have teatime. That's at five o'clock, and say dinner at seven and then go out, if you want to go out – not every night, but when you have to go out, go out. We don't press her to go. She goes out of her own accord. We don't say, 'You must go out tonight,' do we?

SARAH: No, no.

MOTHER: If she wants to go out – she comes home, 'Mummy I want to go out.' I say, 'All right then, go.'

INTERVIEWER: So this business of regularity and routine is obviously something that you feel is –

MOTHER: Necessary in a home – if you want to keep the home up. One should get up at eight, one should get up at twelve, one should get up at four?

And:

MOTHER: I do get cross, I lose my temper. I mean one's only human. I mean she knows she has to go to school and she has to walk to the bus stop and has to have something to eat before she goes. I think it's only right, considering we've paid the fees for a month. And also, when she knows that she has to go. She should know that her responsibility towards herself – not towards me – but towards herself as an adult – she's got to face life and get up. It's not asking much of her. It's a normal thing. Everybody else does it. If everybody said, 'I don't want to go to work,' there'd be no hospitals, no shops – everything would be closed. We'd all be in bed. I mean look at it that way!

And:

MOTHER: Yes, we know she's still got her life ahead of her, but look at all the time that's been wasted; she could have been out and about, led a normal life and *done* something. No matter what it is you do – something! From nine till five.[1]

---

[1] And see, for example, the quotation on p. 95.

They failed to explain why failure to eat regularly and work routinely was illness. To them it was self-evidently so.

They also assumed as self-evident that the highly routine pattern of living should be regulated to fit the time-schedules of others – 'appointments'. Failure to fit the others' schedules was an essential feature of the 'laziness' and 'illness', as we have just seen in the above quotations. The point is further illustrated by the following:

FATHER: The principle of not letting down is very important as well.

MOTHER: I don't think – you must not – if you make an appointment, keep it. You feel you can't get there today – tomorrow – phone them up today, say 'I can't come tomorrow', they can make other arrangements. You must treat *other* people as you would be – as you yourself would like to be treated. I feel I wouldn't like to be let down if someone had an appointment with me. She also wouldn't like to feel that she was let down. Well? Don't you think that's a principle?

FATHER: The whole – the whole picture – the whole thing may alter if she gets married – responsibility might, er, might perhaps . . .

MOTHER: Yes, but a man won't live with a woman who won't get up to give him breakfast every day.

And:

MOTHER: There's a limit to sitting up at night – it's only the routine of getting up early – being normal like everybody. If everybody said, 'Oh, I won't go in today. I feel lazy.' You wouldn't be here, my husband wouldn't be at work. You go into the big stores, nine o'clock they're all by the counters, aren't they? These girls have to clock-in. If they'd all said they were going lay in bed, Bourne and Hollingsworth would be closed, Selfridges, everything would be at a standstill. Why? Because they want to lay in bed. . . . Even the Queen gets up early – when she's got to have an appointment. [Father says something in an amused tone and Mother replies in a similar tone.] Royalty start their lessons at nine-fifteen, the children . . .

And:

MOTHER: But you can't let people down, Sarah, they've also got a living to make.

SARAH: Well I was there on time.

MOTHER: Only by me getting you out – coming out.

INTERVIEWER: You're concerned with the fact that the hairdresser – had a living to make?

MOTHER: No, I wasn't concerned –

INTERVIEWER: No?

MOTHER: No, it wasn't that. What I was concerned was that if she makes an appointment, she should be sensible enough and grown-up enough to keep it. [Father starts to speak.] If you give your word that you're going to somebody –

They never seemed to feel that Sarah might *legitimately* expect others to modify their schedules, even slightly. Or that an appointment, for instance with the hairdresser, could reasonably be cancelled. And though they themselves compromised with her in this respect, they regarded such compromises as essentially illicit concessions.

Bearing in mind the unconscious phantasy meaning for them of laziness, as we have elucidated it, we may infer the logic that unifies the elements of their reasoning about appointments and time-keeping is also a logic of unrecognized phantasy, in which Sarah was implicitly experienced as an infant gut, which was implicitly required to ingest and excrete strictly to a time-schedule regulated according to the convenience of a food-giving other. This inference is congruent with our inference respecting their phantasy about Sarah's economic independence. There, too, we inferred, they implicitly expected her to excrete in relation to what was in effect a regulating other.

Now, Sarah's laziness was as much an expression of her parents' shared phantasy experience as the process from which she was supposed to be suffering. According to her parents, Sarah had for years been living an abnormal life. She had, they said, been lying in bed, sleeping all day instead of going to work. But by empirical standards they grossly exaggerated the problem. Sarah in fact slept less than they did, and they wanted her to sleep more.

MOTHER: Listen, when you don't lead a normal life of course you get tired and exhausted. It can happen to everybody, some of the strong people. 'Course it makes you tired and irritable if you don't get your proper rest. You might stay up one night, two nights, but you can't stay up every night in succession, it's bound to lead to some sort of nervous exhaustion in a person, especially you.

As for her failure to go regularly to work or to college, this dated only from the time she had been inaugurated into a career as a schizophrenic;[1] to be precise, a year after her first admission to hospital, six months before her second. When pressed, her parents did admit that Sarah had worked hard at college, and that though she had to be called a few times in the mornings she was no worse in this respect than John, about whom they were not complaining.

INTERVIEWER: Well, on the last two or three occasions that you've been here, Mrs Danzig, you have painted a picture of this happening or imminently about to happen.
MOTHER: No, no, I think you've got me wrong. What I said was I have *great* difficulty in waking her in the morning to go to school. As I told you, she's got to be there by one-thirty. I've already told you that, and it's best for her not to get up at the last minute and rush, rush. I have difficulty in waking her on the whole, getting her out of bed, but I wouldn't say she sleeps till five now.
INTERVIEWER: My clear recollection[2] of what you said is that if you didn't be at her, she would lie in bed all day.
MOTHER: I think she would probably sleep, think, 'Oh another ten minutes, another ten minutes,' and then go into a deep

[1] Goffman, E., *Asylums. Essays on the Social Situation of Mental Patients and Other Inmates.*
[2] Confirmed from tape-recordings of the sessions in question.

sleep – sleep – I don't mean lay awake sort of – but just sleep and sleep till late and I don't want that to happen again.

INTERVIEWER: And that's what you're afraid will happen.

MOTHER: Yes, but she does get up after a little bit of struggle with her to get up, but this week she's been better, she has got up.

INTERVIEWER: Have you been coaxing her this week?

MOTHER: Well I mean, I have to get her up, I have to go upstairs and tell her to get up and she does get up.

INTERVIEWER: The *difficulty* in getting up, or having to be called a few times to get up – that's common enough.

MOTHER: It is?

SARAH: Yes, it is. Jean Williams[1] used to sleep late.

INTERVIEWER: Don't you know that?

MOTHER [laughing]: I know I have to get up, I get up. I should also like to be in bed. No, I get up.

INTERVIEWER: Don't you know other people who have to be called a number of times before they get up?

MOTHER: Oh yes, yes. Some of my own family, you know – Reg – Auntie Ethel used to have to tell him twice, then he gets up. She has to tell him twice.

FATHER: How about your own son, John?

MOTHER [loudly]: But he does get up.

FATHER: Yes, but you have to call him three or four times.

However, their perception that their anxiety was exaggerated was fleeting. A few minutes later they were again complaining anxiously of her laziness and the danger of her spending the rest of her life in bed.

MOTHER: You mustn't be afraid of life. You've got to face up to it.

It appears that on the issue of working and rising there was a gross retrospective falsification of her parents' and brother's collective memory. Until she had been labelled ill, her parents

[1] Another patient.

had worried only over her thinking, or 'brooding', and the fact that sometimes she did not eat her meals with the rest of the family. This behaviour they had simply called 'lazy'. It was after their decision that she was ill that they experienced her as having lain in bed all day for years 'doing nothing'.

This retrospective falsification of the Danzigs' experience seems to have been generated by a collective panic that was intense and persisting. The panic was an expression of the phantasy in which they were unconsciously immersed. The following excerpt, which demonstrates the retrospective falsification, also conveys something of this atmosphere of panic and phantasy. It gives, too, some idea of the difficulty this atmosphere creates for discovering even the simplest facts.

INTERVIEWER: What do you perceive as being Sarah's illness?

MOTHER: Well I put it down to this. When she left art school instead of going out and making a go of something – do something . . .

INTERVIEWER: How old was she then by the way?

MOTHER: Then she was about eighteen. She used to lay in bed, now this is not a lie, Sarah will tell you that herself. Mr Danzig used to come home at half past seven, 'Where's Sarah?' That was the first thing. She was still in bed sleeping. I used to go in to her at eight o'clock, go in nine o'clock, half past nine – this is all from the kitchen to upstairs – 'Sarah get up' –

JOHN: Yes and she used to stay up all night.

MOTHER: Please John – six o'clock in the morning – [argument between Mother and John].

SARAH: Well I used to get up at six in the morning – half past five.

MOTHER: I said to her, 'Sarah get up.' 'No.' 'Get up, Sarah, it's eleven o'clock, get up. You don't know what daylight looks like. You don't know what the sun looks like. Get up or I'll – get up. Give me a hand with the washing up. Do a couple of beds. Do something.'

SARAH [voice raised]: I do, I do things like that.

MOTHER: Just a moment dear [Sarah interrupting] – Sarah, no.

She used to lay awake and get up at eight o'clock. When we had finished our dinner she used to come and make breakfast – ten o'clock – make breakfast. We used to go to bed at eleven. She used to sit downstairs in the dining-room and read – do things – ironing, washing – the whole house, the whole neighbourhood was dead. The house was so quiet you could have heard a pin drop. She thought and thought and sat and thought and her mind was all the time thinking, and this went on, not for one year but for six – four, five years – not going out to work, not going out weekends. Her friends used to phone. 'No,' she says, 'I'm not going out.' I'd say, 'Sarah, come with me to buy clothes – any shopping. Come with me, we'll spend the day out.' One day I *did* get her out. We went by car and Mr Danzig dropped me in Oxford Street. 'Oh,' she says, 'look, it's only half past nine. Isn't it marvellous?' she says. 'People running backwards and forwards, through the shops, the sun's shining.' I said, 'I know,' I said, 'to you it's a novelty to see daylight isn't it?' I said, 'Do it every day.'

JOHN: Only a short time ago she used to stay up all night until –

MOTHER: She used to stay up all night.

JOHN: Pinning her hair, she used to pin up a bunch of hair literally for an hour.

MOTHER: Yes, one bunch of hair – she was dissecting herself. This went on for so long, but we didn't see the danger – used to say, 'That girl definitely needs a psychiatrist.' Well, at that time we were inexperienced. We didn't know what it was. I thought, 'Oh, she'll get up eventually. She'll come to see the red light.' And I – thinking all these hours, night after night and nobody to talk to all the time, all by herself. It's lack of occupation. Doing nothing all day, when she could easily have gone out and done something – earned something, go to the office. True, she had two years at commercial college, short-hand-typing. She's got all her certificates for passing English, you know, whatever it is that they take in that commercial course. I've got them at home. 'Do something Sarah, go into Daddy's office, help Daddy from ten till six.' No.

JOHN: Anyway, your question was – what do we think the nature of Sarah's illness is?

MOTHER: And she was always miserable and always discontented, never a pleasant word.

JOHN: Well, it's very difficult for us to tell you *how* she is, all we can – or how she is ill, but we can just tell you the facts.

MOTHER: That she didn't lead the natural normal life that a girl of her age . . .

JOHN: She never went out to work, this was over – in the past six months. And when she did go out to work she used to have suspicions[1] that people were talking about her and they were plotting against her.

INTERVIEWER: This was in the past six months.

JOHN: Yes, six months. When she did go out to work, they were talking about her, they were plotting against her, and when she eventually went to work in Dad's office [Mother interrupting] she said they spoke about her and the people were incompetent and didn't ought to be working for Dad and they'd been working for Dad for twenty years and that sort of thing. Finally when she didn't go to work any more –

The intensity of the panic, and the overwhelming nature of the phantasy experience, may perhaps be gauged, too, from the fact that it seemed to have affected the sense of proportion of the persons responsible for clinically examining Sarah at her parents' urgent request. This effect can be seen in the following excerpt from a medical report, which declared that Sarah was ill and should be compulsorily detained in hospital.

'Patient states that prior to her coming here she was studying law[2] in a businessman's office. She says she hoped to be a lawyer, or something like that. She refuses to say what her father's occupation is. She denies having attacked her mother

---

[1] We have already made intelligible these so-called delusions of reference in the earlier account of the family. See Introduction.

[2] She had said that she had been studying the Torah, which she had explained was the Law. The certifying clinician had regarded this as a delusion.

and sister.[1] She is suspicious and resents questioning. She insists she is perfectly well, and keeps asking to go home today or tomorrow. Patient admits to having heard the voice of God, but denies that she heard it over the telephone.'[2]

Thus the problem of Sarah's behaviour dissolves into the mists of her parents' phantasy when the family praxis is examined phenomenologically. However, it had been dealt with clinically. Sarah had been subjected to the degradation ceremonial[3] of a psychiatric examination, in which she had been formally and solemnly invalidated as mentally ill, thus confirming her parents in their panic-stricken perception.[4]

Since Sarah's 'illness' was her 'laziness', and since both attributions were the expression of misperceptions, empirically speaking, we may infer they were perceiving in Sarah their own unrecognized 'laziness' and loss of control. And since they were in phantasy experiencing Sarah as an infant gut, we may infer that in phantasy they had unwittingly identified her with their own unrecognized infant bowels which, in phantasy, they experienced to be out of control.

Now, they had also called 'laziness' her thinking and her occasional failure to eat meals with the others at the 'proper' time. We may infer, therefore, that even before they saw her as sick, they had in phantasy projectively identified her with their own infant gut. Their perception of her as sick seems to have marked a change in their phantasy experience of this projected gut. This changed experience was one of imminent incontinence.

---

[1] She had not attacked them. It was her father with whom she had been quarrelling. See account in Introduction.

[2] This is by no means an isolated example of this type of clinical report. I have other specimens.

[3] For a formal description of degradation ceremonials, see Garfinkel, H., 'Conditions of Successful Degradation Ceremonies', *American Journal of Sociology*, LXI, 1956, pp. 420-24.

[4] For an account of how the diagnosis of mental illness is simply a ceremonial that rubber-stamps a prior assumption by family and psychiatrist, see Scheff, Thomas J., *Being Mentally Ill*, especially Chapter 5.

We can now understand better the Danzigs' confusion between praxis and process. We may infer their phantasy situation to be as follows: The lazy, sick 'Sarah' of their phantasy experience was derived from the period of development when bowel control is marginal, when the agent is only learning to control process. The Danzigs were, in phantasy, still concerned with gaining and keeping control of their marginally controlled infant bowels, in anxious anticipation of the response of a regulating phantasy other, who disapproved of failure to control. For reasons we have yet to discover, when Sarah stepped out of her serial familial role of filial compliance, there was evoked in them a threat of imminent incontinence. Since in phantasy they had already unwittingly projected their infant gut into her, they experienced this phantasy threat in her. And we may infer that in requiring her to behave regularly and routinely they were, in phantasy, requiring her to embody and control on their behalf their projected marginally controlled bowel.

This kind of defence requiring the cooperation of the other is *transpersonal* rather than intrapersonal or 'intrapsychic'.

If our construction is correct we may reasonably infer that the 'public opinion', before which she was expected to behave so properly, was a derivative expression of the disciplining phantasy other. Or rather, it was a function of an early experience of a disciplining other who embodied and mediated a phantasy presence, whose attitude to bowel control implied a pattern of values on behaviour, which was later called the view of 'public opinion'. This inference would explain their constant attempts to placate 'public opinion' by persistently urging Sarah to control herself, despite their view that she was ill.

The inference that their confusion between praxis and process originated in a phantasy of a marginally controlled infant gut is congruent with Mr Danzig's perception of his wife's relationship with Sarah.

He told me he wondered if his wife had caused Sarah's 'illness' through being constantly impatient and irritable with her for her 'slowness' in doing what was required of her.

FATHER: Well she would take a long time in her food, eating, and in her dressing, and in going out, going to school. Lost patience waking her up in the morning. Lost her patience to see her out to school, and when she had meals or dressing, all sorts of things, all this slow-motion business, my wife lost patience – erratic.

Even when Sarah was an infant his wife had been impatient and irritable with her slowness to comply. She was particularly impatient over what he called the 'mess' that Sarah made in the course of learning. She had shouted at her for it, even when she was an infant.

FATHER: Well, Sarah may have been somewhat difficult as a child – all right, every child is difficult. My wife has no patience, she's not – she's got no patience.

And:

FATHER: When she lost her patience – 'Sit down you brat – Don't – don't – don't' – she had occasion to use that word, I may be wrong, I don't know.

INTERVIEWER: How old would Sarah be then?

FATHER: Oh about a year, eighteen months, I don't know – I think, I'm not sure. Maybe it was just a bit of temper, I may be wrong. I'm not quite sure of my recollection of it. Maybe my recollection is bad. You see you've got to understand my wife – she is inclined to be a bit erratic, bit nervous – I don't know. Am I wrong, or am I right?

According to him, he had been highly indignant over her behaviour towards the infant Sarah, and had remonstrated with her for not giving Sarah more time to comply. However, he had not pressed his objections to the point where they were effective. He had apparently been uncertain whether Sarah's failure to comply was due to praxis or process.

FATHER: Frankly, I wasn't a judge of it. I couldn't understand it. I'm not in a position to judge it. I don't understand anything different. At that time I felt – I did say to her, 'Don't be silly, leave the child alone.'

He had apparently never asked himself why Sarah should be expected to do things his wife's way in the first place. Nor had he asked himself whether the 'things' she did and the 'mess' she made were, in fact, wrong. He believed too firmly in 'discipline' to do so.

Now, whether his description of his wife's relationship with Sarah as an infant is accurate we cannot tell, but it was clearly congruent with the way she behaved in the present. Nor can we know whether he had been angry at the time, but there was no doubt that in the present he was very angry about this possible past behaviour of his wife's. He thus appeared currently involved in a phantasy about his wife's relationship with Sarah, and his with both. Its content, from his statement above, is congruent with an experience of Sarah as an infant with marginal bowel control, who should comply with the requirements of a disciplining other. His complaint about his wife was merely that she was rushing the training unduly.

This inference about the phantasy significance of his behaviour is also congruent with his currently mystifying praxis towards Sarah. His description of his tolerance and his ineffectual indignation over the way she said his wife had treated Sarah as an infant, corresponded to his attitude in the present to his wife's response to Sarah's 'ill' behaviour. For now, too, he saw himself as more tolerant than his wife. He was prepared to be more patient in explaining to Sarah where she was going wrong, and he remonstrated with his wife over her 'impatience'. His remonstrations, however, were ineffectual and, worse, they were mystifying, and in two ways. Firstly, because his tolerance consisted in reminding his wife that Sarah's 'lapses' were due to process and not praxis. Secondly, his reminders were made only in private. So that while implying to Sarah he was an ally who saw her as ill, he allowed his wife to speak for both of them when she reproached Sarah for her sick lack of self-control.

CHAPTER 6

The domestic order

One of the complaints the Danzigs voiced was that Sarah disrupted an efficient housekeeping routine. This routine, and the
Danzigs' efficiency in carrying it out, we now consider.

As persons, the Danzigs each appeared to be poorly integrated.
They were, for instance, chronically anxious, and had been so
all their lives. While their manner of speech and pattern of
communication[1] also indicated poor personal integration.

And just as they appeared intrapersonally poorly integrated,
they appeared interpersonally poorly coordinated. Their poor
personal integration and poor interpersonal coordination could
be seen in their domestic arrangements.

Mrs Danzig was concerned to be seen publicly as a competent
cook-housekeeper. We know this was important for her altered
identity as a member of the family for-'the-others'. However, in
carrying out her role she also appeared to be acting under emotional compulsion. For even on occasions when she knew 'public
opinion' would concede she could rest, she continued cooking
and cleaning. For instance, in the course of a discussion on servants
she said even if she had as many as she needed to do all the
work, she would still rise early to cook and clean. Not to do so
would be wrong, whatever 'public opinion' thought. It would
be lazy.

As for Mr Danzig, an essential aspect of his identity as a
successful family man was that he should appear 'domesticated',
and ready to help at home. And so he cleaned and tidied.

[1] This has been described in the earlier study. Numerous examples are to be
found in the present account.

However, it was evident that he, too, acted under emotional compulsion, for he insisted on cleaning and tidying on occasions when he knew 'public opinion' would concede he need not. For instance, when his wife made clear his help was a hindrance.

FATHER: I can't stand untidiness. I can't stand – I like cleanliness in every way, no matter where it is. I'm very particular. In fact they may say I'm mad clean. I like cleanliness, tidiness. Tidiness in manner, in habit, can sometimes indicate a tidy mind. In the home, domestic things – I like tidiness, cleanliness. Even if a cup is *touched* I don't want it to be used again. Or something – I don't want something to be passed on from one child to another. An illustration – a glass of milk will be left, drunk by John or Sarah or Ruth. I don't want that left for tomorrow, and somebody else will drink it. I want to be sick. My wife says 'Save it'. That's a small illustration – gives you an indication. Or I like everything else appertaining to the table to be clean. We differ a lot on that. One of the excuses is 'I haven't got the time, patience', or 'I have no help'. All right, I try to alleviate her worries. I chime in sometimes. I help her. Then she comes back – I have no right to interfere.

INTERVIEWER: From your wife?

FATHER: From my wife. I get erratic. I say, 'No, I like – I'm only interfering when I see something which I don't like.'

We may infer from their compulsive preoccupation with food and cleanliness that they had each in phantasy unwittingly identified their house and domestic arrangements with their gut. This phantasy gut appeared to require a constant expenditure of energy on its pattern of intake and output to prevent its becoming disordered. This is congruent with our inference that they were in phantasy preoccupied with controlling their marginally controlled bowels.

Now, though Mrs Danzig was a compulsive housewife, she was not a tidy one. She always seemed to be fully stretched coping with her work. It was true that there were four persons in the family to look after, but it seemed to me and to other observers she made heavy weather of it, considering she had a daily help and none of the persons were children.

MOTHER: Even at home in the day, I'm busy all day. I don't scrub the floor and things like that because I have somebody that comes in and does all that sort of thing, but with a family there's lots of other things to do. I mean I do all the shopping. I do all the baking, if I feel like it. I do all the cooking for the family, you know, myself, and things like that. But I do *something*.

On visits to her home it could be seen she had the greatest difficulty in organizing her time and delegating tasks. These visits always stretched her to the utmost. For she was in a continual anxious rush trying to coordinate such simple matters as serving tea and biscuits. She appeared, in fact, not very competent as a housewife, and was greatly upset by events that seemed, to me and others, to require minimal alterations in her routine. Thus, judging by her performance on these occasions, she seemed poorly integrated as a person, and appeared to be placed under threat by tasks whose complexity was such that an experienced housewife of her social class and standing should have coped with easily.

This view of Mrs Danzig her husband held too. He said she always had difficulty in doing her housework on time, and so he insisted on giving her his unsolicited aid. But this view was private. He never revealed it explicitly to his wife.

Now, Mr Danzig aspired to be a calm, orderly person who lived in a calm, orderly house. This ideal of family life, he said he was trying to help his wife create when he participated in her work. He told her this. Unfortunately, his manner of helping was extremely erratic. Highly excitable and easily flustered, he seldom did anything with reference to what his wife was doing. And on those occasions when he did make reference, his attempts to coordinate his efforts with hers were quite ineffectual, leading only to quarrelling and increased disorder.

MOTHER: Yes. I don't – it doesn't matter to me. It doesn't worry me. It doesn't matter. It's not so important as to make over it. If I want a thing and I can't find it, I can't find it, I say, 'Where is it? Where the heck is it?', and I sort of get very cross with him. I get sharp when I want it. I've left it, there, and I can't find it; but it's not *that* important. I mean it's not such a terrible thing.

Thus the Danzigs, preoccupied with maintaining tidiness and order, were, by virtue of their poor integration and lack of coordination, continually on the brink of domestic disorder.

And this need not surprise us. For if they had unwittingly identified their house and domestic arrangements with their marginally controlled phantasy infant gut, as we have inferred they had done, we would expect their attempts to keep domestic order to be constantly on the verge of breakdown.

Nor need we be surprised to find that their difficulty in maintaining domestic order was the expression of their poor personal integration. For if, as we have inferred, their continued bowel phantasy difficulty was the outcome of pressure upon them too early in their development, the marginal nature of their control would be a function of not yet being sufficiently personally integrated to feel safe from sudden incontinence.

Our inference that the Danzigs had in phantasy unconsciously identified both Sarah and their domestic arrangements with their own unrecognized marginally controlled infant gut, helps us explain further aspects of their mystifying praxis.

They complained that Sarah stayed in her room thinking, instead of coming down to meals on time. Yet they implicitly encouraged her to stay in her room by giving her meals whenever she asked for them. And they still did this even after it was pointed out what they were doing. They appeared to be acting compulsively.

They had this to say about her thinking in her room.

MOTHER: Well I think that she's sort of living in a world of her own – thinking that everything should be given to her. She wants this, she wants that. When she wants this, she wants that, she gets it; but I mean if you undertake, as she says, in her *own* words – that *she* chose – I didn't say that. And I didn't make her future for her. At the moment, changes could be made of course – at the moment she says, 'Mummy, I want to go to school.' Right, well we booked up. Well, if you're booked up, keep your word and do it.

And:

MOTHER: She's got to face life.
FATHER: She gets married she'll face life.
MOTHER: No –
FATHER: Her husband'll get her up.
MOTHER: No. I don't look at it that way. I look at it that she's – she knows she's got to do a certain thing that's got to be done. If I asked her to get up, say eight in the morning, said, 'Look, Sarah, I'm going to lay in bed and you do all the housework. Scrub the floor, do the dinner and everything.' 'Oh,' she'd say, 'why should I do that? It's your job.' I'm only asking her.
FATHER: Wouldn't be unreasonable either.
MOTHER: She still sort of can't come to grips with life. It's not sort of – nothing is real to her if you know what I mean.
FATHER: Well, she – er –
MOTHER: You've got to come to grips. Now this week it'll be school and from – for one thing leads to another. That's what I'm trying to – it's a sort of routine.

It is evident that, in phantasy, they experienced Sarah as wishing to return to an idealized infant-gut world in which there was no need to comply with the complexities of the cleaning and food-giving routine of the other, and no rhythm except her natural infant rhythm. We may infer that in implicitly encouraging Sarah to return to this world, they were unconsciously encouraging her to enact a similar desire of their own.

Since they appeared, in phantasy, to have embodied their infant gut in their domestic order, any attempt by Sarah to enact their desire to return to an ideal infant-gut world would inevitably evoke their phantasy of imminent incontinence. Their compulsive implicit encouragement of her to act in a way that caused them to experience her as creating disorder was, we may infer, the return of their repressed desire to give up control of their bowels. And since they also reproached her for not complying with their routine, we may infer their contradictory behaviour was the expression of unconscious conflict over this desire.

Our inference that the Danzigs had in phantasy identified their domestic arrangements with their marginally controlled bowels, helps us explain another feature of their mystifying praxis.

Mrs Danzig complained bitterly of the domestic inconvenience caused by Sarah's irregularity, and Mr Danzig reprimanded Sarah for not helping her mother with the chores. But when Sarah offered to help, her mother always refused. Sarah was highly mystified.

To the extent to which Mrs Danzig had identified their home with her bowels, she was under unrecognized compulsion personally to maintain domestic order. She required Sarah to fit in with her routine, not to clean. To the extent to which Mr Danzig had also identified the home with his bowels, he was compelled to make more of those poorly coordinated attempts to create order, which led only to increased disorder. And Sarah, in his scheme, was to be his filially obedient proxy – in phantasy, a controlled bit of himself – doing his work at home when he was busy elsewhere.

INTERVIEWER: I got the impression from you, Mr Danzig, that Sarah wasn't helping.
FATHER: Not in the way she should. I'm not ashamed to admit – I help the wife as well – the little bits and pieces I do for the wife, perhaps I could er – engage my time in other directions.
INTERVIEWER: Do you think Sarah's helping you in the way you regard as the way she should?
MOTHER: Well I'd prefer her to go to school better – I wouldn't like her to stay at home all the time – I'd much prefer her to go and get a profession or a trade –

INTERVIEWER: But when she is actually in the home?

MOTHER: She keeps her own room tidy, I will say that, you know, she – er –

FATHER: But helping you more, helping more –

MOTHER: What do you mean? In the kitchen?

FATHER: Yes – not helping you – no – helping you more than she does at the moment – would you like her to do – do you feel she's not doing enough?

MOTHER: Well I've got someone to help me with the rough work.

FATHER [shouting]: I'm talking about in the home – do you?

MOTHER: Light duties, do you mean, such as wiping up, washing up?

FATHER: Yes, yes, yes.

INTERVIEWER: No, I'm asking you – I'm simply asking. Mr Danzig doesn't think that Sarah is helping you enough. I'm merely asking you whether you're satisfied, or whether you think she could be helping you more than she does.

MOTHER: Well, I suppose she could do a little – wipe up, wash up –

INTERVIEWER: You don't seem to be very concerned.

MOTHER: Well, that is – that's not the issue – the issue is the need to get a regular life –

We may also infer that their joint praxis, which induced domestic confusion through inducing confusion in Sarah, was another expression of the return of their repressed impulse to experience loss of bowel control.

CHAPTER 7

The family secret

It will be recalled that Sarah's parents saw her as lazy for years without seeing her as sick. Only when her behaviour threatened the family reputation did they change their view. This view was, as we have reason to infer, a function of their unrecognized phantasy experience of loss of control of their unwittingly projected and embodied infant bowels. How did Sarah's behaviour come to evoke this phantasy? Firstly, we must clarify the nature of the phantasy expressed in their preoccupation with their group reputation.

We said earlier that their identities were entirely altered. And they were altered because, never having revealed themselves directly in a relationship with another person, they depended for their feeling of being on how they appeared as others to 'the others'.

Since the self they wished 'the others' to see was an entirely successful self – success being the appearance of success – we may infer they were concerned with concealing from 'the others' aspects of their family selves that would reveal them to be failures. If we have been inferring correctly about the nature of their unrecognized phantasy experience, we would expect to find that in phantasy each experienced his concealed failed aspect as an infant bowel with marginal control.

Now, the key feature of an institutionally successful self was the ability to appear 'publicly' as the respected parents of respectful children. In practice, as the competent managers of their domestic affairs, who had successfully trained their children to do as they had trained them to do. As competent managers, they had to show they could maintain a 'public' front of harmony and cooperation with one another. While as successful trainers they had to train their children to maintain the front of family cooperation and harmony, and so demonstrate their parents had successfully trained them to cooperate. Thus, family success was simply the ability to maintain the appearance of group order, no matter what disorder reigned behind the appearance. It involved, for the parents, demonstrating they had trained their children to help maintain the appearance of order.

JOHN: You mean we don't bicker. Well, we don't differ in public, whereas in private we say we do differ.
INTERVIEWER: Well, that's what the impression is.
JOHN: Well, I think it's a natural habit, because maybe we're so conscious of differing among ourselves in private, that for the public we put on a united front.

Their 'public' interpersonal preoccupation was thus significantly similar to the intrapersonal issue with which each appeared to be preoccupied in phantasy. For, as we inferred, each was intrapersonally preoccupied with maintaining control of his bowel contents before a phantasy disciplining other. While in their 'public' social relations they were preoccupied with maintaining the appearance of group order and social control of their children before a critically evaluating phantasy other – 'public opinion'.

The parallel is even closer when we recall that the parents openly regarded their children as the equivalent of property or money to invest. This meant, in phantasy, they experienced the children to be parts of themselves to be controlled. The parents did not, of course, fully realize the implication of their view of the children.

If the parents' preoccupation with maintaining the 'public' appearance of group order was the expression of an unrecognized phantasy preoccupation with controlling their bowels, we would expect that on any occasion when they felt this order was being 'publicly' disrupted they would experience unwittingly in phantasy a threat of imminent incontinence. This, in fact, appeared so.

As we described earlier, the family, structurally speaking, was not the same for the children as for the parents. For the parents it was a pledged group, while for the children it was simply a nexus until they came of age. It was as important for the parents' reputation to be seen 'publicly' presenting a harmonious marital front to the children, as it was to present a united family front to everyone else. The question of the parents' united marital front was a problem that emerged early in discussions involving the whole family.

JOHN: Well, take one of them. Let's take my parents' relationship. I can't expect them to discuss it in front of me.

From the parents' point of view, the family had two 'public' boundaries, and their reputation depended on maintaining both

a = marital
    boundary
b = familial
    boundary

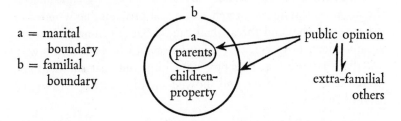

intact. The parents had to maintain 'public' harmony before the children, the children had to maintain 'public' harmony with one another, and the children had to maintain 'public' harmony with the parents.

However, since parents and children embodied 'public opinion' for one another, it was extremely difficult for them to be sure when they were in public and when in private. Indeed, they appeared to have little respite from feeling publicly observed, except perhaps when each was physically alone, and in no danger of being intruded upon. So far as I could gather, the lavatory was the only place where Mr Danzig, for instance, felt reasonably private. There he felt free to break some of the rules of public respectability as he understood them. However, even in the lavatory, there was present an observer, one whom he called 'God'.

The extent to which they felt continually publicly observed may be gauged from the following muddling admonition by Mr Danzig to Sarah. In it, public and private are unwittingly confused.

FATHER: A young lady should have respect for her father and mother irrespectively of what she may think privately, outside the house.

Now if our inference about the phantasy significance of the importance of maintaining the appearance of group order is correct, we would expect that breaking the inner marital boundary would have the same phantasy significance as breaking the outer familial boundary. And this indeed was so.

Though Mr Danzig did not see his wife's nagging and suicidal threats as indicating the presence of a real problem, he wondered if her reproaches and threats had caused Sarah's 'illness'. It soon became clear, however, that what he saw to be pathogenic was not that his wife was unhappy with him, but that she demonstrated it to the children, and showed she did not respect him as head of the house.

FATHER: She has on – she has on more than one or two occasions – I may say so – in front of the children in a moment of temper, in a moment of annoyance or irritation due to all sorts of circumstances – threatened to do herself in – in front of the children. That's not the right attitude of a mother.

And:

FATHER: And I've told her more than often, 'If you've anything to say to me, say it not in front of the children.'

And:

FATHER: I can't – I can't – it's an admission which I can't understand. You see, my wife – she's not a foolish woman – if she *only* realized by showing me a little cooperation with the children – try to cooperate with me – having like a front so far as the children are concerned – things might be a little bit different. Or – we have an argument or we disagree or perhaps – 'Let's assume I'm not so good to you. Let's forget about that issue. We'll adjust that later on. Meantime we've got the children to consider, but don't – Let's show each other a little more respect, I to you, you to me. You try to do things to please me and I will try to do things to please you. So far as the children are concerned we should not show antagonism.' And yet I go for the children because of their attitude towards my wife occasionally, so my wife says, 'Why do you have to do it? I can take my own part.' And I don't like that.

Since Sarah was neither ill, nor was she complaining of her parents' quarrelling, we may infer that the loss of self-control which he experienced in her stemmed from a phantasy loss of control in himself. And since, as we know, he experienced her in phantasy as an incontinent bowel, we may infer he had unwittingly identified her with his own phantasy uncontrolled bowel. Thus, when Mr Danzig felt his relationship with his female partner was 'publicly' seen as disordered, he experienced in phantasy, without realizing it, loss of control of his own bowels.

We may therefore infer it was this phantasy that was expressed in his preoccupation with the appearance of group order. This inference is strengthened when we note, in the example just given, that his interpersonal experience is once more significantly similar to his intrapersonal situation. We may reasonably infer that, in phantasy, his female partner was identified with the passive aspect of himself expressed through his bowels. When she appeared 'publicly' uncontrolled he experienced in phantasy loss of control of his own bowels. He appears to have dealt with his anxiety by unwittingly projecting his loss of control into Sarah, who was here embodying 'public opinion'.

As for Mrs Danzig, she tried to organize herself according to a schedule of clockwork regularity. To do less was to risk being labelled 'publicly' as lazy. And she expected everyone in the family to cooperate routinely. On the 'public' appearance of domestic clockwork familial cooperation and order depended her reputation as a successful, conscientious housewife and parental trainer. So important was it to maintain this 'public' appearance that after her daughter had failed to cooperate 'publicly', she tried to hide the fact, so ashamed did she feel before 'the others', and such a failure.

INTERVIEWER: In terms of your feeling of shame about this –
MOTHER: Frankly I feel I've failed somewhere, that – why do other people's girls and boys lead a normal life? Why doesn't my daughter – John gets up to go to work every morning. – He's working now in a firm. He knows he's got to be in by a certain time. I have to coax him once or twice, say. You know. Give him a push, say, 'Come along, John. Hurry, it's getting late.' But he gets up.[1]

Indeed, so intense was her fear of being 'publicly' shamed that for years she had been trying to prevent it by hiding Sarah's failure to cooperate in maintaining domestic order.

MOTHER: My relations used to come sometimes for tea. 'How's Sarah? Where is she?' What could I tell them? 'She's in bed?' They wouldn't blame her. They would blame me. They would say, 'What, let a girl of seventeen lie in bed all day? It's not natural.'

And:

MOTHER: Well they wouldn't say ill. They would put it down to sheer damn laziness. Yes, they would blame me. I'd be ashamed. I'll be quite candid. I didn't want them to know.

This discovery validates our earlier inference that the Danzigs' preoccupation with appearing successful expressed a concern to conceal from 'public opinion' aspects of their family praxis which would reveal them to be failures.

However, during the years of concealment Mrs Danzig had not seen Sarah as sick, simply as lazy.

[1] And see quotation p. 6.

MOTHER: And I tell you, and I told you last time. And I'll always say it. It was my fault more than my husband's, because I should not have let her sleep all those years, day in and day out. *I* must have been mad. *I* should have gone to see a psychiatrist myself.

FATHER: Well I won't say it's anybody's fault –

MOTHER [voice raised]: No, it's my fault.

It was only when Sarah acted 'publicly' in a way that threatened to reveal her mother's shameful domestic secret that her mother concluded Sarah's 'laziness' was illness. In revealing the shameful secret, Sarah risked bringing 'public shame' on herself and her mother. And in her mother's experience anyone who risked this must be ill, for she was sure no sensible person would ever risk public opprobrium. And so Sarah was ill because she was scandalous.

However, she was scandalous, not because she was her mother's shameful secret. She was scandalous because she 'publicly' revealed herself as the secret, and because in so doing she revealed her lack of filial respect. There was thus a double occasion for scandal. The 'public' revelation of the secret, and the public revelation of filial disrespect implied in the revealing. Not the existence of the dirty linen, but its public display, and the failure to keep it private was scandalous. Such behaviour the Danzigs unquestioningly experienced to be illness.[1]

And Sarah's protests to the contrary were taken as proof of the validity of their view. For how could anyone deliberately risk her

[1] Just how automatically they experienced her as a non-agent when she publicly stepped out of her serial filial role is clearly shown in two exchanges in Chapter 13. These exchanges of approximately equal length occurred in my presence during the first family session.

In the first exchange the topic of discussion is defined and closely controlled by the rest of the family. Sarah, who is conforming to their pattern, is regarded as behaving well, and is seen as an agent.

In the second, which followed a few minutes later, Sarah has stepped out of her serial role of respectful daughter of a loving father. She has said she is afraid of him. She is immediately experienced as a non-agent. In the course of the exchange her family make seven attributions invalidating her experience and agency. These attributions were all empirically unvalidated assumptions.

reputation by saying her scandalous behaviour was deliberate? Thus, her parents' perception of her as ill protected her reputation, and theirs. And later they were confirmed in their view clinically.[1]

But Sarah was not ill. And we have seen that Mrs Danzig's experience of her as ill was a function of having projectively identified her in phantasy with her own imminently incontinent infant gut. Thus, this phantasy of incontinence was evoked when Sarah 'publicly' disrupted the appearance of domestic clockwork cooperation and order, threatening her mother's alterated group identity.

How did Sarah's behaviour come to evoke this phantasy experience of imminent bowel incontinence? Since disruption of the Danzigs' alterated group identity evoked in them this *un-recognized* phantasy, we may infer that their identity served the double function of freeing them from ontic anxiety and instinctual anxiety.

The Danzigs were respectable people. They also felt they were

[1] The clinical view is based on an assumption similar to that made by the Danzigs. This assumption is expressed in the concept of the need to adapt to what is clinically called 'reality'. Patients who learn to 'adapt' and not mention views which they have learnt their psychiatrist calls delusions, are soon reclassified as 'remitted' or 'socially recovered'. There is controversy over whether it is legitimate to call such people 'cured'.

In his novel *Ward 7*, Valeriy Tarsis describes a Soviet writer, Almazov, who was sent to an asylum as a political lunatic. Almazov's illness was not the thoughts he thought. Thinking what he thought appeared to be common enough. It was that he revealed his thoughts publicly, i.e. abroad. This brought the danger of scandal, for the Soviet management feared they would gain a reputation as barbarians. Labelling Almazov mad was, from the clinical viewpoint, perfectly logical. It was assumed without question that Almazov, like the psychiatrists and the governmental managers, was identified with the Soviet group-for-the-(foreign) others'. The 'herd', Almazov called it. To damage the group reputation meant damaging his own. Only a madman would do this. Almazov's reproaches to the psychiatrists, that they were cynical jailers, were countered by the attribution of illness, again perfectly logically in terms of psychiatric assumptions and the structure of psychiatric experience and consciousness. Almazov continually underestimated the extent of psychiatric self-alienation. Alarming though it is, labelling dissenters mentally ill is, culturally speaking, an advance on killing them or leaving them to starve or die of exposure. Just as the institution of slavery was an advance on killing prisoners-of-war, as Marx pointed out.

good. To be respectable was to be good, for respectability implied goodness. Indeed, goodness was central to respectability, for it had preceded it. Respectability dated from the time they came of age, while being good dated from childhood.

Now, goodness had been to the Danzigs as children what respectability was to them as adults. For being good, like being respectable, was a function of living an altered identity as ordered and orderly persons. It was not a group identity, however. It was the child's interiorization of his being a particular other-for-the-parental-other-embodying-'the-others'. This being other was called, in Mrs Danzig's case, 'being a good girl', in Mr Danzig's, 'being a nice boy'. We shall call it generically 'being a good child'.

Being a good child was depassed towards being a respectable person when the good child came of age. For his identity as good was then dissolved into, and preserved in, his new identity as respectable. This occurred when the good child obediently interiorized the parental ordered family group-for-'the-others', forming for himself an altered family group identity. This interiorization *was* his coming of age, marking as it did his definitive affirmation of the family pledge. And this had happened with the Danzigs. The good girl and the nice boy underwent the ontic transformation that marked the birth of reputation. Each became identified with the parental family group-for-'the-others'. Each developed an altered group identity, with the good child still present. And though their identity was further modified as they passed through the stages of institutionally respectable group being, viz. being a partner in a respectable marital partnership, and being a parent in a respectable ordered family, the good child continued implicitly present and central. Just how present may be gauged from the fact that, fifty years after the identity had been allocated, they still spoke proudly of having been good children.

Now, a good child was regular and orderly, rising early and complying with the routine of the parental order. The Danzigs, who expected their children to be like this, had been like this themselves. In addition, regularity and order were right. And a good child was regular and orderly because it knew it was right. However, its knowledge was not a function of reflection and understanding. It was a function of being a good child. For instance:

MOTHER: Because I knew it [failing to rise early] would have been wrong. I knew the difference between right and wrong. I'm not clever, but I know the difference between right and wrong.

And so the Danzigs were good because they were regular. They were regular because they knew it was right. They knew it was right because they were good. Thus, they were good because they were good. Their good regular behaviour was a function of their altered identity as good.

They also said they were regular because an alternative never occurred to them. Not clever, at least they were good. Thus being good children kept them unaware of an alternative to regularity and order. Their altered identity as good, therefore, determined their behaviour by radically restricting their experience to one possibility, which was designated right. This possibility was being regular. We may infer that the interiorized parental-other-embodying-'the-others' originally designated regularity as right.

Since the Danzigs' preoccupation with regularity and order was the expression of an unrecognized chamber-pot morality, we may infer that their altered identity as good children func-tioned to protect them from being aware of any impulse to forgo control of their marginally controlled bowels. And since this altered identity was central to their altered group identity, we may infer that their group identity functioned similarly. Thus their altered group identity appeared to function against both instinctual and ontic anxiety.

This inference helps clarify a statement by Mrs Danzig about her need to live and work routinely. Failure to fulfil her family role as an orderly housewife evoked an experience of muddle and nothingness. We may infer that in phantasy she was experiencing herself to be exposed to the double threat of incontinence and non-being.

MOTHER: No, but on the whole, apart from anything else, you must have a regular life, otherwise you're in a muddle all day. Your life's in a muddle.

One had to rise early regularly and get on with it, otherwise:

MOTHER: It's not a day. What is it? It's nothing.

Now, an altered identity seems generally to have a twofold defensive function. If the identity is successfully established, no instinctual impulse is felt.

The split between what may be termed the personal and the animal appeared to be a function of the Danzigs' social experience. We may infer it was encouraged by an interpersonal transaction that went something like: 'You are a good boy, [because] you would not think of not controlling your bowels.' As the transaction became internalized the position became: 'I control my bowels, because I am a good boy.' Becoming later: 'As a good boy, I control my bowels.'

Presumably as the Danzigs grew older the split in their experience between the animal and the personal became more definitive, until it was no longer a simple case of a relationship of mutual opposition. For a point appeared to have been reached when there was no longer any obvious relationship between them at all. The animal simply became lost. It was simply assumed by the Danzigs no longer to exist. This assumption about oneself and one's family is a public feature of respectability.

It was, of course, the loss of animal instinctual experience that made the Danzigs dependent for their feeling of being on their altered identities. For they progressively came under social pressure to relate in a non-instinctual way within a highly institutionalized social system. Since they were so divorced from the animal in them, they had no spontaneous experience, and so no experience of their own. They depended entirely for their feeling of being on how they felt they were perceived as others by others in the system. Their feeling of being, thus, came to depend to a significant extent on enacting specific patterns of non-instinctual behaviour (social roles). It depended on that which divorced them from the possibility of an authentic experience of being.

CHAPTER 8

The household gods

Our discovery of the nature of the double threat to the Danzigs' security helps us to clarify further aspects of their mystifying praxis.

The Danzigs regarded themselves as Orthodox Jews. They said they expected their children to comply fully with ritual observances. Yet when Sarah, even before she was labelled ill, tried to follow tradition and remain home on the Sabbath meditating, they violently opposed her. They said she was lazy. Later they said she was sick. They also mystified her by continually lecturing her on the dangers of sitting thinking instead of rising early and regularly on such occasions as holidays and weekends, when by ordinary standards there was no need for her to rise early. Failure to rise early on these occasions was also called 'laziness' and later 'sickness'. An illustration of their praxis occurs in the following exchange, which took place while Sarah was waiting at home for the college term to start. Though when it began she attended promptly.

MOTHER: I mean, I get up – get up. I mean she's got to get up and get into a normal routine. You know what I mean? It's not good having dinnertime when it's breakfast, and so forth. Well, you've got to sort of come down and get washed, have breakfast and have lunch and then tea, supper, finished. It's getting up. I don't know if she's – seems – she tells me she feels very tired – not that she doesn't want to. She says she feels tired.

INTERVIEWER: What time do you actually get up, Sarah?

SARAH: Well most days it's around about twelve.

INTERVIEWER: Uh-huh.

MOTHER: It's late, isn't it? I mean, makes it – and then at night, if she gets up so late, she may find it's difficult to get to sleep again. [Sarah breaks in.] Pardon?

SARAH: I don't find it difficult to get to sleep.

MOTHER: But you shouldn't get up so – I should only have to wake you twice – I've got a little girl of fifteen – quarter to seven she gets up every morning – regardless if she has a late night or – like Friday night – like Saturday and she gets up quarter to seven – wake her once and she comes down and runs off to get the bus – you know she has to change six times to go to school – three times there, three times getting back. She knows, she says, she's got to get up and she gets up – and if *I* get up early, so can Sarah.

INTERVIEWER: What do you feel about that, Mr Danzig?

FATHER: It is a problem – getting her up, but I should think perhaps in due course it might er – right itself. It's possible.

Their behaviour becomes intelligible if we recall our earlier statement that the Danzigs were in the position of serving two masters, 'God' and 'public opinion'. 'God' they served with compulsive activity, which in phantasy warded off their instinctual impulses, while they served 'public opinion' by complying with institutional *mores* for the sake of their ontic security. So long as 'public opinion's' requirements were of a kind to allow them to work compulsively, there was no problem. But when its requirements contradicted those of 'God', they were in a dilemma.

Such a dilemma happened on the Sabbath, and on holidays. They had no fear that 'God' would punish them for working on the Sabbath. It never occurred to them to wonder at this. Their fear was before Jewish 'public opinion', and they dealt with it by compulsively insisting that Sarah, who was trying to meditate, should carry out the routine of regular rising and active ordering from which they were precluded by fear. That is to say, Sarah, into whom in phantasy they had unconsciously projected their marginally controlled bowels, was expected in phantasy to embody and control these bowels on their behalf. She was allocated the position of family safety valve, relieving the pressure of their enforced rest.

And, because they had no dialectical awareness, there was no check on their doing this. For without such awareness they could neither empathize with Sarah's dialectical project of self-understanding, nor could they reflect on their own impulse to act as they did. They simply felt tense, while finding her behaviour unintelligible. And their fears and phantasy had unchecked sway.

However, their way of coping with the conflict between 'God' and 'public opinion' only made matters worse. In expecting Sarah to embody and control their infant bowels her parents had placed themselves to a significant extent in her power. The more they were not themselves, the more they felt threatened by that from which they were alienated. The more they felt threatened, the more they projected. The more they projected, the more they were alienated from themselves, and the more they became dependent on 'the others' for reassurance they were not that which they were trying to escape being. The more they were dependent on 'the others', the more they were vulnerable to the others' response to the other into whom they had in phantasy projected the forbidden, and so the more they were dependent on how the other embodied that which they had projected. And the more they depended on the other embodying that which they had projected, the more they had to collude in being what the other wanted them to be. And if the other wanted them to be in a way that contravened the formula of regular work and routine living, then they were in an intolerable position, caught between 'God', 'public opinion', and the other. This, we shall see, happened with Sarah. It was another factor in her parents' decision to continue to supply her with food according to her convenience and their great inconvenience.

Our discovery that Sarah was allocated the position of family safety valve is congruent with our earlier inference about the

Danzigs' motive in implicitly encouraging her to stay in her room thinking. She was a means of indulging their own unacknowledged 'laziness' without conflict with 'God'. For through her they were vicariously gratified. Sarah as a safety valve functioned to allow her parents to experience in phantasy forbidden pleasures. She was a vehicle for the return of their repressed impulses in derivative form.

This discovery deepens our understanding of their decision to conceal her 'laziness'. Since Sarah's 'laziness' was incompatible with their family reputation as successful, she had to be hidden from 'public opinion' if she was to be a source of gratification. Hiding her thus served both their phantasy (bowel) instinctual needs, and their ontic needs.

Sarah as a source of vicarious gratification helps explain why, during those years of 'laziness', they never sought medical help or attempted to discuss the matter with their Rabbi. It was only when Sarah herself broke the family front that they sought outside help. Their failure to seek such help earlier could not have been out of fear for their public reputation, for the matter would have remained confidential. We may infer that their motive in hiding her contained an unclarified desire for her to remain as she was.

This inferred unrecognized component to their motive also explains another aspect of their praxis. Though they complained bitterly of the trouble Sarah's self-indulgence caused them at home, they repeatedly failed to cooperate in proposals I made to find her an alternative place to stay. They said she was too sick to live away from the family, and besides, they said, she did not want to live away. It seemed they compulsively retained her at home for motives they had not clarified.

We may conclude that Sarah, as a family safety valve, fulfilled the double function of allowing her parents at times to gratify in phantasy forbidden instinctual impulses without conflict with 'God', while at other times allowing them to defend themselves against these impulses without conflict with 'public opinion'.

How are we to understand this 'God' who was at times in

competition with 'public opinion'? Like his rival, he was an experience in phantasy unrecognized as such.

Since the Danzigs derived from 'God' their sense that regularity and order were right, we may infer that in phantasy this 'God' was a god of the chamber-pot. This inference is congruent with what else we know of him. For instance, in his rivalry with 'public opinion' he often came off second-best. Only in the lavatory he reigned supreme. There his dominion was unchallenged, for 'public opinion' was completely excluded.

INTERVIEWER: Well I was very struck by what you were saying earlier, Mr Danzig: not so much to give an impression to the Almighty, but to give an impression to other people. That seemed to me a rather strange statement.

FATHER: Well – well, shall I say this. If I want to smoke on Saturday, nobody need see me, I can go to my toilet – take a cigarette and smoke, nobody sees me, just me myself, so that I'm only answerable to myself. But there's a certain amount of discipline in my mind that I've got to observe certain laws and regulations according to the Torah, if you believe in the revelation of the Almighty you accept that – then, smoking is prohibited. Who sees me? Only One – One God sees me.

The lavatory was the only place in the Danzigs' home where each member of the family was entitled to be physically alone after a certain age.

We may infer, too, that the 'God' of their experience was an expression of the disciplining phantasy other, before whom in phantasy they were controlling their marginally controlled bowels. This inference is congruent with Mr Danzig's furtive disobedience under the nose, as it were, of 'God'. His particular acts – striking a match, and smoking a cigarette, both of which are forbidden to Orthodox Jews on the Sabbath – indicate a phantasy libidinal (i.e. anal masturbatory) component to his disobedience.

We know, too, that the Danzigs' knowledge that regularity was right was a function of their altered identity as good children. We may thus infer that their experience of 'God' was a function, too, of their interiorized parental-other-embodying-'the-others'. This inference is congruent with the fact that, except for the lavatory, everywhere 'God' was 'public opinion' was too.

We may also infer that 'God' was an experience that maintained their continuity of being between the stage in infancy when they related to the world of the not-self exclusively through their gut, and the time when they started being aware of other ways of relating to the not-self world. Presumably in the gut period they were predominantly aware of the disciplining other, and hardly aware of 'the others' this other embodied. Hence 'God's' un-challenged lavatorial dominion. As their experience of self and others grew, presumably they became aware of 'the others' too. Hence, outside the lavatory, everywhere 'God' was there were 'the others'.

Since 'public opinion' was experienced everywhere outside the lavatory, it may be asked how they were able to conceal Sarah's 'laziness' from the time she was thirteen until twenty-one. The answer lies in the fact that 'public opinion' was always felt to be embodied in others as others. In a place where no others could be, there they felt free from observation.

Now, in their house certain rooms were sometimes completely private. Their house comprised a ground floor and a first floor. On the ground floor were two reception rooms (dining-room and lounge), morning room and kitchen. These were always public. Here the Danzigs were a family before extra-familial others, and the parents a couple before these others and the children.

On the first floor were four bedrooms and the bathroom (bath and lavatory in one room). The parents shared one bedroom, and the three children had a room each. The parents had the right to enter the children's rooms at any time, and the right to investigate their wardrobes, drawers, cupboards, and any of their possessions. The children were forbidden to enter the parents' room which housed the parental pair in privacy. Outside the four walls of their room the parents were always a couple before 'the others', whether embodied by their children or others.

However, only their partnership was private within their bedroom, not each personally. Only in the lavatory did they feel personally private. There each could be alone with his God.

During the years of concealment, the main extra-familial embodiments of 'the others' were the daily help, and visiting friends and relatives. All the bedrooms were public places, Monday to Friday, from the time the daily help arrived until she left at 4 p.m.

Before she was labelled sick, Sarah's 'laziness', we know, took the form of thinking in her room – 'brooding', and occasionally not coming down to meals on time. Since her thinking took place after she returned from school or college, or at the weekend, the daily help knew nothing of it. And since it occurred in her bedroom, visitors knew nothing of it either. And so her 'laziness' remained private, hidden within the family.

CHAPTER 9

Family religion and the religion of family

Since the question of religious observance was an important problem in this family, we must consider this issue more closely.

Sarah was extremely mystified over the practice of religion in general, and Judaism in particular. Her mystification was a function of her family's mystifying religious praxis, itself the expression of their own deep unrecognized confusion on the matter.

Her parents called Judaism their family faith, received, they said, from their parents, whom they saw as more faithful than they. But the family faith they practised seemed mostly faith in family.

Now, the Danzigs' parents had immigrated to Britain at the end of the nineteenth century, fleeing from persecution in Eastern Europe, choosing to leave their old home rather than enter the Christian family as their persecutors urged them to do. The parents' parents had many brothers and sisters, some of whom emigrated too. Others had stayed behind because there was not enough money to pay the fares of everyone. These died in Eastern Europe, most of them from natural hazards, the remainder with their children, grandchildren, and other relatives[1] in German gas chambers, fifty years later.

---

[1] Three descendants are alive. One is a cousin of Mrs Danzig. He had apparently been called 'the madman'. He had gone to Palestine as a member of one of the early communal settlements in which groups of men and women tried to evolve a way of living together that avoided both the distortions of family life, and the alienation from their primary source obtaining under capitalism. The other two are children of Mr Danzig's cousin. They survived the Second World War, and are now also in Israel.

Mrs Danzig's parents met for the first time in this country. Mr Danzig's were already married with two sons when they came over. A third son, Mr Danzig, was born shortly afterwards, and a fourth was born three years after him. There were no other children.

When Mrs Danzig's mother landed in this country she had been a girl of thirteen. She had gone straight to work. She worked as a tailoress until she married, and after marriage continued to work, now as a housewife. Mrs Danzig's childhood memories of her mother were almost exclusively of her as a tireless worker, whom she still regarded with respectful awe.

Her father, too, had been in his teens when he came over. He was a tailor's apprentice. For years he worked for others until he saved enough to open a business of his own. Even then he had to struggle hard, because competition was fierce. It was many years before he felt he could afford to marry, so that when Mrs Danzig was born her mother was already thirty and her father thirty-five. She was their only child.

Now Mrs Danzig's father had been Orthodox because, according to her, he had believed in Orthodoxy. Her mother, too, had been Orthodox, although her mother, unlike her father, had not actually believed in Orthodoxy. Or rather she had not believed in what Mrs Danzig understood her father believed in when he spoke of Orthodoxy. Her mother had believed in pleasing her father, and her father had believed in this too. So her mother had been 'Orthodox'.

Like many Jews, Mrs Danzig's father had discovered that strict observance of all the ritual regulations placed him at a disadvantage in the struggle for business survival. In Eastern Europe the Jews, mostly poverty-stricken artisans and marginally existing small traders, had lived in close-knit communities, surrounded by hostile neighbours. Their way of life had begun to emerge from the pattern of the Middle Ages only in the course of the nineteenth century. This pattern, in which there was no great disjunction between their intrafamilial experience of themselves and their extrafamilial, was closely governed by religious tradition.

This tradition regarded business or work merely as a means of providing one's living expenses, while one concentrated on the main purpose of life, which was to study and live the Torah.[1] Consequently, one was required to spend no more time on business or on earning money than was necessary to provide for oneself and one's dependents those conditions that facilitated the proper end. Providing such conditions was the prime duty of a father to his family.

Since the business of most Jewish businessmen was either conducted exclusively amongst Jews, or was to a significant extent dependent on Jews, any businessman who tried to gain advantage over his competitors by disregarding religious tradition risked severe communal sanctions and economic ruin. In Britain, however, this did not hold.

In Eastern Europe the economy had been, to a significant extent, still a peasant economy. But in Britain the Jews found themselves suddenly precipitated into the mill of a highly developed industrial capitalism. This system, little deterred by any traditional religious teaching about the rights of its victims, had killed and maimed physically and emotionally, millions of its people. It had disinherited them, ruthlessly destroying their communal and family life, subjecting them for a century now to a social persecution as sustained and destructive in its own way as any communal persecution the Jews had suffered over a similar period in the East.[2] Such an attack the Jews now came under.

No longer subjected to communal persecution, their communal and family life was far more radically undermined by the system of industrial capitalism than by the physical attacks and communal exclusion they had formerly suffered. In a society exclusively organized as an industrial army, they were communally atomized into a serial mass, a series of isolated individuals competing with one another to an extent hitherto unknown for the relatively

[1] Synonymous with Teaching, Instruction, Direction, Way, Law, Divine Principle.

[2] Of course, capitalism had freed great productive forces, and, particularly in its early phases, had also been a power for social emancipation.

few[1] jobs and business orders that were available. And though they could carry out the rituals of their religion unhindered, in practice they were expected to have no identity other than their rank order, no loyalty except to the system, and no responsibility except to the boss, he who gave the jobs or orders, himself no more than a rank.

In the panic of the struggle for survival, many Jews began to align themselves with the ideology of the system. For they increasingly experienced their traditional religious framework to be irrelevant, or even a hindrance. And though others continued trying to carry out their customary observances, they found them becoming empty of content. Those who wished to maintain their Orthodox tradition placed themselves under the guidance of their institutional religious authorities, but these were as lost in dealing with the situation as the Christian Church was. Many Jews in desperation began to disregard their traditional religious customs, and some with businesses found that, far from suffering, their businesses prospered. Mrs Danzig's father had been one such businessman. He had learnt how to 'stretch a point' as he put it, and his business had begun to do well. With success came confidence, and before long he started to be his own Rabbi, stretching further points that had nothing to do with business at all.

However, he made no open break with tradition. He still regarded himself as Orthodox, but inevitably a change had occurred in his observance. He no longer performed certain ritual acts, nor observed certain customs and laws. Instead, he ritually performed these ritual acts and ritually observed the customs and laws.

Mr Danzig's father had not been a businessman. He had been an officer in the local synagogue, which had been too small to have

[1] Relative to the numbers seeking them, the relative shortage being an integral part of the state of affairs. For a discussion of the significance of scarcity for an understanding of history and social organization, see Sartre, J.-P., *Critique de la Raison Dialectique*. For an exposition of Sartre's statement, see Laing, R. D. and Cooper, D. G., *Reason and Violence*.

a Rabbi of its own. He had been given the honorary title of minister and had supervised certain communal activities, and officiated at certain ceremonies, though always under the direction of rabbinical authority. He had a small local reputation for learning, piety, and holiness, to which he had apparently further contributed by his vigorous denunciations of backsliders. He was regarded as highly respectable.

FATHER: My father was a very learned man, a great Hebrew scholar. My father was a nice, respectable Jew.

He and his wife were much more meticulous in their observances than Mrs Danzig's parents.

MOTHER: He [Mr Danzig's father] used to get up at five in the morning, I can remember at the time I used to live there. When we first got married our house wasn't ready, so we lived there for four months. We used to come down at half past seven – they had already eaten and been to the synagogue and back again. They kept a very kosher house, much more than my parents did, much more – um – Orthodox, and I used to come home and tell my mother. 'Well,' she said. 'I can remember my mother doing that, but,' she said, 'it doesn't matter,' and I used to tell my father, and 'Well,' he said, 'we can stretch a point or two these days.'

As for his father's character, Mr Danzig saw him as strict but just, and a perfect family man. Similarly, his mother was a perfect mother, always neat and clean, an excellent housewife who taught Mr Danzig not to be ashamed of housework. His parents never quarrelled. Their relationship was ideal. And the four sons, too, got on well with each other, the older helping the younger. Parents and children lived in complete harmony. It was the model of a Jewish family.

However, there were signs that the picture was not as bright as Mr Danzig painted it. It seems his parents did quarrel, and there were resentments among the sons. For instance, Mr Danzig complained that though he frequently helped his younger brother with loans, his brother showed little gratitude. Though, he hastened to add, he did not want any.

It seemed that in conveying this picture of his family of origin Mr Danzig, as the respectful son of his respectable parents, was automatically continuing to play out his serial familial role.

Now, Mrs Danzig's parents had wanted a son-in-law who believed in what they believed in, and Mr Danzig had been their choice. It seems, however, they were not so concerned that he practised what he and they agreed they believed in, so long as he said he believed in it.

Mrs Danzig had not objected to her parents' choice. As their respectful daughter she had been happy to agree, and besides, as she said, it had not been important compared with security. It was true that Mr Danzig was perhaps rather inconveniently Orthodox. Many of the ritual regulations were a nuisance, but she complied to please him as her mother had done to please her father. And when she did break regulations, as she not infrequently did, she did so secretly, never in front of her husband. As a respectable and Orthodox housewife in a reputable partnership it was her duty to show respect for her husband and comply with Orthodox regulations. But since in practice Mr Danzig decided which regulations were Orthodox, being an Orthodox housewife, for Mrs Danzig, simply meant complying with the regulations her husband laid down. Her compliance was part of her contribution to their joint reputation as successfully married.

As for being Jewish, she felt this to be more fundamental than being Orthodox. She experienced it as part of her essence.

MOTHER: I do agree to a certain extent that if you're Jewish you keep to the Jewish religion. You *go* to synagogue on Saturday, there's no harm in going to a synagogue on Saturday. That's all right. I mean you can't run away from the fact that you are what you are.

But even being Jewish had little to do with religion. Apart from agreeing it was desirable for her husband and son to attend synagogue on the Sabbath – she never attended because she said her husband told her it was not necessary for a woman – it consisted in almost nothing other than keeping to the dietary laws. And even those she broke by eating, for example, in non-kosher, forbidden restaurants when she felt they were not likely to be observed by Jewish 'public opinion'.

MOTHER: Well I knew when I got married to Mr Danzig I would have to keep a kosher house which I myself – as a matter of fact I like to keep a kosher house. The kitchen is my business and it's no business of his where I get my meat from[1] – whether I get it from Tom Jones or whether I get it from my own kosher butcher. That's nothing to do with a man at all. A woman who runs the home, shops where *she* likes. In any case I do keep my meat and everything separate, as it should be. That's the way my mother did it and I think I like it that way. We never eat anything – what the children do I don't mind, I can't answer for them, if they go out or are on holiday, what they eat I don't ask them. But when we go out we stick to our kosher diet, and if we can't get anything kosher we have an omelette or fish.

In observing or failing to observe the regulations in the way she did, she was simply being her Jewish mother's Jewish daughter. Her Jewish identity was nothing other than an altered group identity. That is, she perceived herself as a member of a family perceived by 'the others' as Jewish. And she felt perceived as Jewish because she and her family ate more or less according to certain dietary regulations. Or, if they did not eat according to the regulations, they took certain precautions not to be seen not to be eating in this way. This designated the Jewish family-for-'the-others' she had internalized.

Mr Danzig was more particular about observing ritual regulations than his wife, but for him, too, being an Orthodox Jew was primarily a 'public' role. It was a role in which one gave the impression of self-control through appearing to observe ritual

[1] In an Orthodox house it should be the concern of the head of the family that his wife buys only ritually pure food and keeps to the dietary laws.

law meticulously. Indeed a Jew who did not give this impression was not even religious. He was what Mr Danzig called 'an atheist'.

FATHER: You want to smoke – well, you have to create the impression, mostly about yourself, as certain respect is based on self-control. I'm not saying there are plenty of Jews who smoke on the Sabbath who are very nice people, nice gentlemen, but they're not Orthodox, they're atheists.

Though others could be nice respectable Jews without observing ritual regulations, this was not possible for Mr Danzig. For he indicated that if the children of an Orthodox Jew publicly failed to demonstrate self-control ritually, they would jeopardize their father's reputation, causing him to die quickly of shame. This respectful ritual demonstration he called Orthodoxy, and even Judaism. In being an Orthodox Jew Mr Danzig was protecting his Orthodox Jewish father's family reputation by being one of a family seen by 'the others' to be Orthodox Jewish. In other words, he experienced himself as an Orthodox Jew when he felt himself seen as a member of his family ritually demonstrating the self-control he believed the son of an Orthodox Jew was required by his father to demonstrate. When he was seen like this he was also a respectable Jew. For Mr Danzig, being an Orthodox Jew was an altered respectable family group identity.

And publicly observing ritual regulations suited him well enough, for they allowed him to express his compulsion to regularity and order. Thus, being an Orthodox Jew usually allowed him to serve 'God' and 'public opinion' at the same time.

It is true there were times when such combined service was not possible. 'God' then took second place.

FATHER: You've sometimes got to create an impression, more so to people than to the Almighty if you believe, and you read the Bible. And you [Sarah] are so much engrossed in reading the Bible. Often you've got to create an impression with *people* who *don't* understand certain things. They don't want to understand or *cannot* understand, not *prepared* to understand. So you've got to avoid giving them something to talk about. Am I wrong in my thinking?

But there were times when combined service was completely possible, though this service appeared to have little to do with the tradition of Judaism.

FATHER: Yes, that's right. He [the minister] did it.[1] There are people who might see him would think, 'Ah, you're not a Jew', who don't understand it, don't understand what's happening.

INTERVIEWER: But I'm saying the minister is obviously prepared to be misunderstood for the sake of doing what he thought was right.

FATHER: Well, therefore I – I like to feel I'm not giving people any wrong impression, any opportunity to think I have done something which should not be done on a Saturday.

INTERVIEWER: You haven't heard what I said, Mr Danzig. I said the minister was obviously prepared to risk being misunderstood to do what he thought was right. Whereas you're saying you're not prepared to be misunderstood.

FATHER: I want to avoid being misunderstood.

INTERVIEWER: That's right. The minister was prepared to be misunderstood for doing what he thought was right.

FATHER: Well, as it was the minister people might have realized that it must have been a very serious matter if he could leave the service. But as an individual, a layman, I may not be viewed the same way.

INTERVIEWER: So your whole concern is about what people are saying.

FATHER: By standards – yes, by certain standards. I don't want to be misjudged by desecrating certain standards – by breaking certain standards.

[1] The minister used his car to visit his sick daughter in hospital on the Sabbath (see p. 20).

INTERVIEWER: Ah, but your standard at this point becomes public opinion.

FATHER: Public opinion.

INTERVIEWER: I mean, I haven't understood that to be – that the standard of a religious person is the standard of public opinion.

FATHER: To a very large extent, religion and public opinion. A minister has very often got to show certain examples or certain Orthodox Jews in a community who enjoy a certain reputation have got to observe certain standards.

We can now understand another aspect of the Danzigs' mystifying praxis in relation to Sarah. Before her first admission to hospital she had started to read the Bible and to meditate on what she found there. Her parents, far from welcoming this, had vehemently opposed it. They said she was not being a good Jewish girl. When she returned home after her first admission she resumed reading the Bible, and her parents' opposition became even more intense. She was being sick.

Their praxis becomes intelligible in the light of our discovery that their family faith was their faith in family. This faith, as we know, required them to maintain a public front of family harmony. In reading the Bible, Sarah disrupted this front, for she stepped out of her serial family role of daughter.

SARAH: The funny thing is, when I read the Bible they object.

FATHER: I don't object.

MOTHER: It's not natural for a young girl to read the Bible. Do you think so, Doctor? Not for leisure. She should read something a little lighter, not the Bible. My father was Orthodox, as you know, and I never read the Bible.

FATHER: There's nothing wrong with reading the Bible, it depends on the circumstances under which you read the Bible. Er – I can assure you it's not. I don't try to make religion an issue to such an extent, that it must be, the house must do a certain thing because I want them to. It's nice to conduct – to have a Jewish atmosphere at home.

In an Orthodox family as her parents saw it, it was not her place to read the Bible. It was her father's. In reading the Bible, she was experienced as usurping his position. Her act was thus an act of filial disobedience, which threatened her father's *raison d'être*. She threatened his altered group identity as a respected parental manager making an orthodox success of the business of family.

FATHER: It's [refraining from reading the Bible] not asking very much. I'm entitled to have a certain amount of say in my own house. If I've got no say as far as that is concerned and my wife doesn't want to listen to me and my children don't want to listen to me – what pleasure do I derive from the home? So I've outlived my usefulness to my wife and to my children. I'm not asking very much. It's a business deal – I look on it as a business deal, you want to look on it from a business point of view.

CHAPTER 10

Sexual life and manners

As we now know the Danzigs had been worrying about Sarah's improper behaviour for years without calling in a doctor. The incident precipitating their action was her assertion she had been sleeping with a boy. This generated such panic that their perception of her became retrospectively falsified. They became lost in a timeless phantasy of perpetually imminent crisis.

How are we to understand this sequence of events? In the darkness of the Danzigs' world of shared phantasy, what was the relation between Sarah's possible sexual experience and the 'laziness' they saw in her?

The Danzigs felt sexual behaviour was more dangerous than any other form of 'ill behaviour'. Sarah's 'laziness', though potentially scandalous, could be hushed up, but sexual behaviour was different. It was much more worrying. It would almost certainly lead to scandal.

FATHER: Because if he's in trouble, gets in trouble, God forbid – as you might know, Doctor, the first thing that happens reacts on parents. Or the daughter gets in trouble. Well now whatever the trouble may be, its very worrying. I want my children, my daughter particularly, my daughter –

However, to see Sarah's sexual behaviour as bad was not possible without affecting their reputation. Like their attribution of process to her 'laziness', the attribution of illness to her sexual behaviour was facilitated by the nature of their phantasy about her possible sexual experience.

Their statements on her and John's possible experience showed they assumed their children would engage exclusively in relation-ships that were illicit, furtive, dirty, disgusting, and dangerous. They saw them led astray into a 'Chelsea' underworld of bad people who tricked and seduced the unwary, causing them to lose control of themselves, so that something scandalous occurred. At no time did they speak of their children's possible sexual experience as a joyful expression of mutual love and direct reciprocity. For instance:

FATHER: I'm interested – this is a general statement my wife and I are making – I'm not specifying any particular part of their life or conduct. We've discussed it in a general way. I'm interested, very keenly interested and concerned that my son and Sarah, my daughter, should not do something which might cause a lot of complications and unnecessary worry. If my wife feels – and she may be justified – that Sarah is capable of looking after herself, when she is well – but I know human nature is – one of the things you can't mould is human nature. If she mixes and meets with the right company it's possible, but the danger lies if she may meet the wrong company. That's why I'm concerned that she should mix with the right company, the right kind, the company, so she'll not get into trouble.

And:

FATHER: I'm concerned knowing your actions, knowing your movements. If you go out – by all means go out. Have a good time; but if you're going out to an all-night party I don't think it's unreasonable to say I should know where you're going. If you get into trouble the first thing that will happen, I shall be informed about that trouble.

JOHN: What sort of trouble do you visualize?

FATHER: You might get mixed up with a woman, the wrong woman, the wrong company – with men, young men in coffee bars, in restaurants, in other places – confidence tricksters.

And:

JOHN: I should think what Daddy means, get mixed up with a

woman. What he's thinking is that if I had an affair with a girl and gave her a baby without being married, this is what he means. Isn't it Dad?

FATHER: Not only that. You can probably contract some sort of disease as well in that way – also get mixed up with black-mailers as well and bad company. It might be 'illegal' women.

And:

FATHER: I'm concerned that you *should* because you might be inclined to believe certain things and certain people at certain times and on certain occasions and I want to guard against that possibility – based on one thing, discipline of the mind, discipline in certain things in life, a high standard of living in every way.

And:

FATHER: The modern trend is, if you're engaged to a young man, it's all very well to go to bed. I've seen it. I've heard about it. It's disgusting. Well if that's the way it is I can't –

MOTHER: It's almost back to *Lady Chatterley's* –

FATHER: No wonder then that *Lady Chatterley's Lover* was passed.[1]

The nature of the Danzigs' anxiety can be gauged from the fact that though they were worried stiff in case Sarah had a baby, they did not worry to anywhere near the same extent over her catching 'a disease'. Though this was an important feature of Mr Danzig's worry about John.

We may reasonably infer their assumptions about the nature of their children's possible sexual experience was the expression of an unrecognized bowel experience in relation to bad, seductive, and completely anonymous others or part objects. This experience would cause them to become orgastically incontinent in public ('. . . the first thing that will happen, I shall be informed . . .'), particularly Sarah.

This inference is congruent with our earlier inference about the

---

[1] And see, for example, quotations pp. 142-4, 150-1.

nature of their phantasy experience of Sarah's 'laziness'. We inferred they experienced her retaining her pleasurable faeces until she became incontinent.

But why did Sarah behave in the way she did, asserting to her parents that she had been sleeping with a boy? An examination of her parents' sexual relationship is relevant here. This examination will require us to consider their relationship with John.

The Danzigs' marriage contract was, we said, purely a business arrangement. Apart from the procedures needed to produce children – children were required by a reputable family firm – it was a contract from which sexuality was clearly understood to be excluded. Lack of sexual pleasure was not even a basis for discussion, far less an occasion for the expression of dissatisfaction. For instance, the following exchange occurred after Mr Danzig had complained to us in private about their lack of sexual harmony.

INTERVIEWER: What you're saying, Mrs Danzig, is that you don't believe that any quarrels were in terms of your own relationship with Mr Danzig.

MOTHER: Oh no, we never quarrelled over money or anything like that. No, she [Sarah] knows it.

INTERVIEWER: What do you say, Mr Danzig? Do you agree with your wife there?

FATHER: I, er – frankly my mind's a blank. I can't go back so far. I can't remember. I always take – I don't mind – let quarrels remain too long. What I've got to say – say it right away until I've finished it. I don't court a grudge, or carry a hate in my heart against anybody. I may be somewhat inclined to be a bit sharpish sometimes. It can't be helped.

INTERVIEWER: You would say that your relationship with your wife was a harmonious one?

MOTHER: Oh yes.

FATHER: Nothing very serious.

INTERVIEWER: And that this marriage that you have is a happy marriage?

FATHER: Er – as marriages go, yes [laughs] as marriages go, yes.

INTERVIEWER: Uh uh, that's an extremely cautious answer.

MOTHER: Yes, well I mean, there's no hundred per cent in any-thing is there? Not in a business or anything – in a partnership of any kind?

FATHER: Well, I'm no Venus. I'm no beauty. I'm not going to kid myself that my wife fell head over heels in love with me, and I wouldn't bluff my wife that I fell head over heels with her.

On another occasion Mr Danzig hinted obliquely he was not sexually satisfied. His wife reacted with alarm and indignation. This was no ground for complaint. As far as she was concerned the bargain had been fulfilled.

MOTHER: Has he told you what it is about? Have you asked him? Can he lay a finger on what? That's the way of getting it out. Has he told you what? Has he said specifically what? Or has he not? I mean, two people come to talk to the Court and the Judge says, 'What is this argument over?' One says, 'This man owes me money and I want it back,' and the other says, 'No, I've never lent him any money. No, I've never lent him any money. You've got nothing to prove I've lent him any money.' What has Mr Danzig ever said to you that should give you the inkling, that there's sort of something, something solid to go on.

Besides, she was making no complaint about him. In the face of her response Mr Danzig did not try to press the matter.

They both seemed to feel that a sexual relationship was in-compatible with maintaining their contract, though they were not opposed to sexual relationships in theory. They agreed it would be thrilling and natural to let oneself be carried away by one's feelings, but they thought it was highly dangerous. It would probably turn out bad. It could lead one to defy one's parents, and besides it would mean being in love with a blackguard.

INTERVIEWER: But the question I was asking was, being *in* love,

which isn't necessarily the same thing. Would you regard yourself as the sort of person, Mrs Danzig, who would have let
her heart rule her head?

MOTHER: Yes, I think that would have been very thrilling. I
think that would have been most exciting, and very natural.

FATHER. That's what I think.

MOTHER: You see and I was very practical when I was single,
you see. And you do sort of weigh the pros and cons, and you
have to be sensible about marriage as well. I mean don't fall
in love with a blackguard, that's sheer infatuation.

FATHER: Well, in fact it's the blackguards they do fall in love
with.

MOTHER: Well I wouldn't fall in love with a blackguard. I was
too practical for that. Afterwards they turn out nasty, well
that's just one of those things.

And so, for the sake of 'security' they felt it best to control out
of existence their sexual feelings, by applying the practical logic
they had derived from their parents. They had done so even before
they met. For they had never had a relationship with anyone based
on sexual attraction.

Their anxiety over possible sexual experience is congruent with
a phantasy of orgastic incontinence in relation to seductive faecal
objects ('thrilling', 'nasty', 'blackguards').

However, though they had precluded themselves from having
a sexual relationship with each other, the issue of sexual experience
was alive, and made itself felt in ways that were devious.

Mr Danzig had agreed with his wife that sensible people considered only 'practical' matters in judging a marital partner, but,
as we said, he privately complained that his sex life was unsatisfactory and always had been. He had never derived any satisfaction with his wife. According to him, this was her fault, for he had
tried to raise the matter with her, but she became excited and
nervous and refused to discuss it. She lacked self-control. On the
other hand, he said, possibly the fault was his. It could be. He
did not know. He was prepared to admit that was possible.

Perhaps his wife was not his ideal in marriage, but then maybe he was not hers. His wife may be a fine woman, and he may be a very fine man, but together perhaps they may not be a suitable partnership.

It emerged that this was not a new thought. It had occurred to him before, a long time ago, practically on the day of their wedding, in fact. Not that he would ever think of leaving her. What one said in moments of annoyance, one would not do in one's sane moments. Not under any circumstances would he do that.

His wife, too, had complaints, he admitted. She bemoaned her unhappy life with him, how sorry she was she married him, how she felt like doing herself in because she was fed up. He usually tried to pacify her by saying jokingly, 'What, are you going to leave such a lovely house? I'll get a nice young lady.' And she usually replied. 'I thought that a long time ago. I knew you'd do that.'

He was very puzzled by her attitude. He wondered whether she was irritable because she was feeling less secure in his love. She may have felt he did not love her, although he could see no reason why she should think that. After all, he did not ignore her existence altogether. On the contrary, he was very careful, he said, not to make it apparent, for he did not want her to feel entirely insecure. Really, he did not know what she expected from him. Maybe she wanted him to 'Darling this' and 'Darling that', and kiss her, and perhaps put his arm round her. Or maybe she expected him to make a fuss of her, or make love to her. But, frankly, well it was a funny thing, but he did not feel that way, never had.

He had, occasionally, and in a very general way of course, tried to raise the matter of their sex life with her; but no, she refused to discuss it. There was nothing he could do about it. And so the question remained unsolved. However, when I tried to explore the matter further he said hastily it was not really important. Nor could he be induced to discuss it on any other occasion. When it was raised he simply became evasive.

However, I did learn that his sexual feelings were highly

tenuous. His interest in sex was only some four or five years old. Even before his marriage he had never felt the slightest interest. But recently he had begun to feel some stirrings, because, he explained apologetically, when you got on to your sixties you naturally thought of these things.

Apparently, therefore, some guilt-ridden sensations, mainly in the form of feelings of frustration, had in recent years begun to percolate through to his consciousness. These were the years of Sarah's adolescence, and the period of her so-called laziness. It was also a period of increased quarrelling and tension between the parents.

What was the nature of these sexual feelings that were irritating Mr Danzig? He thought they were heterosexual, but his identification appeared to be strongly, even predominantly, feminine. For instance, he appeared identified primarily with his mother, not his father. This mother was an other who was mainly a housecleaner.

FATHER: I'm not a lazy man. I was brought up – my mother, we were four brothers. We were brought up domesticated, to fend for ourselves. My mother wasn't very well, so we always helped in the house with anything. I'm not ashamed to admit that. Naturally we would not get down and clean the floor, but we were not cripples in the house. Naturally I'm not going to admit to my wife that I'm domesticated. I wouldn't do that.

His reference to Venus (see p. 117) also implied he experienced himself as a woman, though not as a sexually exciting one. While sexual confusion was evident in his idealized ambiguous experience of his father.

FATHER: My father was a very fine man in character, never insulted a person in his life, hated to hear discussions about other people talking about somebody else. He used to jump down people's throats for discussing or criticizing other people. He was a diamond of a man, a man with no badness in him. He was a fine man, and a fine-charactered individual, a man who thought well of people. He used to treat my mother like a gentleman and Mother used to treat him as a lady.

Lastly, his phantasy of the 'nice young lady' was not derived from a heterosexual phantasy. A man of fifty-six with a sexual history like his, who thought he could win a heterosexually active young woman, was as far removed from heterosexual reality as anyone could be. Assuring me that he would never think of leaving his wife for another woman simply indicated how removed he was. Of course, his wife may have thought he might carry out his threat. But if she did, it would simply indicate how far she was removed from heterosexual reality.

Mr Danzig had an explanation for the absence of relationships with women before his marriage. He had been seeking his ideal; but he apparently saw nothing incongruous in a quest for an ideal woman which involved refraining from seeking her in the real women who existed. And since he never sought her, he had precluded himself from becoming disillusioned. And in precluding himself from disillusion, he had avoided any occasion for questioning himself and his existential projects, and so precluded himself from the possibility of discovering who he was and who she was.

And now he was once more thinking actively of his ideal woman. She took the form of a 'nice young lady' who was neat, orderly, and attractive, a perfect wife and mother. She was the antithesis of how he experienced Mrs Danzig, with whom he constantly quarrelled for not being like her, in effect.

FATHER: I wanted her to go out more often with me. My complaint with my wife is that she doesn't – she doesn't – um – she's always tired out and then can't go out with me. I want to take her out. I want her to look smart and presentable, and go out with me oftener. It's necessary for general make-up. It's necessary for the mind as well.

And:

FATHER: I want her to dress very nicely, very neatly and cleanly and smartly. I want to go out watching her. She doesn't care. She's indifferent to this. I don't like that. I say, 'Whatever position arises between me and you privately or otherwise, publicly, come out clean. Go out occasionally. It's not nice for the children. It gives an example to the children if you go out occasionally.'

It may well be perhaps, shall I say – I may even go a bit further than this. It may well be, and I've often thought about it, it may well be that *I* may not have been her ideal in marriage – and I'm going to admit to you that *she* may not be *my* ideal in marriage . . .

We may infer the 'nice young lady' of his imagination was his divorced, projected, but unembodied *anima* or *Shechinah*.[1] Or to put it slightly differently, we may infer that she was his denied split-off, externalized,[2] and idealized femininity. Bearing in mind our inference that he avoided sexual experience because of an unrecognized phantasy fear of orgastic bowel incontinence, we may further infer the ideal woman was an expression of his phantasy-controlled bowel self. Imagining her, while confining himself to imagining her, appeared to be the compromise expression of unrecognized conflict over desire to experience his passive (feminine) sexuality, the conflict being a function of anxiety over becoming orgastically incontinent.

This is congruent with his preoccupation with the nature of John's sexual experience. In phantasy, he appeared to experience John's experience as homosexual. For instance, he experienced John as likely to be 'mixed up' – confused – with a woman (see exchange with John, p. 114).

As for his wife, we may infer she was experienced as an

---

[1] Hebrew (-ch- pronounced as in the Scottish lo*ch*). In the Jewish mystical tradition the following synonyms are used for *Shechinah*, depending on the experiential and emotional circumstances: the indwelling presence of God, the Inner Divine Presence, the Queen, the Sabbath Bride, the Supernal Mother, the Virgin of Israel. In other traditions the term is synonymous with the Holy Mother, the Holy Virgin, Virgin Mother, Soul, Anima Mundi, the Shakti of Siva, Mother Nature, the presence of healing emotion, healing emotional experience.

[2] That is, experienced by him as external.

incipiently disordered bowel. This inference is congruent with his perception of her as lacking self-control, and with the anxiety he felt all the years of their marriage that she would scandalously disrupt the marital front by quarrelling with him 'publicly'. We may further infer he had identified his wife with the uncontrolled aspect of his own bowel. This is congruent with our earlier discovery that he experienced, in phantasy, loss of control of his bowels when his relationship with his female partner was 'publicly' seen to be disordered.

Now, Mr Danzig was chronically anxious quite apart from his fear of scandal. He was continually alert for signs of ridicule. Even in circumstances when he knew there was no question of his family reputation being at stake he constantly felt people did not respect him and were making a fool of him – his brothers, customers, business associates, other synagogue members. He felt they did not take him as seriously as he deserved, considering he was head of a family. He constantly felt the respect of 'the others' was highly marginal. His reputation seemed always in the balance.

For comfort he repeatedly sought his wife's point of view. He asked for reassurance that the other had no right to make a fool of him. However, her reassurance was highly ambiguous. For while she seemed to say the other simply acted compulsively, she said so in a way that left the matter in doubt.

MOTHER: He worries, not so much worries, but things upset him easily. He's very sensitive. If anybody should ever say anything to him he'll come home and say, 'Now look, I want to tell you something.' He'll say, 'Do you think it's not very important, do you think Gerald,' that's an associate of his, 'should have said this to me?' 'Well,' I said, 'you know Gerald's been a colonel in the army for so many years and still thinks he's in the army, and he's using the same tactics to you, but I don't think he means anything,' I said. 'It'll blow over by tomorrow.'

He appeared repeatedly to invite the ridicule of others without realizing he did so. His praxis becomes intelligible when we recall his alterated identity functioned to prevent loss of control of his marginally controlled bowels. In placing himself in situations where his identity was called into question, we may infer he was, in phantasy, placing himself in a position where 'the others' allocated him an identity as an other who had lost control of his bowels. We may further infer that in phantasy this position was one in which his lack of control had been demonstrated by the other penetrating him anally (upsetting him by using army tactics).

This construction is congruent with our inference that he was unwittingly in conflict over desire to experience orgastically his anal sexuality. We may infer the desire was to experience orgastic incontinence, since he repeatedly placed himself in a position wherein, in phantasy, he appeared to experience himself allocated an identity as incontinent. In seeking reassurance from his wife, he was apparently, in phantasy, seeking reassurance he was an other who did have his sphincter under firm control with no thought of relaxation. This is implied in his perceiving 'the others' as entirely to blame, and not seeing that he placed himself in a position to be ridiculed. In other words he was, in phantasy, seeking confirmation of his alterated identity as a good (bowel-controlled) boy.[1] This identity shielded him, as we know, from becoming aware of any alternative to controlling his bowels.

Mr Danzig's reputation as a successful family man depended, as we know, on appearing 'publicly' as the head of the house. It meant appearing to direct and control the complex of intra-familial relationships. We know, too, he expected his family to cooperate in maintaining the appearance of control. But he also expected them to help him feel in control. In particular he wanted John to help. He wanted to feel John respected him. Unfortunately, Mrs Danzig and John, though careful not to humiliate him 'publicly', cooperated only intermittently at home. Mrs Danzig agreed her husband had a right to expect John to cooperate, nevertheless she encouraged him to defy his father, especially in

[1] We may infer that at one stage in his life 'the others' were embodied by his brothers, and he had sought reassurance from his mother.

matters over which his father thought it important to be obeyed. This, as we shall see, was a tactic designed to evoke Mr Danzig's anxiety. Not surprisingly, therefore, her husband constantly felt that affairs were liable to get out of his control.

FATHER: Oh well, I suppose I can't control the present family events. It's very worrying.

Paradoxically, this anxiety was shared by Mrs Danzig and John. They seemed afraid they would press things too far and disrupt the family publicly. Yet they persistently failed to co-operate privately. They seemed to be acting under compulsion. They seemed to be engaged in a form of brinkmanship.

However, the game was much safer than it first appeared. The parents in particular had been at it for years. All three, father, mother, and son, knew the rules perfectly, and in practice matters never got out of control. The game they played was as follows:

Mr Danzig wanted to be allowed to teach John religion and moral control. But when, for instance, he demanded that John should daily recite the morning prayer and accompany him to synagogue on the Sabbath morning, John refused, and his mother backed him. In her view, Mr Danzig was being intolerant. He was expecting too much of a young boy. Her husband defended himself, usually angrily. He insisted his demands were reasonable. As a father he was entitled to expect his son to please him. And he criticized his wife for criticizing him before John. Mrs Danzig defended herself in turn. She insisted Mr Danzig was very unreasonable, and a row usually developed, with Mr Danzig hard put to justify himself.

However, from the point of view of the religion the three of them explicitly professed, Mr Danzig was perfectly right in expecting John to pray and to attend synagogue regularly. John, at twenty-one, had long passed the age when an Orthodox Jew is expected to take up the religious rights and obligations of an adult. Since he was engaged in no other tasks of spiritual validity which took precedence, reciting the morning prayer daily, and attending synagogue on the Sabbath morning, were in the circumstances the least he could do. But this correct stance Mr Danzig never adopted, for the simple reason it had never occurred to him. His expectations of John precluded him from seeing it. While the expectations of John and Mrs Danzig similarly precluded them. For the last thing any of them wanted was for John to become a sexually mature man. John was still a boy, and John saw himself like this. There had been a time during his adolescence when, in alliance with Sarah, John had considered breaking away from the family and its ideology. But he had panicked. The world was a big place, and it was frightening to be outside the fold. The worst punishment John could envisage was 'excommunication'. So he had affirmed the family pledge, and stayed a boy.

Now, Mr Danzig's insistence that John should obediently learn from him was a function of Mr Danzig's experience of 'public opinion'. Though he sought comfort from his wife about how 'the others' saw him, her reassurance was second-best. 'Public opinion' for him was masculine, and a woman's reassurance would not do. Apart from his ideal, women in his world had inferior status. They lacked self-control,[1] unlike men. A man was always controlled. Indeed the criterion of manliness was control of self, as the criterion of fatherhood was control of the family. And only a man could confirm another as self-controlled. In getting John to obey him, Mr Danzig could kill two birds with one stone. For John as a male and a member of the family could confirm him doubly. In letting himself be taught self-control, he would be confirming his father in his alterated identity as a man and a father. But this meant John had to stay a boy, for only a boy would allow himself to be controlled.

John was prepared to stay a boy. But this brought complications, for John had his own expectations of his father. These led to continual sparring in which John, to his father's dismay, disobeyed him.

[1] This experience of women was expressed in his view that his wife was more to blame for their quarrels than he, and in his greater concern over Sarah's sexual behaviour than John's.

However, though John disobeyed him, he did so as a boy. He appeared to be provocatively tantalizing his father, simultaneously confirming and disconfirming him in his manliness and ability to control, but without seriously challenging him. This was most evident over John's sexual behaviour.

John led a sexual life which was an open secret between him and his parents.

JOHN: But I have my parents reasonably well-trained now, when I go out [smiling]. [Slight laugh from Mother.]

And:

JOHN: Well when I go out – say I go out and Dad says, 'Be home at one.' I hate to promise a certain time, because I can't always keep to this promise. And over the weekend, Saturday night, I don't mind if I go out to an all-night party. I don't like to say what time I'll be home because I don't know what time I'll be home. But they're well-trained, I come in, there's a little bit of a row in the morning if it's after midday, but it's quite er –

But there was no great joy in his sexual life. He was haunted by a fear of seeming unmanly if he did not do what the girls seemed to him to want him to do. His sexual relations were, to a considerable extent, an expression of bravado, and of desire to show off to his friends. He therefore had intercourse with various girls; but his parents, particularly his mother, determined its nature, in effect. It was quite forbidden to engage in a genitally mature love affair in which he and the girl seriously considered marriage. His intercourse was to be entirely for self-gratification, a kind of intravaginal masturbation or, since his parents' phantasy of his experience was a bowel phantasy, an intra-anal or intracloacal masturbation.

It was also implicitly understood that he should only have intercourse with non-Jewish girls. They were good enough for such an unclean purpose. In fact he had had intercourse with Jewish girls, but this he kept secret.

INTERVIEWER: Have you had intercourse with any girls?

JOHN: Oh yes.

INTERVIEWER: You wouldn't tell your parents this?

JOHN: Oh no. My mother I wouldn't tell. She knows by implication if I stay out all night and I come back with a story in the morning. She'll know. She won't mention it. She might make a little joke about it. Even my father makes a little joke about it, now he realizes I'm twenty-one and have my own life; but I wouldn't *ever* discuss it. If ever I got into trouble with a girl, I would *never* come to my parents with that sort of problem. Go to friends but not my parents.

INTERVIEWER: Would you – have you been out with non-Jewish girls? Had intercourse with them?

JOHN: Oh yes. Yes.

INTERVIEWER: Would you ever marry a non-Jewish girl? You wouldn't?

JOHN: No. I wouldn't consider it. And my father knows I wouldn't. I would go out with a non-Jewish girl for a considerable time.

INTERVIEWER: Yes. You say by implication your mother knows you must have been sleeping with a girl if you've been out all night. Do you think she might think it might be a non-Jewish girl?

JOHN: Oh yes.

INTERVIEWER: She would know that. By implication you think she knows that?

JOHN: Oh, I don't think she knows that, but I think she's got a bit – she seems to view Jewish girls through rose-tinted glasses. So the reason she would think it would be a non-Jewish girl would be because she wouldn't think a Jewish girl would do that.

As for marrying a non-Jewish girl, that was totally and absolutely forbidden, but for reasons that had nothing to do with religion, as we know from his mother (see p. 40).

Marrying a non-Jewish girl, as opposed to furtively having

intercourse with her, would have been an autonomous use of his penis, and would result in his being unequivocally expelled. He was to be, with his parents' permission, a pseudo-genital, self-gratifying little boy, and this he had settled for.

At home he put up a provocative show of protest against his father's attempts to exercise his authority, but it was only a show, as he admitted. For instance, though he protested against his father's entering his bedroom to 'tidy his drawers and fiddle with his things', he granted his father's right to do so, because his father paid for the things. For the sake of his feeling of ontic security he was prepared to maintain the family system by playing the role of respectful son, even if it meant foregoing genital maturity and existential autonomy. However, this compromise brought difficulties.

Giving up the attempt to attain existential autonomy and genitality merely increased the importance of other diversions and interpersonal projects. These were expressed in expectations he had of his father. These expectations gave rise to certain contradictory complaints described in the earlier study of the family (see pp. xiii-xxxv).

For instance, he said he was jealous of Sarah. His father had spoilt her by being lenient with her, and he joined his parents in criticizing her for being spoilt. But he also said his father was lenient with him, and he reproached his father for this. This contradiction becomes intelligible if we clarify his unconscious phantasy in relation to his father.

He said he wanted his father to be strict with him.

FATHER: I think I made everything too easy for him. I wasn't insistent. I wasn't strong enough. I should have kept on bullying him. I should have said to him, 'You've got to go to school. We're not going to have this. You've got to do it. You've got to do that.' I was too easy.

JOHN: No, I wasn't frightened of Dad and I think that if – I know that in books, the modern books they say a child shouldn't be frightened of his father, but I think in his younger years he *should* be. If he's a bit uncontrollable he should be scared of his father so he does well at school, because of the fear that if he doesn't do well, he'll get a clout. And if I'd known that if I didn't do well I'd have got a clout, I should have done well.

FATHER: I should have clouted him more.

MOTHER: Oh – no.

JOHN: No, probably [Mother protesting]. I honestly think if Daddy had hit me, if he'd used physical violence to me when I was young –

MOTHER: A poor way of getting work done.

JOHN: I know, but that was the only – there are some people it works, and with me it would have worked.

He recalled that as a small boy he used to mess his pants, and he had continued to do so until one day his father had thoroughly spanked him. This, he reiterated, ignoring his mother's protests, was the kind of firmness he wanted.

Interpreting, we may infer his defiance was the expression of unrecognized conflict over a phantasy desire to be anally penetrated. It expressed the desire and the resistance. It was a compromise whereby he experienced vicariously the thrill of sexually tantalizing his father in phantasy, daring him to penetrate him. This inference is congruent with his acquiescent protests when his father entered his bedroom to tidy his drawers and fiddle with his things.

It is also congruent with the implications in the following exchange, in which John is provoking Mr Danzig. John implies that he (John) has illicit sexual fantasies[1] ('never dreamt'), and says in as many words that he believes his father is more like him than he is prepared to admit. He implicitly experiences his father's illicit fantasies as homosexual ('another woman'). Since he implies his father is like himself, we may infer his illicit fantasies are also implicitly homosexual. And we may further infer the unrecognized phantasy expressed in his provocative way of discussing illicit sexual behaviour is also homosexual.

[1] We are here following the psychoanalytic convention of spelling fantasy with an 'f' when we mean 'imaginings' in contrast to 'unconscious phantasy'.

JOHN: You're not – in fact you're such a good example you're too good to be true. You're a perfectionist and you want your children to be like that –

FATHER: I don't want –

JOHN: You've led a strict life, you've always been very religious, you've led an extremely strict life regarding moral behaviour and all sorts of other behaviour, and you want your children to conform to that sort of life –

FATHER: No, no, no.

JOHN: But you do, Daddy – you've always – you've told me many a time that you would never have dreamt of sleeping with another woman before you got married, you wouldn't have dreamt of it – it was completely against your moral ethical code, and you want your children to conform to this sort of thing. If your children don't conform *exactly* to what you want them to be, in your mind, they're not worth –

We may also infer from the following that sometimes in phantasy he experienced his father to be trying to penetrate him, and that his resistance in phantasy was evoked because he experienced the attempt to be made too aggressively. He and his father were again discussing illicit sexual behaviour.

JOHN: No, it's because Dad states an opinion. [Father protests.] No, listen Dad – he states an opinion – Wham! – This is the opinion! So I feel immediately I've got to go the opposite. If he put forward that opinion in a more easy relaxed attitude, and just put the opinion forward, instead of pushing it on you, I wouldn't feel so inclined to argue with him.

That John's provocative behaviour towards his father was, phenomenologically speaking not the expression of a heterosexual, i.e. Oedipal,[1] phantasy is borne out by the fact that he never

---

[1] By *Oedipal phantasy*, I mean a triadic phantasy relationship in which the child experiences himself or herself in rivalry with the parent of the same sex for a privileged genital relationship with the parent of the opposite sex.

John's behaviour does not preclude the existence of an Oedipal phantasy at a deeper level, as it is called. But, phenomenologically speaking, its existence at this

showed any sign of envy of his father's position or prestige, or of his father's claim to religious or moral superiority, nor any sign of jealousy of his father over his father's relationship with his mother. Nor did he ever fight with his father over his mother. Even when his parents were quarrelling he never espoused his mother's cause. Nor did he ever criticize to us his father's behaviour towards his mother. Nor did Mr Danzig ever complain that John sided with Mrs Danzig against him. John and his mother were in alliance against Mr Danzig, but this was because Mrs Danzig intervened on her son's side against her husband, not because John intervened on his mother's side against his father. We shall be discussing this mother-son alliance shortly.

As for John's attitude towards his father's relationship with Sarah, he invariably sided with his father when she was reprimanded. He never acted as if he was his father's rival for his sister's affections. He appeared rather to be unconsciously in sexual rivalry with his sister for his father.

But John had to suffer frustration in his relationship with his father, for his homosexual phantasies remained unconscious. Even in derivative form he had to suffer disappointment. For no matter how provocatively he behaved, his father failed to respond decisively. His father continually laid down the law on sexual behaviour, issuing warnings about disease, confidence tricksters, and 'young men, villains and crooks who cross the door every day and give him a nice smile'. But when John defied him, though he flustered and blustered, he made no attempt to impose any of the sanctions it lay within his power to impose. There was thus never an unequivocal clash, nor, of course, an open discussion.

Mr Danzig failed to respond forcibly to John's defiance, partly

---

stage must remain speculative. And it may be that as John became more conscious of his homosexuality, his pattern of behaviour and experience might alter in such a way that it would be phenomenologically valid to infer the existence of an active Oedipal phantasy. But on the basis of his current behaviour and experience, there was no evidence of an active phantasy of Oedipal rivalry. This appeared to be in part due to the fact that his father had, in phantasy, surrendered Mrs Danzig to John. We shall discuss this shortly.

in order to avoid a clash with his wife. Only a response that clearly and definitively prohibited illicit sexual behaviour would she not oppose. For then, the matter would be out in the open, and her own ideology would preclude her from supporting John. This was evident during one family exchange. Mrs Danzig had been implicitly encouraging John to continue with his illicit sexual activity. But when the issue seemed about to come clearly into the open it was she who intervened to keep it under cover.

JOHN: I have a habit of, for the sake of – I'm very argumentative when it comes to issues with Dad, and he seems to be argumentative when it comes to me. If he states one opinion, I go on the other opinion, just to have an argument, just to be contrary. In actual fact I agree with Dad to a certain extent, but for different reasons. But to say I disagree with him because I prefer to have an easy life, my own personal life I prefer to be easy. But also because I have the habit of going contrary to Dad's wishes – as a matter of perverseness.

MOTHER [alarmed]: What – in practice or theory?

JOHN: No, only in talking.

MOTHER [relieved]: Oh.

And so, though Mr Danzig needed to be confirmed as a man and a father by John, he never definitively laid down the law in a way that would have stopped his wife interfering and ensured John's compliance. Each time he lectured John on self-control, John with his mother's encouragement argued back. Consequently, the inconclusive quarrelling continued, with Mr Danzig constantly anxious in case things got out of control.

How are we to understand Mr Danzig's inconclusive praxis, his failure to lay down the law definitively? We must examine his phantasy experience in relation to his son.

Though Mr Danzig required John to confirm him in his manliness, he did not appear to see him as a rival for his wife's affections. For, though he complained that John did not obey him, he never complained that John sided with Mrs Danzig against him. Nor did he complain that Mrs Danzig showed too much affection for John. On the contrary, he seemed to concede that mother and son should have an especially close relationship. He appeared to have no special interest in his wife's affections.[1] This is congruent with what we already know of the parents' relationship; that, in Mr Danzig's view, it was justified for mother and son to have an especially close relationship, is evident from the following account of his relationship with his own mother. For the sake of his relationship with her he had been prepared to risk even the scandal of divorce.

INTERVIEWER: When did you start feeling this, that you weren't suited to your wife, and your wife wasn't suited to you?

FATHER: It must have been quite a long time.

INTERVIEWER: Ten years?

FATHER: I would say, yes. Maybe for quite a long time. It started a long time ago. It started in nineteen thirty-four before the children were born.

INTERVIEWER: What happened then?

FATHER: I lost my – I got married in nineteen thirty-three. My father died in nineteen thirty-four and my mother was left a widow in a house that they had just moved in. So my house and my mother's house were within about five or ten minutes' walk. So one of my brothers and I discussed the question of my mother, and realizing that the question of a daughter-in-law came into the picture, living with one or other of us – so we decided to let my mother stay where she is – not uproot her, but that we should go to sleep with her alternate nights. One night I go, one night he goes. And as I'd no children, I would go with my wife to my mother's at the weekend, Fridays to Sundays, or bring my mother home to me. My mother was never left alone. Hail, rain, or snow, my mother was never left alone. On occasions when my brother went – it was supposed to be fifty-fifty, but I did most of the going. When I went during the week my wife wasn't alone. I never left my wife alone. Either my father-in-law or my mother-in-law was there, or the lady of the house was at home. This went on from

[1] We shall show how this played a crucial part in his relationship with Sarah.

nineteen thirty-four until the war, and then we were evacuated, and Mother with us. One day, on several occasions, my father-in-law, we had no children for five years – Sarah was born five years after our marriage – my father-in-law kept on saying, quite rightly perhaps as a father or father-in-law, by my going to my mother, I commit a breach. I thought, 'What do you mean?' He showed annoyance about my going to my mother. So I felt that if he showed annoyance, instead of extending some admiration for me, or at least some consideration for not neglecting my mother – I took exception to this and I did pass a remark, and I'm not going to say I regret it. I said, 'Look, a wife you can get one, another one, but not a mother.' He took it *very* seriously. It upset him; but things were peaceful after that. He realized he could not meddle with me, just like that. I told him, I said, 'Not under any circumstances will I leave my mother-in-law just like that – my mother – people would have complaints if my Elsie was left alone,' I said. 'Where I go, Elsie goes with me. Where I sleep, she sleeps.'

INTERVIEWER: That's your wife? Elsie is your wife?

FATHER: Yes. I said to my father-in-law, 'If you can't come' – and there was no maid then – 'Elsie will go with me.' Never leave her alone. Whatever, the matter – no matter what weather, if accident or otherwise. So it went on. And then of course, naturally my wife goes shopping to the grocery shop and she hears all sorts of nonsense, where some of those un-desirable women keep talking a lot of nonsense to other women. So my wife comes home with a story that she's heard from so-and-so and so-and-so, whether it was a real story or not, or a made-up story – 'She wouldn't allow her husband to leave her and go to her mother.' Just like that. 'She would under no circumstances. She wouldn't allow it. I think I'll go to the Rabbinical Court, and see what they say.' I said, 'Look Elsie. You're excited. Now go to the bedroom. It's very late at night,' I said. 'Look if you want to get me to the Rabbinical Court and get a ruling on what I do, I'm quite prepared to go to the Rabbinical Court – out of respect to them. As a public official[1] I must respect the Rabbinical Court. I'll go. If you take me to the Rabbinical Court, I will go. But remember, whatever the decision of that Rabbinical Court, and as soon as we go out of the door of the Rabbinical Court into the street, that is the last time you'll see me. So make up your mind. You go to the Rabbinical Court, or not, one of the two.' And nothing was said about the Rabbinical Court after that. So I don't know if that has any bearing on the present situation.

This incident is congruent with Mr Danzig's being so tied in an unconscious incestuous relationship with his mother that he was unable to transfer any sexual desire to any other woman, including his wife. And we may infer that it was because he had never experienced any such desire for his wife that he never experienced his son as a sexual rival.

What, then, was the nature of Mr Danzig's phantasy experience in respect of his son?

Mr Danzig felt emphatically that moral character was his strong point.

FATHER: Now, I was ill, I was ill with pleurisy, before I got married. Opposite there lived a Dr Hicks. I had pleurisy, a very bad attack – this side I think it was – and he came in and discovered it was a serious illness, and he put on a hot poultice – hot towels, one off, one on for a good hour. The purpose of that I don't know, and I was in great pain and great, er – I wasn't well, and he said one of the main reasons why I was able to – [he hesitates, and John prompts 'resist this illness' – he has obviously heard it all before] resist this illness was because he could see from examination and, er – his feeling – I had led a clean and upright life and not abused myself [sternly] or I wouldn't have that resistance – to resist that complaint. I've always thought about that.

It was self-discipline above all that he wanted to be allowed to teach John, particularly sexual self-discipline.

FATHER: Religion, no religion, conduct in life in every way –

[1] He had a minor position in his local synagogue.

your discipline, discipline the mind, character – character holds all the time. If you have strength of character and you realize – it's not religion, it's *discipline*. I say 'Do you say your prayers?' It's not because I want you to say your prayers, because you don't feel about it, but a form of giving somebody some satisfaction – a pleasure. If you are in the army and you are sent on a mission to another country, if your Sergeant-Major or your General or Commanding Officer can't stand by you all the time doing your job. But if you've got that discipline in your mind that you've a duty to perform, you'll do this sincerely and conscientiously, irrespective of whether you like it or not. You've got to carry out a discipline – duty.

JOHN: From what you say I gather that you think I'm likely to fall into these pitfalls you mentioned [Father breaks in] – Yes, but if you're obviously concerned, why? If you thought I wouldn't fall into them you wouldn't be concerned. So you are concerned because you think I *would* fall into them. Number two is that you don't think I have the strength of character – you said *if* I had the strength of character – so in other words you don't think I have the strength of character –

FATHER: I'm concerned that you *should* because you might be inclined to believe certain things and certain people at certain times and on certain occasions – and I want to guard against that possibility – based on one thing, discipline of the mind – discipline in certain things in life – a high standard of living in every way.

JOHN: And where I disagree with you, and where we have arguments, is that I don't –

FATHER: Religion –

JOHN: You want me to self-discipline myself – in other words do something that pleases somebody even though I don't believe in doing it –

And:

INTERVIEWER: Would the wrong step involve actually sleeping with a woman?

FATHER: It could be, and mixing with bad company – could be going into – in perfectly good faith – going to a party, meeting the wrong type of individual there – one thing leads to another, can lead to another. I'm concerned – I'm not imposing my will on him, but I'm gravely concerned. It doesn't necessarily follow that I've got no faith in his ability or his character, or that he's a low cad – he's not – I want to guard against him getting that way. They say I'm prying or nosey – it's not prying or being nosey, I'm concerned.

JOHN: But your method of shielding me from these pitfalls is to shield me from the sort of places where I might encounter these pitfalls. So far I gather that is your method of protecting me from these pitfalls, to shield me from the places where I might encounter them. Quite frankly, what I say to you in return is that you're trying to shield me from the main part of life, because you're [sighs] –

Since Mr Danzig equated self-control with manliness, and lack of self-control with femininity, we may infer that in phantasy his erect penis was identified with his controlled anal sphincter ('clean and upright life'). This inference is congruent with the pride he invariably displayed when he discussed his self-control. In excitedly insisting he wanted to help John by teaching him to discipline himself and do his job regularly and conscientiously, we may infer he was defending himself against both a phantasy excitement over John's anal sexuality ('pitfalls') and his envy over John's possible homosexual freedom. However, his excitement was not the expression of an unconscious desire to penetrate John. It was the expression of a desire to inspect and smell John's regulated anus and stool ('nosey', 'prying'). His phantasy, therefore, did not mesh too well with John's.

However, they appeared to have reached a compromise in their verbal sparring. For the sparring was not entirely unsatisfactory to Mr Danzig, as we may infer from the fact that though he could have finally settled this contest at any time with a definitive prohibition on illicit sexual behaviour, he chose not to.

Their sparring appeared to allow them to share implicitly and unavowedly an interest in John's sexuality. We may infer that while it enabled John to experience vicariously the thrill of sexually tantalizing his father in phantasy, it allowed Mr Danzig to experience vicariously the phantasy thrill of incipient loss of bowel control.

There were times, however, when John's provocative defiance seemed in danger of going over the brink. Mr Danzig then became anxious that things would get completely, i.e. 'publicly', out of control. But John by himself never carried matters that far. He did so only when his mother encouraged him. She appeared to take advantage of their quarrelling. However, matters never actually got out of hand, for she always stopped John short of the brink. How do we understand Mrs Danzig's praxis?

John's expectations of his father appeared to evoke his mother's jealousy. On the few occasions when Mr Danzig seemed provoked enough to try to act forcibly, his wife stepped in to prevent him. For instance, though she encouraged John to see his father as favouring Sarah, she stopped Mr Danzig being as strict with John as John wished.

MOTHER: I don't like it when you speak sharply to them. I mean the things are not even worth it. You do lose your temper with him. You seem to vent it all on him. He's a bit thick-skinned but still he doesn't like it. I know you don't mean it. We know, but still –

FATHER: My actions towards him, they're not mean or silly things.

MOTHER: No, but he's your son isn't he, and you do your duty as a father. A child wants love from a father.

FATHER: Well, I do.

MOTHER: No, no, no, not when you bully him all the time.

FATHER [voice raised]: No, you can still love a child by being a bully occasionally. Couldn't you?

MOTHER: You have to give and take. It can't be all take. You've also got to give a little. They are a different generation with different ideas from the way we've been brought up. You were brought up Victorian the same as I was. I think it was wrong. That's why I don't do it with my children.

Mrs Danzig described herself as a referee between John and her husband. And as referee she felt superior to both. In her view, she was more tolerant and broadminded than Mr Danzig, and, particularly in private, she was patronizingly disparaging about his 'religious obsession'.

MOTHER: But still, praying doesn't make one bad, praying doesn't make one good. It is what you do yourself, but Mr Danzig says, 'No,' he says, 'let him grow up. Let me teach him what to do,' he says. 'When he gets married and has a home of his own then I can't control him, but,' he says, 'while he's here, it's a little thing to please me. Let him do it.' Well I agree with Mr Danzig. I tell John, for the sake of peace and not having a quarrel. – All right, he does that. Now then it comes to Saturday morning. Mr Danzig likes going to the synagogue. He likes to hear the Rabbi deliver a sermon. He likes it, and he understands, I suppose, what he's saying. Well John, if he does go it's under pressure. 'Oh,' he says, 'honestly, Mummy, it's so boring,' he says. And I say, 'Try and please Daddy,' because on Saturday morning I expect there'll be fireworks.

She compared her husband unfavourably with her father, who had apparently regarded Mr Danzig's interpretation of religious tradition as a rather unintelligent fanaticism. For her father, unlike her husband, had been prepared to turn a diplomatic blind eye towards what he saw as minor breaches of the Law. Such a minor breach had been a breach of the laws of the Sabbath.[1]

MOTHER: Well my father was also Orthodox, and my mother only did it to please my father the way I do to please Mr Danzig. But I never did anything in front of my father that I thought would upset him. But he gave me a lot of freedom. If I said I

[1] A breach of the laws of the Sabbath for trivial reasons is, of course, regarded by religious Jews as a major breach.

wanted to go out on Saturday – in the summer, you know, we used to go out to town or a show or go out somewhere. I never used to ask him and he never used to ask when I came back where I was. He knew I was out from three till twelve. I used to eat out. He knew very well I had to carry some money with me, that I wasn't taking sandwiches, but he never said anything and he never questioned me. He was sort of diplomatic about it.

And so she intervened to mitigate her husband's excessive religiosity and 'Victorian outlook'. Unfortunately, her interventions were markedly biased. One of the rules of the game was it should always remain a sparring match. It should never become a title fight. But the referee, in demonstrating 'tolerance', showed signs of disputing the title for herself.

For instance, Mr Danzig claimed that as head of the family he was responsible for any trouble that occurred in it. To criticize himself on any occasion for failing in this role was, of course, to define himself as head. But when he did criticize his leadership in respect of John, Mrs Danzig immediately dismissed the criticism in a way that implicitly dismissed the claim on which his right to criticize himself was based.

INTERVIEWER: I have the impression, Mr Danzig, that you seem to feel that you, because you're the head of the family, that this is a position[1] that you have to take on yourself.

FATHER: Yes, yes, I could say – it could be said that I may have failed in leadership. On that point and in my house –

MOTHER: No, I'll tell you what it is – no it isn't that. When your father and mother were alive – I'm talking about when we were both single – your father and mother used to, I can remember now – in those days, what Mother said, what Father said, it went for the children. It was *their* opinion. Now the same thing applied to my father. They were also what you call Victorian parents. Now, looking back on it, I think if I had my life over again I would never have stuck it out. I would have told them outright what I think is right, and, well I mean,

---

[1] I.e. of being responsible for the trouble in the family.

they give you advice, what they think is right, they did for the children, as right. Let the child also have an opinion sometimes. You see they thought everything, but today children are allowed to think more for themselves.

FATHER: You can't let children run riot, run wild.

MOTHER: I'm not saying run wild. If ever John says something he's always got a reason for it. There's always something behind his statements. He's no fool.

However, though she was full of admiration for John's intelligence, and implied that he was too grown-up to be expected to do things just because his father told him, what she actually said amounted to no more than demanding that his father should allow him to *say* what he thought.

MOTHER: Don't you underestimate his intelligence.

FATHER: I'm not –

MOTHER: He's not babyish for his age. He's quite intelligent. In fact it's not only that I've learnt from his conversation – that other people have come and told me. In fact a reverend from the synagogue – he met him at a friend's house and he asked this chap, he said, 'Who is that boy?' 'Oh he's Danzig's son.' He said, 'Honestly, he's such a nice boy,' he said, 'I'd love him to come to the house and have a meal.' Do you remember? He wrote John a lovely letter, said he would like to meet him again, you know, if convenient for him – would like to meet him again. He's not a fool. I mean, when he says something you say, 'Look, John, you've got no opinion.' That kills him. Don't say it [Father interrupting, Mother raises voice] – *Let* him have an opinion. *Let* him say what he thinks.

Caught between her desire to champion her son against his father, and her fear of destroying the family system, she used her position as referee to lay down rules. These rules, while not threatening the continued existence of the family, implicitly allowed her to control her husband and son. Her interventions usually had a fourfold effect. They encouraged John to defy his father, they prevented Mr Danzig from taking effective counter-action, they demonstrated to John his father's impotence, and they allowed Mrs Danzig to vent her spleen.

Now Mrs Danzig, we saw, worked compulsively from morning to night to have everything clean and tidy on time. To do less was to be lazy and careless. Leisure, enjoyment, recreation were possibilities she hardly dared entertain for herself. As for sexual pleasure this, as we have said, had no legitimate place at all. It was not even a subject for discussion. When we tried to discuss it with her she minimized its importance, but in a way that implied that problems existed.

MOTHER: Probably been married so long we take each other for granted. We know each other's failings.

As far as we could judge, she seemed to have very little, if any, genital awareness, and very little idea of what to expect in a mature sexual relationship. Apart from her father, her husband was the only man with whom she had ever had any kind of relationship. Speaking of their sexual relationship, she said:

MOTHER [laughing]: It's a bit late in the day. I don't know what you mean by – what – whether he's an ideal husband. I don't know. I can't compare him with anybody else. I don't know how other people live. I don't know what they do privately. It's something you don't ask other people, do you? Unless you're told, and if you're not told you're not meant to know, are you? I mean, it's something very very private, isn't it?

Though she would not discuss her sexual life, there were indications that she felt bitter and disappointed with her husband over it. For instance, she bemoaned marrying him, and she disparaged his authority on sexual morality, though she did not do so on her own behalf. She did so on John's. Nor did she do so directly, merely implicitly; but in a way that encouraged John to enter into sexual relationships.

JOHN: What it boils down to with me, is that when I go out you would like to hear me say to you, 'Where are you going to-night, John?' 'I'm going to a bazaar.' 'Where are you going tonight, John?' 'I'm going to a charity committee.' Those are the things you'd like to hear me say. But if I say I'm going to an all-night party in Chelsea, you don't like to hear that. Because all you believe is that loafers go to all-night parties in Chelsea. You *are* concerned about what happens to me, but you're more concerned about the places I go to.

FATHER: Even if you go to Chelsea, how do you know who's in Chelsea? Are you a – a friend of yours takes you to a party in Chelsea. Have you seen the papers? Do you know what happens in Chelsea?

JOHN: I was saying you don't approve – what it boils down to is, you don't approve of the places I go to.

MOTHER: There's another question to this. I think John has enough common sense, at least I think he has, that if he goes anywhere and he sees – he doesn't think it's just so, if he doesn't think it's right or good, I think he'd just go out again.

JOHN: Well, mind you, what I consider right is a different thing trom what Daddy thinks is right.

MOTHER: It's up to you.

JOHN: I don't come home drunk. I don't drive the car drunk. I refuse every form of drink before I drive.

MOTHER: In that case children should be tied to their parents.

FATHER: That wasn't what I was suggesting. Have a good time by all means.

MOTHER: Perhaps your good time's not their conception of a good time.

She also disparaged her husband's claim to authority on religious matters.

Thus, though she could not, and presumably dared not, compare her husband with anyone else sexually, in disparaging his religious and moral authority she was implicitly comparing him unfavourably with her father in precisely the area where Mr Danzig most wanted his masculine authority to be recognized.

And though she did not deny his right to expect John to comply with his demands for sexual abstinence, she entered into an unavowed collusion with John, encouraging him to disregard his father's demands, just as her father had entered into an unavowed collusion with her to allow her to disregard furtively the demands of traditional authority.

We may infer, therefore, that Mrs Danzig's bitter complaints about marrying her husband were the expression of sexual disappointment, deriving from an unclarified desire that may be reconstructed as follows: Though it was 'publicly' forbidden to show interest in sexual experience, she had secretly hoped her husband would enter into a publicly unavowed collusion to disregard privately the sexual prohibition and initiate her into a sexual life. He failed to do so in a way that satisfied her. Because her ideology precluded her from complaining, she could only attack him by comparing unfavourably his claims to authority with her father's. This inference is congruent with Mr Danzig's speculation that possibly his wife was complaining because he had never made love to her.

It is also congruent with their responses in the following exchange. Though sexual experience had no legitimate place in her marriage, Mrs Danzig fleetingly became almost vivacious when she spoke of falling in love. And speaking of her parents' marriage, she recalled with warmth how they had been in love. The terms of their marriage had apparently not precluded satisfying sexual experience. Mr Danzig's response to her enthusiasm was to pour scorn on it, and a row quickly developed.

INTERVIEWER: Do you think your parents ever were in love?
MOTHER: Oh yes, oh yes. My father loved my mother. That's the thing that – everybody knew that.
INTERVIEWER: Can you remember the time that they were actually in love?
MOTHER: Oh rather. He used to give in to her.
FATHER: Give in to her? He was afraid of her.
MOTHER [angrily]: He *wasn't* afraid of her. No, no, no. He

wasn't afraid of her, but he was very much in love with
her.

FATHER: He liked her very much.

MOTHER: I mean she was a very very very poor girl, wasn't she?

FATHER: Very obstinate.

MOTHER: Well, I'll say she was obstinate. She liked her own way.

FATHER: On the twenty-fifth of June she used to make the old
man wear two gardenias and a red carnation.

MOTHER: Oh no, that was when he became ill. No, he became ill.
She thought that would sort of [argument over this – then, to
Interviewer] – No, he became ill, you see. He became very ill.

FATHER: It's a very complicated issue, isn't it? It's a very complicated issue here.

MOTHER: Well, your mother was domineering and your father
used to give a lot in to your mother and you know it.

Judging by Mrs Danzig's response, interest in possible sexual
experience could still be evoked. Judging by her husband's
response, this interest could evoke in him a reaction to turn her off.

Animosity towards her husband was not her only motive for
colluding with John. From her smiles, gestures, movements, and
paralinguistic responses while John was discussing forbidden
sexual activities, it was evident that she was deriving considerable
vicarious gratification. It was similarly evident from John's
responses that he derived pleasure from their secret sexual understanding. This is congruent with our earlier statement that in
phantasy John had been conceded a privileged sexual position
with his mother by his father.

With no sexual satisfaction from her marriage, John was Mrs
Danzig's only source of sexual gratification. Therefore, it was of
the greatest importance to her that nothing should interfere with
their continuing relationship, neither a relationship with his
father, nor any relationship with a girl that threatened to remove
John from her orbit. Though she envisaged John marrying one
day, it had to be a Jewish girl, and one of whom she approved.
This requirement, as we know, had nothing to do with religion.

146

But we have reason to believe that sexual experience for Mrs Danzig was, in phantasy, an experience of orgastic incontinence, and that this was an experience she unconsciously feared. How then could she tolerate the vicarious excitement of her relationship with John? We must further examine the nature of her phantasy of sexual experience.

Her reply (see p. 117) to her husband's hint that he was sexually dissatisfied showed that she implicitly experienced their sexual relationship as one between two men, one of whom was trying illicitly to get something – 'money' – out of the other, which the other was retaining. She was primarily identified here with the victim.

Bearing in mind her defensive alarm as she replied, we may infer that, in phantasy, she experienced sexual intercourse as an anal attack in which the victim was made to give up his bowel contents to the attacker. This, of course, is congruent with our earlier inferences about the nature of her phantasy experience of intercourse. This phantasy attack appeared to be a penetration of the anus of one by the other ('laying a finger' on it to get it out).

Her reply shows, too, she had a strong masculine identification (the plaintiff attacker calls the other a man). It also shows her to be identified with the male attacker (confusion of borrower with lender – 'I've never lent him', instead of 'He's never lent me'). We may infer, therefore, that in phantasy she was in some measure identified with a penetrating object – a penis – and that in phantasy it was possible for her to identify with the one who penetrated. This inference is congruent with the part she played in colluding with John over his sexual behaviour. In this relationship she was identified both with John and with her father. It is congruent with her animated reference to her parents' sexual relationship, in which she spoke from the position of her father, not from that of her mother. She spoke of her father loving her mother, not of her mother being loved by her father.[1]

And she appeared to see John, too, as the active one who penetrated in his sexual relations. For instance, in the earlier exchange

[1] Her sexual confusion is also evident in her statement quoted on p. 46.

(see p. 144) she sees him as able to withdraw from any sexually illicit place if he felt it too dangerous. We may thus infer she derived her vicarious gratification in her relationship with John through identifying in phantasy with his penis, and not with his anus. This inference is congruent with her contempt for, and dissociation from, the non-Jewish girls, who were good enough for dirty, sexual purposes.

CHAPTER 11

The brink

And now we must ask why matters had gone over the brink. Why had Sarah behaved in a way that had brought about that which her parents had been fearing all their married life, a scandal that shook them and their system to the foundations?

In the brinkman game that John and his mother played with Mr Danzig, they were careful not to press matters too far. The game was a compromise that enabled them to obtain some libidinal gratification, while still maintaining the system that ensured their ontic security. But it was much less satisfactory for Mr Danzig than it was for the others. With no sexual interest in his wife, the sole object of his frustrated desire was the nice young lady, the ideal woman of his phantasy. But where was he to find her?

Now, concerned as Mr Danzig was about John's morals and behaviour, he was even more concerned about Sarah's.

He and Sarah were very fond of each other, and he wanted her to enjoy herself; but he was continually worried in case she was seduced.

FATHER: Well one of the reasons why I personally was interested in her social life is not because I was prying into her private affairs; I was mainly interested in watching that she shouldn't be impressed by funny stories, by all sorts of – all and sundry – I realized she was a very sensitive young lady, very highly impressionable, and that she should not be impressed, to get wrong impressions. Because there are so many young men around with glib tongues and fancy themselves and able to get hold of a girl like Sarah and tell her all sorts of funny stories, and can lead to a lot of complications – that was the main reason why I was interested in her social standing and social life. But I wasn't interested to pry into her private affairs.

He insisted she ought to go out with young men, but he insisted, too, on stressing the moral dangers:

FATHER: But I understand, I fully understand a young lady and a young man enjoying themselves – they enjoy flirting or necking what they call it, and young men, I understand that – I'm human – I was once young myself – I'm still young but –

However, neither he nor his wife taught her how to recognize these dangers. He simply issued vague and ominous warnings about the places where she might meet boys.

FATHER: I'm expressing my concern, I can't watch over – I can't run after you –
JOHN: I appreciate your concern –
FATHER: Concern – I'm concerned – I'm concerned about Sarah. I can't tell you 'Don't go to this, don't do this' – but I am expressing my views. I *am* concerned – as a father, I'm concerned, very much concerned.

Nor did either parent help her make a relationship with anyone outside the family who might teach her about the dangers. She was thus left completely in the dark on how to conduct herself when alone with a young man.

For a time John had been a confidant, but he now simply followed his parents. He had been won over by his mother when she helped him deal with his father's prohibitions.

However, phenomenologically speaking, we must not assume that Mr Danzig was lying when he said he wanted her to enjoy herself. If he stressed the moral dangers, it was simply because he was anxious things should not get out of control.

FATHER: I'm not saying it occurred or it has occurred or it will occur. But I can assure you there's – it's not an issue at all.

We have never quarrelled about this. I'm just expressing my – my views in no uncertain terms and that I – it's not because I want to disrupt their life or interfere with their life or dictate to them how they should conduct themselves or impose my will. It's how strongly I feel. I want them to grow up, and – grow up a bit older with a certain moral responsibility, knowing the difficulties and the pitfalls that they have in life. Have plenty of fun, by all means have plenty of fun. Enjoy yourself. I too like enjoyment – too, within limits. At the same time, watch your step in every way. Rather – rather be sorry than er –

And so, he put pressure on her to bring all her boy-friends home. Not because he wanted to pry into what they were doing, but because it was natural for a father to watch over his children, particularly his daughter.

FATHER: My interest in her was not because I was trying to encroach on her private life. It's a natural feeling for a father to be int – to watch over his daughter.

And:

FATHER: I want to watch their movements – not because I'm prying into their private affairs, not that I'm nosey, using their language, I'm nosey – or mind my own business. A young man, if he's good enough to meet outside he's good enough to come into the house. If you're going out to a party or a dance, all right, you've got a home, invite him into the home. If you're ashamed of your father and mother, all right, I'll go upstairs, but get him into your house.

All he wanted was to be allowed to ensure her young man acted properly.

Unfortunately, he never attempted to vet the young men discreetly. As her moral guardian, he felt a closer watch was required. He got his wife to question her about her relationships, while they both opened her letters and listened in to her telephone calls.

JOHN: But I don't want you to get the impression that Dad hangs over like an eagle and tries to control Sarah's social life. Before she was ill he was always very careful about his intrusions into her private life, because he knew that if he did make an obviously nosey approach she would *flare* up, so therefore we tried to – very very carefully about her social life – the questions, if there were any, were always put by Mum, put in a sleeky way, sometimes or [protest from Father about the word 'sneaky'] – I didn't say 'sneaky', I said 'sleeky' – a silky sort of way [Mother tries to calm Father, explaining John's statement to him]. By sheer – by continuous nagging on Mummy's part – 'give a name' – whether it was the right name or not, she gave a name – that satisfied her.

Though in Sarah's own interests they took care to watch her as secretly as they knew how. For they understood a child could not enjoy itself when it knew its parents were looking on.

MOTHER: You know what, John? Not really – I feel – I know how I used to feel, that if you went anywhere, if parents are onlooking you can't behave naturally. There's a lot in that.
JOHN: Oh I know.
MOTHER: I also couldn't do that – I also felt the same way. When I went anywhere and my mother and father were there – half the enjoyment went out of life.

However, Sarah found out about their watching and was resentful. But when she accused her father of prying, he indignantly denied it. And his wife and son backed him. He did not feel he was being contradictory, for he knew he was concerned only for her welfare. Her reputation demanded he should properly fulfil his familial role as guardian, while her happiness required she should not feel she was being watched. So they continued watching her while denying they were doing so.

Not surprisingly, Sarah became highly mystified. In the face of the others' alliance, she gave up going with boys altogether and stayed at home. Her family was puzzled. And when she accused her father of not wanting her to go out, their bewilderment deepened. And later, when she began to keep to her room, they started to worry in case something wrong was happening which they did not know about. Her father, in particular, worried in case she was smoking in bed. She might mess up the carpet with burnt cigarette-ends, he said, or might be burning without his knowledge. This greatly upset him. For if she burnt they might burn too. And so, as her guardian and as the head of the house, he had to keep a watch on things. He entered her room to investigate, and simply could not understand why she became angry, and shouted. She seemed to think he had no right to enter. After all he never went in when she was getting dressed. He always knocked, at least when he remembered.

Mr Danzig's praxis is congruent with our inference that, in phantasy, he had unconsciously projectively identified Sarah with his own marginally controlled bowels, for her to embody and control on his behalf. It is also congruent with our inference that he was unwittingly in conflict over desire orgastically to abandon control of his bowels. His phantasy experience may be construed as follows:

Mr Danzig was consumed with unacknowledged curiosity to see what was happening between Sarah and her young men. We may infer that, in phantasy, he was preoccupied with desire to witness a primal scene wherein he participated orgastically in the excitement of Sarah, with whom he was identified through his bowels. We may infer it was in the woman's excitement he wished to participate, because he did not put pressure on John to bring home his girl-friends so that he could watch John. However, he was also afraid of his possible phantasy incontinence. This was expressed in his compulsive attempts to control, in phantasy, what he experienced to be happening between Sarah and her young men. Encouraging Sarah to enjoy herself with boy-friends while he watched was thus the expression both of his desire to become orgastically incontinent, and the defence against its fulfilment.

This inference is congruent with the form and content of his injunctions. These were vague and obscure, ambiguous and difficult to grasp – as we would expect if they reflected semi-liquid bowel contents threatening to emerge incontinently.

FATHER: I didn't say coffee bars generally – there can be certain coffee bars which are very dangerous to visit as well. I'm not particularizing *any* coffee bar, *any* restaurant, *any* dance-hall, or *any* place of amusement – I'm making a general statement how much I am concerned about *both* of you.

His praxis thus appeared to be a compromise, the function of which was to allow some measure of vicarious gratification.

Our construction also implies Mr Danzig implicitly experienced Sarah as the embodiment of his nice young lady, sexually exciting but controlled. This is congruent with the fact that his recent sexual stirrings dated from the time of her and John's adolescence. This was also a period of increased tension between the parents.

If Sarah was the unacknowledged embodiment of his ideal woman, then as a source of vicarious gratification she was his only feasible sexual release. This is congruent with our earlier conclusion that she functioned as an instinctual safety valve in the family. Further, as his only sexual safety valve, it would be important for him not to lose her. We would thus expect him to discourage any action that might take her away from home. And, indeed, this is what happened. He acted in a way that discouraged her from making any autonomous relationships, even those with girls and women, and non-sexual relationships with men.

When Sarah in despair retired to her bedroom, his phantasy had even freer play as expressed in his prurient curiosity about her feelings, and his anxiety that these would get out of control and affect his reputation. His anxiety that he and the others might be burnt by her (passionate) disorder expressed the intensification of his phantasy. And so he tried to intrude on her. His action expressed his desire and his defence against fulfilment. However, the more he intruded, the more Sarah excluded him. The more she excluded him, the less he could evaluate his phantasy. The less he could evaluate his phantasy, the more excited and anxious he became. The more excited and anxious he became, the more compulsively he insisted on his right to intrude. Thus, a spiral of reciprocal mistrust evolved, in which the actions of each confirmed the unformulated fears and suspicions of the other.

How did his relationship with Sarah come to get out of hand in this way? We must examine the part played by Mrs Danzig.

Mrs Danzig acted as a referee between John and his father. But in the relationship between her husband and Sarah she made no attempt to mediate. On the contrary, she acted in a way that intensified Sarah's mystification. For instance, she joined her husband in blaming Sarah for being spoilt by Mr Danzig. She also blamed Sarah for bringing her illness on herself through being spoilt. Mrs Danzig's reasoning appeared to be that Sarah's laziness had caused her trouble. And Sarah had caused her laziness by being spoilt by her father. Mrs Danzig also reproached her husband for spoiling Sarah, but she did so only in Sarah's absence. In Sarah's presence she blamed Sarah. Since her husband did not contradict her when Sarah was present, Sarah was made to feel responsible for being spoilt and for being ill. She was responsible for not being responsible.

How did this situation between mother and daughter develop?

According to Mrs Danzig, Sarah had been a model baby and a model child. Apart from a little difficulty over weaning, when Mrs Danzig had been worried about getting her to eat, they had got on 'wonderfully well' together. Sarah had been good, sweet, and obedient, sharing everything with her – 'a lovely child' with a 'jolly good mother'. But when she was thirteen Sarah began to change. She started going out with boys. Her mother encouraged her and discouraged her at the same time. She told her that she should go out.

MOTHER: I often used to tell her, I said, 'I think you ought to go out and meet boys and meet girls. You should go out more and get dates and get to know people and go somewhere else.

You meet them if you already know somebody. If you have seen them before you can approach them. You feel you've seen them once before, you know them and it doesn't make you so shy.'

It was a social obligation for a normal girl to go out, but she should go out in the right way.

MOTHER: Well, I would have liked her to go out with boys. I think it's very normal for young girls to go out with the opposite sex, and I think it's the right thing that she should go out with the opposite sex, in the right way of course, to go out socially, yes.

Unfortunately, Mrs Danzig did not explain what she meant by 'the right way' that was implicitly sexual and yet 'social'. She seemed to feel that Sarah should know without being told. She also expected Sarah to continue to confide in her, though only 'little things', she said, such as:

MOTHER: When she's been out with a boy, what they've said, things like that. Little things you see. What she thinks about them, you know, her opinion regarding them.

Sarah did continue confiding, and then stopped. She told her mother she wanted to know too much, and 'withdrew'. Mrs Danzig was disappointed. She would have liked to have known a few things, but she 'understood'. She continued to urge her to go out with boys, though only 'socially', of course.

Now, though Sarah had stopped confiding intimately about herself and her boy-friends, she still asked her mother's help in evaluating social and sexual cues. Shy and lacking self-confidence, she asked her mother what to wear, did she look nice, had she acted properly in a particular situation, did her mother think the boy would like her, and so on – the kind of advice a girl might ordinarily expect from her mother. But Mrs Danzig had lost patience. By the time a girl was sixteen or seventeen, she should have acquired social graces. She should not need such advice. And when Sarah persisted in asking, Mrs Danzig would exasperatedly 'reassure' her. 'People don't bother about you. They forget you the minute you go out of the room, or when they stop talking about you.'

Not surprisingly, Sarah stopped seeking her mother's help. However, Mrs Danzig was extremely surprised. And when Sarah lost all interest in social activities, as we have described, her mother found it unintelligible. Could it be laziness? Mrs Danzig decided it was. What else could it be? She and her husband then redoubled their efforts to 'encourage' her to go out. But the more they 'encouraged' her, the more she did not. For while they complained of the inconvenience she caused them, they took food to her room and provided meals any time she demanded.

Sarah then began to stay up late, reading the Bible and 'brooding irritably'. We know this meant simply she was trying to think matters out for herself, and resented her parents' intrusions. However, Mrs Danzig, like her husband, did not see it this way. She became alarmed. She did not know what was happening; but she assumed the worst. And this meant she would be blamed by 'people'. This was most unjust. She felt bitter. Sarah's trouble was not her fault. She knew a girl of fifteen whose mother had died, and whose father remarried. The girl had never accepted her stepmother and they were always quarrelling. Yet that girl had not gone like Sarah. So how could Mrs Danzig be to blame? Her husband was to blame, and Sarah. Her husband had spoilt and indulged her. He had made her dissatisfied with what her mother gave her. He had bought her expensive toys. That had made her think she was entitled to anything she wanted. It had encouraged her to become demanding, so that no matter how her mother tried to please her, it was not good enough. If you brought her anything to eat, she either left it or shouted at you for bringing it. She had Mrs Danzig running up and down stairs fifty times a day. Children did not need expensive toys. Her husband said it gave him pleasure, giving toys to Sarah, but Sarah did not need them. Mrs Danzig had never expected toys from her father. Even if she had, she would not have got them. But her parents had loved her just the same.

Mrs Danzig's behaviour, like her husband's, is congruent with our inference that she was unwittingly projectively identified with Sarah through her marginally controlled bowels, which she expected Sarah to embody and control on her behalf. Her position in relation to Sarah appears to have been as follows:

For the sake of the parents' reputation, Sarah had to be seen doing what her parents believed to be the socially normal thing for her age. This involved meeting people outside the family and having relationships with boys. At the same time she was required not to be seen engaging in any relationship that had sexual overtones. However, Mrs Danzig, like her husband, secretly wished Sarah covertly to experience sexual excitement ('enjoy herself'), and like her husband, Mrs Danzig wished to participate vicariously. Since her participation was based on her bowel identification,[1] she was exposed in phantasy to conflict over orgastic incontinence. She attempted to deal with the problem by controlling Sarah. Like her husband, she issued injunctions; but these, reflecting her bowel conflict, were contradictory, shifting, and mystifying. At the same time, because she was closely identified with Sarah without realizing it, she expected Sarah to know as well as she did, how to behave with boys without being told.

Sarah, finding it impossible to discover where she stood with her mother, stopped confiding intimately in her. Mrs Danzig now felt excluded, and resented it, particularly since Sarah and her father had begun to draw together. Spitefully, Mrs Danzig refused to help Sarah evaluate the behaviour of boys and others. But she still urged her to go out, while continuing to warn her. Sarah's self-confidence, which had never been high for reasons I shall explain, was undermined. It was completely undermined when her mother began criticizing her for lacking self-confidence, and for being favoured by her father over John. Mr Danzig was

---

[1] Although her words and actions indicated she was actively defending herself against pre-genital impulses, it is possible that in the course of a successful analysis of these impulses she might become aware of genital strivings. But this must remain conjecture at this stage, since our data points, phenomenologically speaking, only to an active phantasy of a pre-genital nature.

also privately criticized for favouring Sarah. At this point, John, who had been backing Sarah, deserted to his mother's side. Sarah was left only with her father. But he, in the excitement evoked by their closer relationship, was acting in the way I have described. Sarah, now totally muddled about the validity of making any kind of relationship, gave up going out socially altogether. She stayed home, and excluded her mother more than ever.

She still attended college regularly. But she had no social life there, though this was not necessary. For the institutional identity, 'being a good student', mediated by the college establishment, did not require her to have a college social life. Nor did her parents. In their schema, being a good student was practically synonymous with being a good schoolgirl. Thus, attending college actually offered some relief from the pressures on her.

Since Sarah, like everyone else in Mrs Danzig's world, was simply an object of unrecognized phantasy embodying or failing to embody serial institutional roles, Mrs Danzig could only experience Sarah's non-serial behaviour in terms of her own phantasy experience. And the phantasy expressed in her evaluation of Sarah's behaviour was that already active in respect of her.

When Sarah withdrew from her so completely, Mrs Danzig experienced her in phantasy as an infant gut that failed to ingest and excrete regularly and routinely. She then began playing the role of a mother with a recalcitrant infant. She bribed Sarah with food, while complaining of the inconvenience. For a time Sarah colluded and allowed herself to be babied. An equilibrium was thus established that allowed Mrs Danzig to regain something of her original primacy in her relationship with Sarah. It also allowed her to gratify vicariously her own unconscious desire to be an unregulated infant. Her complaints as she babied Sarah were in part the expression of her unrecognized conflict over this desire.[1]

The equilibrium was shattered when Sarah began angrily to reject her mother's babying. This deprived Mrs Danzig of the gratification she derived from their relationship. It also threatened

[1] They were also the expression of physically determined inconvenience in the ordinary social sense, and of anxiety for her reputation as a successful parent.

her alterated identity as a good, i.e. successful, mother in a way that it did not threaten Mr Danzig's reputation as a father. This difference was experienced by Mrs Danzig as an unjust act of discrimination by 'them'.

We may infer, too, she felt she was being blamed for implicitly encouraging Sarah to be a baby. For she began gratuitously to deny seducing Sarah, while blaming her husband for having done just this. She appeared to experience him as a rival for Sarah, and Sarah as a rival for him. In phantasy, she seemed to experience him as seducing Sarah with his penis (= toys), making her dissatisfied with her mother's breast (= food). Her anger with Sarah seemed partly a function of experiencing Sarah, in phantasy, to have deserted her for Mr Danzig's penis, and partly a function of experiencing her as an incestuous rival with prior sexual rights. This is evident from her story of the girl and the intruding step-mother. It is evident, too, in her remarks about her own father. She seemed here to be denying a feeling of chagrin that appeared in phantasy to be an expression of being given to understand she had no right to expect to participate in experiencing his penis.

Now, in a sense Mrs Danzig was right when she said Mr Danzig had spoilt Sarah through being too lenient, causing her to act as she did. But she had not been spoilt in quite the way Mrs Danzig understood it to have happened. And certainly its effect was not as she understood it. Its effect had been to mystify Sarah, who consequently maintained her withdrawal. The matter was as follows:

Mr Danzig saw himself as Sarah's ally and felt very lenient towards her. But he would not support her in rebutting her mother's reproaches, as her mother backed John in rebutting his. However, he did reproach his wife in private for being intolerant, saying, though Sarah was not behaving properly she should not be coerced, because she was still young. She was not fully respon-sible, for she could not properly understand what was required of her. His wife, who already found it difficult to cope at home because of Sarah's irregularity, found that her husband's tolerance added to her burden, which he had recently further increased by an unsolicited act of filial piety by proxy. Overriding his wife's protests, he had invited to stay with them her old mother, who was showing clear signs of organic decay of the brain.

Mr Danzig's tolerance appeared to be a repetition of the ineffectual tolerance he said he had expressed when the infant Sarah failed to comply with her mother's time schedule (see pp. 73-5). It was ineffectual in that it did nothing to help Sarah. But it was effective in hindering his wife, making her feel guilty and resentful. She took her temper out on Sarah, reproaching her angrily for not being responsible. When Sarah was formally labelled 'ill', Mr Danzig saw this as validating his policy of leniency. It allowed him to make things even more difficult for his wife.

Now, Mr Danzig refrained from criticizing his wife before Sarah because he felt it important for the sake of their marital relationship to maintain a united front in the children's presence. But we know he did quarrel with his wife in front of the children. How do we understand this contradiction in his and her praxis?

Though they quarrelled before the children, they did not seem so worried about John seeing them as they did in Sarah's case (Ruth was too young to count). For instance, when John told us in their presence that they quarrelled they did not deny it. But when Sarah said so, they told her she was imagining things. It was evident they experienced Sarah to embody 'public opinion' to a greater degree than John. Sarah, in fact, had been allocated the role of keeper of the family's conscience.[1] And before her, they felt they had to maintain a front at home. One expression of this experience of Sarah was their persistent adoption of a conspiratorial tone and manner when she was around.

However, allocating Sarah the role of domestic 'public conscience' brought certain advantages. It allowed their persecutory 'public' anxiety about the others to crystallize round her, enabling them to tolerate more easily each other's presence. Of course, living as they did under the same roof as Sarah, it was impossible for the parents constantly to maintain before her the front of

[1] We shall discuss this in more detail shortly.

marital harmony. This problem they resolved by telling her their quarrelling was not quarrelling at all. And if she insisted they quarrelled, they told her she imagined it. They told her this even when extrafamilial others were not present. Thus Sarah, who functioned in so many ways as the family safety valve, also helped them minimize their feeling of being constantly in the public eye at home.

CHAPTER 12

Expulsion

And what of Sarah herself? Where was she in this play of shadows? She was hardly anywhere, for to tell the truth she barely existed. Mistrustful of everyone, she distractedly haunted the fringes of her family. Expected to say and do only as her parents wanted her to say and do, she had, when I met her, practically given up saying anything to anyone. Instead she fled fearfully from the presence of others, or repelled them angrily if they tried to probe. Required in phantasy by her parents to embody and control on their behalf their projected personal disorder, she was expected to live the ideals of respectability they did not. She was to be the living public proof of their success and solidity as a family. She was to be 'an untarnished daughter of Israel', a talisman against evil repute, to be discarded if she did not fulfil her function.

INTERVIEWER: Both Sarah and John have implied that sexual relationships with people is the main part of life. How do you feel about that Mrs Danzig?

MOTHER: I think that's wrong.

INTERVIEWER: You think that's wrong?

MOTHER: Yes.

JOHN: If my parents learnt that Sarah had had extramarital relationships with a boy they would be very disappointed. They would view upon it I should think that she's now – instead of being an untarnished daughter of Israel, now she wasn't even worth having as a daughter of Israel.

Sarah was to see no evil, hear no evil, speak no evil, and feel no evil. She was to be pure behaviour. To her parents, with no reflective self-awareness, pure behaviour was implicitly behaviour pure of experience, the behaviour of an automaton. She was to be simply an alterated role, without even the furtive feelings her parents and brother had. The living proof of her parents' family success, she was to be the ideal child, embodying all the virtues of filial respect and respectability. She was to be entirely good, experiencing nothing spontaneously, having no opinions other than those the familial others thought she should have.

Speaking for instance of her protests at her father's intrusions, John said:

INTERVIEWER: You also used the word 'intrusion', which implied something that your father had no right to do.

JOHN: Well then I meant intrusion. From Daddy's point of view it's not intrusion, from Sarah's point of view it *is* intrusion.

INTERVIEWER: And from your point of view?

JOHN: From my point of view when it comes to *Sarah* it's not intrusion – when it comes to me it *is* intrusion.

INTERVIEWER: How do you make that out?

JOHN: Because it's completely illogical.

INTERVIEWER: Yes, but how do you justify it?

JOHN: I can't. Quite frankly I can't. It's just the natural selfishness in me. I can see the situation objectively when it comes to Daddy and Sarah – which is not me – and I can say Daddy's perfectly justified in wanting to know who she's going out with.

She was not to register the brinkman game the others played, even when played in her presence. She was not to see her brother implicitly encouraged to act according to his feelings.

INTERVIEWER: Now your parents wouldn't know that you were necking in those early days?

JOHN: I don't think so, no, I don't think so. I think they suddenly realized it when I was about sixteen.

INTERVIEWER: Do you think your parents would have looked with more, or less disapproval, on your necking than Sarah's?

JOHN: Oh, they would have looked with more disapproval on
   Sarah's.
INTERVIEWER: So in this respect they were more – they were less
   supportive to her?
JOHN: Yes, yes. In this respect. I mean Dad always used to give
   her little lectures which amount to – 'lead not thyself into
   temptation'. Those sort of lectures.
INTERVIEWER: Never to you?
JOHN: Once or twice.
INTERVIEWER: And how about your mother?
JOHN: No, never at all.
INTERVIEWER: To you?
JOHN: 'Don't do anything stupid', she'd say to Sarah – to Sarah –
   not to me.

She thus grew up a model child, whose behaviour was absolutely predictable, experiencing for the most part only what her
parents mediated to her. However, her behaviour was the
expression of a compliant false front, developed to preserve her
integrity. It was a shield behind which she sheltered to maintain
herself in a state of equilibrium with her parents, especially her
mother, until adolescence.

With adolescence the equilibrium was disturbed. Two sets of
forces, intra- and interpersonal, began to impinge. Sexually she
began to mature, while familially her parents required her to
change her behaviour.

As their successful product, she was now expected to play the
role of a respectful child coming of age; one who had affirmed
the family pledge. Among other things, she was required to
relate 'independently' to extrafamilial others, though in a manner
that maintained her parents' reputation.

Unfortunately, though she was of ordinary intelligence, she
had been made extraordinarily naïve socially. Discouraged from
developing a point of view of her own, she was lost in the new
extrafamilial situations she was required to enter.

JOHN: I think, she was self-conscious in a different way. She didn't worry so much – um – what people *thought* of her but she was self-conscious of – I think she maybe was, but she used to keep it to herself. She was very, very quiet. Used to read – considerably – a lot. I mean, now – I can never see what she saw in reading – we used to call her a bookworm. *Now*, I read, but I mean she used to read a fantastic amount. When she was very young and she would rather stay with a book all day than, say, go out. Yes, she was always a very quiet and very sensitive girl.

Dependent on her parents for evaluating social cues, she turned to her mother. And she was maturing sexually. This further complicated her relationships. She again sought help from her mother. But her mother's attitude was ambiguous, and Sarah stopped confiding in her sexually. Instead, she and John tried confiding in each other.

JOHN: No, she used to talk to me and I used to talk to her. We used to have this sort of exchange. When we were young we used to go to the same clubs, and when we used to come home she had a feeling of lack of confidence at what she'd done over that evening, and she'd ask me and I'd give her my opinion, because I was too young to appreciate a big problem and vice versa. I always thought she was exceptionally intelligent in appreciating my problems. And when she did go out, sometimes she used to ask me to come and reassure her, but I think invariably if I went out, she was at the same place, or I had a certain situation to deal with, social situation. I used to come to her for *her* advice *far* more than she used to come to me [pause].

They exchanged sexual confidences, though with considerable anxiety.

JOHN: No no no, but I always – um – she gave me her views on virginity which seemed to be quite emphatic, they seemed to be quite reasonable views – um – they seemed to be intelligent opinions and I thought – I always thought that she would never deviate from these opinions being an intelligent girl.

And:

JOHN: Once, about two and a half years ago, I was very curious about one boy she was going out with, didn't really like him – and she told me. I think she was – I didn't ask – I didn't ask for details but she gave me the details without probing for them.

INTERVIEWER: She gave you the details?

JOHN: Yes.

INTERVIEWER: Has she ever given you details on other occasions?

JOHN: No.

INTERVIEWER: This is the only time she's given you details?

JOHN: And they weren't particularly *full* details, they weren't what you'd call in detail. Relatively speaking from a 'yes' and 'no' – I asked her how far did you let him go and she said, 'Well everything but . . .' And that's all there was you see. Twice – three times she told me – three times she told me.

And:

INTERVIEWER: Now have you ever told Sarah about your affairs with these girls?

JOHN: Yes, once or twice.

INTERVIEWER: Have you described them?

JOHN: No.

INTERVIEWER: Once or twice you've told her, not very often?

JOHN: No . . . well I felt it was *my* personal experience and – not to share it.

INTERVIEWER: When did you tell her? How old would you be?

JOHN: Um – about thirteen, thirteen, fourteen – fifteen. I mean she'd ask. She might ask. She would say, 'Was she easy?' So then I'd say 'yes' or 'no'. And from this she'd imply whatever she wanted it to imply.

INTERVIEWER: You, thirteen, fourteen, fifteen – you stopped doing this?

JOHN: Oh, yes, yes.

INTERVIEWER: When did you stop doing this?

JOHN: Oh, when I was about sixteen. Sixteen – seventeen when I met a girl I felt a little bit – a genuine liking for.

INTERVIEWER: So you weren't prepared to discuss them in this way.

JOHN: Yes. I might come – she might ask me point blank if I slept with her and I'd come back point blank and answer 'yes' or 'no'.

INTERVIEWER: But that was until the age of sixteen.

JOHN: No – all the way through.

Unfortunately these confidences roused Mrs Danzig's jealousy and resentment. She felt excluded, as we described.

Sarah also drew closer to her father. She tried to comply with his interpretation of ritual requirements. This pleased him and he took an indulgent pride in her. However, this roused John's jealousy, while Mrs Danzig's was so intensified that she implicitly incited Sarah to break the Sabbath laws as Mr Danzig understood them.

JOHN: I think she [Sarah] was indulged a bit more, I think Daddy was more strict with me. He wouldn't have allowed me to do certain things which he allowed her to do. For example, he wouldn't have allowed me to stay in bed. Well, I don't dislike her. I feel a little jealously towards her, particularly about the age, I think, of seventeen. She's been a bit of a nuisance, I consider her a slight nuisance because she used to interrupt my life. If I want to go out, I have to give her a lift. Well, I don't mind that, but she used to be an half-an-hour late which would make me late for my appointment. And then Dad used to insist upon me collecting her from wherever she went and I find it unreasonable two or three times a week, and when I do collect her she's not ready on time. Or when I go out on a Saturday evening and Dad wants me to collect her at about eleven o'clock and my engagement is to be out until one or two.

And:

MOTHER: If she wants to go out with a fellow on a Saturday, I

don't think it's such a terrible thing. She's not doing anything
immoral. She's not doing anything very bad by going out with
a girl or a fellow asks her to go out on a Saturday.

Mother and son formed an alliance against father and daughter.
They ceased helping Sarah to evaluate social and sexual cues. This
stopped her dead. John's desertion in particular was a knock-out
blow. With her maturing femininity, the opportunity had arisen
to divest herself of her compliant model front and express herself more truly. But this required confirmation of her sexual self
by another. Neither of her parents was possible, but John had been
to a certain extent. Unfortunately, he, too, was now acting in a
way that had the effect of undermining her. For instance, though
he regarded himself as more highly sexed than Sarah, he now
implied that her interest in sex was exaggerated, and an expression
of sickness.

INTERVIEWER: Would you call yourself more sexed than she is?
JOHN [after a pause]: Yes, I think so, yes.

And:

JOHN: Sarah does seem to be slightly, although she gets into these
    passions she seems to be slightly obsessed with sex, she was
    mentioning sexual words and all that sort of thing to Daddy
    in her temper.

Relying on John to help her evaluate her sexual relationships,
his desertion left her with the sole possibility of maintaining a
purely altered identity. This meant radically betraying her bud-
ding self. She might even have done so if she had been allocated
a feasible, i.e. consistent, identity by the others, particularly by
her mother. But she was not allocated such an identity. Her father
had begun to take a prurient interest in her developing sexuality,
while her mother supported him. As we know, he urged her to
enjoy herself, while uttering his vague and ominous warnings.

Because her parents appeared to encourage her to experience
her sexuality, she did not destroy it. And because they seemed to

forbid her to experience it, she dared not express it. She thus became completely muddled over its validity.

She was also urged to grow up and become independent. But genuine autonomy required the establishment of her sexual self. Since there was no one at home to confirm her sexuality, she tried to obtain confirmation from persons outside the family. These attempts were aborted for her by her parents and brother, when they were not abortive through shame and guilt.

FATHER: My concern – I want you to understand, my son and daughter, my concern about them, my anxiety about their moral conduct, moral behaviour and discipline is not because I'm prying into their affairs, or I'm nosey or sneaky. And – or I should mind my own business, or a young man rings up for Sarah, 'Don't ask his name', or a young lady rings up. I mustn't ask his name. Why not?

JOHN: I never say 'Don't ask the girl's name.'

FATHER: If a young man rings up for Sarah, and I ask, 'What's his name?' and he says, 'Mind your own business,' I'd bang the receiver on him. He's no gentleman. After all he talks to my daughter, although my daughter may express annoyance over it.

JOHN: You've never heard me say, 'Don't ask her name.'

FATHER: That's beside the point. [Mother and John chorus 'no'.]

JOHN: You've asked me after, 'Who is Sandra? Who is Fiona? Who is Janet?'

FATHER: As far as I'm concerned I'm talking about, if I'm on the phone and my daughter has occasionally stated that I shouldn't ask, 'What's his name?' I don't understand it. Ask his name and if he says to me 'Mind your own business' it doesn't matter? That point my daughter raised to me. I think I'm entitled to ask his name.

She tried to revenge herself on her brother by telling her parents he had had sexual intercourse. But her parents invalidated her statement, treating it as a sign of an abnormal preoccupation with sex.

Sarah was now trapped. Too terrified of the world to renounce the protection of her family, too terrified of being excommunicated if she expressed her secret self, she was completely isolated.

She tried to resolve her dilemma within the limits possible for her. She retired to her bedroom, attempting to establish this as an area of privacy and autonomy. It was also a way of revenging herself on her parents for she began acting like the child they experienced her as being. She became unpredictable, insisting on having meals according to her own convenience, playing on her mother's fear for her reputation.

However, this move failed too, as it was bound to do. Her mother's resentment grew with her exclusion, while her father insisted on his parental right to intrude. Her mother also blamed her father, and she revengefully encouraged Mr Danzig to continue to intrude. Father and daughter were thus set against each other by Mrs Danzig. And when Sarah said the intrusions got on her nerves, her mother remarked spitefully that anything got on Sarah's nerves, and anyway she could not understand why Sarah was so angry with her father, because Sarah never told her anything. She seemed oblivious to the fact that Sarah had told her she was angry with her father because of his intrusions. Her failure to understand Sarah's anger seemed clearly a function of Sarah's excluding her.

Sarah's father, too, found her behaviour unintelligible. Nothing Sarah said seemed to have the slightest effect on how either parent saw her.

MOTHER: I agree with you! – I am sharp because my nerves are bad and – I – I think I've had more trouble than most people have had with their daughters –

FATHER: You're sharp generally – you're a bit on the sharp side, at least unconsciously –

MOTHER: I suppose I've been sort of hard done by –

SARAH: What about those delinquents that go around, and the girls that leave home?

MOTHER: So why class yourself with them?

SARAH: Well you're –

MOTHER: Why class yourself?

SARAH: I don't class myself. Well you know there's a middle way – consider me just ordinary.

MOTHER: I did say – I do say you're ordinary – there's nothing that you do bad, and nothing that you do good that I can –

SARAH: Well that must make me ordinary, mustn't it?

Nor is it surprising that Sarah's protests had so little effect. Since she had hardly been other than an object of unrecognized phantasy to them, the situation was essentially no different now from what it had always been.

As Sarah maintained her withdrawal, her parents became increasingly anxious. But their attempts to deal with her made matters worse. For the object they dealt with was not the person Sarah felt herself to be. They tried explaining, and she contested them. They tried cajoling, and she rejected them. They tried bullying, and she excluded them. They did not try leaving her alone. They seemed compelled to do things to the object of their phantasy. It was as if all their repressed brinkman impulses were now compulsively concentrated on her.

Sarah now became desperate. Caught in this web of phantasy with no one to turn to, she began to read the Bible, seeking there a clue that would help her make sense of her experience. But this, too, was an unintelligible act. To read the Bible was not her place.

MOTHER: Well, she couldn't find the Bible, raised havoc out of the bookcases – 'Where is it? – That one's got it – this one's got it' – I said, 'Who wants to read your Bible?' I said, 'Is it normal for a girl to sit up all night and read the Bible all night?' I also think it's nice to read. I read. I might read a magazine or a book, but I never read the Bible. I've never heard of it. If I saw another girl read the Bible, I would come home and say, 'That girl's got a kink somewhere' – Yes, know about it, look at it for five minutes – just a glance through, but you never make a study of the Bible. I could never sit down to read the Bible for two to three solid hours. I don't think she reads it. I think she just glances at the pages.

INTERVIEWER: I'm a little surprised at this, I had the impression that this is what your husband would like.

MOTHER: What, to read the Bible all night? Oh no, Oh no, Oh no, Oh no. He likes to get down to things. He thinks every girl should know, you know have natural accomplishments. I used to teach her music. She didn't want to practise – all right, we'll drop that. And now with television, they don't want to. And she used to play – all right, don't learn. He likes her to go out with boys. He likes her to mix, to go to socials, you know, like debates. She used to like to go to debates, they used to have special film shows, you know, interest – show it to a group of people – Oh, he likes her to have an interest in all these sort of *normal* things. We used to go very often, the four of us, not Ruth, she was too young – go out at night to the cinema or to a theatre – the four of us, and we'd go out and have dinner. Oh he's not – I tell you – he's been brought up – his father was very religious, he was an officer of the synagogue and a great Hebrew Talmudist . . .

However, she was not explicitly forbidden to study. She was merely given vague but ominous warnings. Consequently she became muddled. This was reflected in further angry outbursts, which so increased her family's alarm that, when John began explicitly to moot the idea that Sarah was ill, he was simply voicing what they had been thinking secretly for some time. His mother was the first to agree. Bringing in the doctor was a serious step. But there was no need to be ashamed of nervous illness nowadays, if she was ill. Her father resisted. After all, she was not noisy. She was fairly quiet. She often spoke sensibly. His wife and son attacked him: 'Murderer, she needs treatment.' 'No,' he shouted, 'she's quiet. I won't let her be sent away without rhyme or reason. I won't let her be sacrificed just like that.'

The climax came shortly after her twenty-first birthday with an incident that resembled a key aspect of her relationship with her parents. It involved a man who failed to respect her in her bedroom, and her mother who refused to support her against the man's action. The incident was as follows:

Her bedroom was being redecorated as a birthday present from her father. The decorator failed to follow her instructions. When she protested he became insultingly familiar. She complained to her mother, but her mother failed to back her. She ran out of the house greatly distressed, and returned the following morning saying defiantly she had slept with a boy.

This desperate attempt to open up the issue of her existential growth was completely misunderstood. For her parents, threatened in phantasy by loss of control of their bowels before the disciplining phantasy other, panicked. Sarah, their ideal child, had gone over the public brink. She was out of control.

Their next step followed logically. They jointly made an alienated attempt to regain control of the embodiment of the bowel from which they were alienated. They called in the doctor. As the agent of society who claimed to know the difference between praxis and process in the behaviour of adults and infants, he could safeguard their reputation by exonerating them before 'the others'. He arranged for the swift removal of the excremental object into one of those places[1] made to receive the malformed products of society, rejected, because having no commodity value they disrupt the smooth businesslike functioning of the system.

Two weeks later, when Sarah returned, her family received her with a mixture of shame, guilt, and apprehension. She was radically changed. She was dull and apathetic, withdrawn and spiritless. She said she had been raped. There had been no confirmation in the mental hospital, except confirmation of the right of others to intrude on her fundamental human right, the right to be treated as a person. She had been processed as an object to make her conform to the stereotype of a productive social unit whose duty was to let her possibilities be exploited by others.

More isolated than ever, with the label of madness attached, she

[1] Colloquially called 'bins' in this country by the doctors who work in them.

retired once again to her room and immersed herself in the Torah.

Her family looked on without comprehension, but her presence haunted them. Utterly alone, day and night she studied, sometimes quoting to them what she found, in the crazy hope they might help her understand the issues over which she was so desperate. But torn between guilt at what they had done to her and to themselves, and fear for their reputation, they simply scolded and shouted.

What had she found? We are required to become complete, which is one. Male and female, each was created, and the Sabbath, the memorial of Creation, the pious Jew was required to celebrate in sexual joy. For sexual joy is a religious joy, and he should be as zealous in achieving this as in taking pleasure in the Sabbath harmony. For, in and through fulfilling his obligation to seek a harmonious relationship with his female partner, he becomes aware of the need to reconcile the conflicting[1] male and female aspects of his nature in a new unity, himself whole and re-created, able to worship in sexual harmony. For harmonious sexual union and sexually harmonious union redeem the Divine Presence from exile, transfigure the everyday, and through the experience of the healing awakening of consciousness orgastically reveal to Adam and his partner the transcendental unity of all experience and being.

But Sarah's parents had long given up any attempt to discover, far less redeem, their degraded sexuality. And when she spoke they simply grew guilty and afraid. In her despair she became a living reproach, a challenge to everything they stood for, the very embodiment of the Shechinah in exile.

As the Days of Awe approached, the Ten Days of Penitence which culminate in the Day of Atonement,[2] Sarah began meditating

---

[1] Eve, generally described in English as Adam's helpmeet (Genesis ii. 18), is called in Hebrew *c'negdo*, which literally means 'as one who is opposed or opposite to him'. Thus Eve is one who helps in and through contradicting and opposing.

[2] The Sabbath of Sabbaths, in Hebrew *Shabbat Shabbaton*, 'Sabbath of solemn refraining' (Leviticus xvi. 31). Sabbath, from the verb *Shabbat* (desist or refrain, not rest).

on repentance and sacrifice. Repentance, she read, is greater than sacrifice, yet repentance is sacrifice.

On the Day of Atonement Israel is required to examine itself openly and confess its sins; the penitent is required to examine reflectively[1] before another his experience and actions. On the Day of Atonement Israel is required to refrain from eating, working, and gratification; the penitent is required to refrain from pursuing phantasy ends. Repentance and atonement bring redemption and reconciliation between man and the Holy One; refraining in reflective awareness facilitates reconciling the contradictions of experience and action in a wider practical synthesis, the penitent healed and unified. This is sacrifice (Leviticus i).

The animal is moved by forces in ways it cannot understand; the sinner acts in phantasy without knowing he so acts. The offering must be dedicated to JHWH (Truly Being);[2] the penitent must be committed to the truth of himself. The holiest offering[3] must be flayed, dismembered, and totally burnt; the penitent's life and being must be radically analysed and called into question. The animal must be brought for sacrifice to a priest;

---

[1] The Hebrew for repentance is *t'shuvah*, literally 'turn back' and 'turn away from'. It thus carries the connotations re-flect and refrain. *T'shuvah* is also one *sephirah* (grade, potentiality, level of experience and being) in the pattern of human perfection in the tradition of Kabbalist mysticism. It is understood as return to the womb, carrying the connotation of regression in the ordinary psychoanalytic sense of rediscovery, through the undoing of repression, of early patterns of personal experience, and the connotation of rediscovery of the primal source of personal being and experience, in and through return to a state of pre-personal unintegration and undifferentiation. This return to pre-personal experience I term *reversion* (see Appendix on Reversion).

The doctrine of *t'shuvah* also refers to a graded pattern of progressive existential training, self-realization, and personal liberation adapted to a community comprising persons ranging from the most ignorant to the most redeemed. This pattern of being of persons and groups is also called *Torah*.

[2] JHWH is translated 'Lord' and pronounced in Hebrew *Adonai*. The term is derived from the Hebrew verb 'to be', and among other meanings carries the connotations of timeless, boundless, self-existent presence revealing Himself in whatever way He is manifest, always fully present and truly realized in whatever way He is. This is implied in the Hebrew *Ehyeh Asher Ehyeh*, translated as 'I AM THAT I AM' (Exodus iii. 14).

[3] The burnt offering.

176

the questioner must be open to mediation by the other. The smoke of the flesh rises as *re'ah* (savour), a synthesis of the experience of eating and breathing; in radical repentance, instinctual being is sublimed in a synthesis with *ru'ah* (Holy Spirit or experience unifying).

Man, the true sacrificial animal, may come to realize in personal renewal the presence of the Divine, in and through seeking to reconcile the contradictions characterizing his human being-in-the-world, the tension between animal darkness and reflective experience.

However, the Danzigs were bewildered by Sarah's meditation. And gradually the tension in the family grew. Once more they thought to have her removed, and once more her father resisted. But the day came when they could stand it no longer. A sacrifice was needed to placate the idols of their haunted darkness, a sacrifice for their guilt and a sacrifice for their fear. Sarah had begun quoting from Ezekiel.[1]

The prophet tells of a seed, the house of Judah, planted in a fruitful land, sustained by the waters of the Divine Covenant, protected by the wisdom of the Torah. This seed grew into a lowly vine, a vassal state unimportant by the standards of worldly power, but free to live by the Covenant and the Laws of Divine Truth. And this they were required to do. For they were to become a stately vine, a holy people united and independent, a redeemed community of redeemed men, an example of the beneficence of the Torah.

But the King of Judah disowned the Covenant, and refused to watch, work, and wait on his destiny to unfold. Pursuing an opportunist policy of short-term gains, quick satisfaction, and immediate returns, he sought to take advantage of the split between Egypt and Babylon, playing one against the other. But, says the prophet, the laws of being cannot be transgressed with impunity. They who will not seek to become what they are created to be, will inevitably suffer consequences. He goes on:

---

[1] From Ezekiel xvii.

Say thou: Thus saith the Lord God: Shall it prosper?
Shall he not pull up the roots thereof
And cut off the fruit thereof, that it wither?
Yea it shall wither in all the leaves of her spring.

For the Danzigs, riven by dissension, utterly alienated from themselves, this was more than they could bear. On the Day of Atonement, the day on which the High Priest in ancient times took a pure white goat for *Azazel*, which means 'the one to be sent away',[1] and symbolically casting out the sin of self-righteous casting-out, confessed over it the sins of Israel before having it led away into the wilderness; on this day of open confession and reflective self-examination the Danzigs, pretending to arrange her passage to the Holy Land, sacrificed their daughter Sarah, sending her into the desolation of a madhouse.

[1] Not scapegoat. See Appendix on the Azazel.

178

CHAPTER 13

Epilogue

MOTHER: You sleep at night now? You don't stay awake all
   night now, do you?

SARAH: No.

MOTHER: You can't. There's no light on [smiling].

FATHER: [something about a woman].

SARAH: Oh thank you very much.

MOTHER: I've got you some – um – all those sort of things you
   wanted what was it?

FATHER: I'm pleased the flowers arrived. Did you like the
   flowers?

SARAH: Oh they're wonderful.

MOTHER: What flowers are they, Sarah? What are they, chrysanthemums?

SARAH: Chrysanthemums, yes.

JOHN [interrupting] –

MOTHER: How do you know?

JOHN [laughing]: I sent them –

MOTHER: Carnations.

SARAH: Beautiful flowers, everybody loves them. I love them –
   beautiful flowers.

JOHN: Sarah, when did they come?

SARAH: They came this morning – this afternoon.

FATHER: That's right, this afternoon.

MOTHER: This afternoon.

SARAH: I was right in the middle of sleeping and Sister came and
   woke me up.

MOTHER: Were you pleased to see them?

SARAH: Yes.

MOTHER: Flowers are nice, aren't they?

JOHN: Last time we saw you, you weren't out of bed, you know.

SARAH: I wear my clothes now.

MOTHER: Much better for you.

JOHN: Don't you feel better walking around?

SARAH: Yes.

MOTHER: Do you watch television at all, Sarah? Where is the television?

SARAH: Yes, in the ward. When you come into the ward.

MOTHER: Do you watch it?

SARAH: It's there just when you come in from the hall.

JOHN: When you first come in?

MOTHER: Do you like it Sarah? You see some programmes?

SARAH: Yes. Last night I saw Jimmy Edwards.

MOTHER: Oh yes he's funny [laughs].

FATHER: Do you like him?

MOTHER: Did you see Hughie Green?

SARAH: No, I didn't see him.

MOTHER: Saturday night – they're quite clever you know, most interesting.

FATHER: Do you listen to the political discussions? No? That's too late of course for you.

SARAH: Labour's coming in I think, the Labour party.

MOTHER: Why don't you have stockings on? You'll feel cold.

JOHN: If you've got socks on, it's all right.

MOTHER: You've got a pair of stockings, haven't you?

SARAH: Yes, but they're laddered.

MOTHER: Well, I've a new pair for you.

FATHER: If you like the colour we'll get some more.

MOTHER: They're wearing very dark colours now. Do you know that?

SARAH: I don't like dark colours.

MOTHER: No, well I brought you a pair. If you don't like them I'll get you a different pair. You know Betty? She says she'll change them for you.

A few minutes later the following exchange occurred after the issue of Sarah's fear of her father was taken up by the interviewer. Her experience and agency were immediately invalidated. Her family appeared to experience themselves as experiencing her experience and also her non-experience ('she's unaware') or process.

MOTHER: Frightened of what?

JOHN: Frightened of Dad. Frightened *of* him.

INTERVIEWER: Mm.

FATHER [incredulously]: No! [Mother laughing.] I am an easy individual to get on with. All I ask – all I ask of my children is just to try a little more self-respect for their Jewish identity. They don't have to be Rabbis or to be ministers. I built up my business on a certain standard. I don't want that standard to be destroyed – just like that. I go to synagogue every Sabbath. [*Explicitly invalidating her experience.*]

JOHN: Well, Dad is not difficult to get on with if you take him out of the house. Unfortunately, in the house he does insist upon us observing certain religious standards which in *my* mind I think is too high. Nevertheless I do try and comply with his wishes. I *try*. I don't always succeed, but I do try. And Sarah does try sometimes and –

FATHER: I don't make unreasonable demands.

JOHN: Not unreasonable but –

MOTHER: You mean the fear of him personally, Doctor, or a fear of his religious views?

INTERVIEWER: I don't know.

JOHN: Oh I don't think she's frightened of – [*Explicitly invalidating her experience.*]

MOTHER: She's not afraid of – when you say *afraid*, I mean Mr Danzig never – [*Explicitly invalidating her experience.*]

JOHN: He's not violent. I mean he won't come up and –

MOTHER: He won't hit her.

JOHN: He won't threaten you with excommunication or anything like that. He might shout at you if you don't comply with his wishes over religion. It's me more than anybody else. He'd never shout at Sarah.

FATHER: Sometimes a child has to go to synagogue now and then – sometimes [voice raised] –

JOHN: He doesn't nag Sarah – and he doesn't nag Sarah at all over religion, but *me*. But I'm nothing to do with Sarah. But he won't nag Sarah over religion. If she played certain good records in front of Dad – he doesn't like her smoking on the Sabbath so I don't smoke on the Sabbath; but Sarah puts a cigarette in her mouth in front of him on a Friday evening or a Saturday. He'll get annoyed, but he won't abuse her for it. He asks Sarah to put it out, and she says 'no'. He'll go out of the room. He might fume internally, but he won't do it in front of her. I don't think she's got any reason to be frightened of him. [*Implicitly invalidating her experience.*]

FATHER: I don't think she smokes intentionally. I think normally she's unaware that she's doing it. Because there were times when she never smoked on Sabbath. [*Explicitly invalidating her agency and experience.*]

JOHN: And I think it's a – we try to – you asked us if we think Sarah's got any cause to be frightened of Dad. We're trying to give you one aspect where we think she might be frightened, the religious aspect. I personally don't think she's anything to fear, I think, over religion. Anything else I can't say.

INTERVIEWER: How do you mean, 'frightened over religion'?

JOHN: I think if she *could* be frightened of Dad it would only be, to my mind, over religion. That's the only thing he does ever insist upon, insist upon – nothing else. [*Implicitly invalidating her experience.*]

INTERVIEWER: You mean she'd be frightened of his insistence.

JOHN: *If* she is frightened at all, this is the only part where I think she can be frightened – over religion. But I don't think she cares so much for religion, I mean she does now. But even if she reads the Bible she doesn't worry about all the little things. [*Explicitly invalidating her experience.*]

PART II

Interexperience and interaction

CHAPTER 14

Dialectical science:
science of social intervention

With the new presentation of the Danzigs complete, we have finished Part I of this report. Part II comprises a discussion of the method of study and the principles involved.

The problem of understanding the Danzig family praxis was one with which Sarah Danzig, too, had been wrestling. Indeed, she had been desperately preoccupied with it. Though she had not thought of it in my terms. She had seen it as trying to make sense of her muddling family situation. Unfortunately, the others had been greatly alarmed, because trying to open up familial issues seemed to her family completely irrational. For by no means of reasoning available to them could they see the point of doing so.

Making sense of one's social situation requires a form of reasoning that is dialectical. But only through trying to make such sense does this form of rationality become available. Sarah's parents, who had never made the attempt, were radically estranged from it, and so found no sense in her faltering attempts. Indeed, they found them so senseless that they acted in a way that functioned to undermine her possibility of reasoning dialectically, thus helping to seal her in her situation.

What is this form of reasoning that Sarah required to bring to bear?

DIALECTICAL SCIENCE AND NATURAL SCIENCE

Dialectical reasoning is the principle of what may be termed *dialectical science*, which is to be distinguished from *natural science*.

By dialectical science, I mean the study of the reciprocities of persons and groups of persons in contrast to the study of natural events, which is the province of natural science.

In relating to his field of study, an observer of others may adopt either of two stances. He may see the pattern of events to be due primarily to a mechanically determined sequence, or he may see it as primarily the expression of the intentions of the persons comprising the system. The movement of an arm may be seen primarily as a pattern of flexion and extension of muscles and joints, or it may be seen primarily as striking a blow. In the first case its movement is explained in terms of anatomy and physiology, in the second in terms of the intentions of the person to whom the arm belongs.[1] In the first instance we deal with process, in the second, praxis. The first stance is appropriate to the study of things and organisms, the second to a science of persons.

Persons are always in relation. These relations are, in a sense, active. Natural entities, too, may be in relation. These relations are, in a sense, passive. Persons relate through establishing relations with each other and to natural events, while things and organisms appear not to relate so.

In relating, persons experience the situation in a particular way. They experience it as their situation. They relate, they experience themselves relating, they experience the possibility of relating, and they experience the possibility of knowing the form and nature of the relations they make. They experience themselves, the relation and that to which they relate. They experience, too, relating as their possibility.

This pattern of relating and experiencing may be termed the *form* of personal relating. It constitutes the relationship as personal, for through it the person is constituted.

In being aware of oneself relating to an event, personal or natural, one experiences and constitutes oneself separate from the event. This separating in and through experiencing oneself separate is crucial to personal being.

[1] This is a shortened version of an example given in Laing, R. D., *The Divided Self*.

But one is not simply a person. One is also this particular person. One has an identity. One's identity is established in and through the way one relates to the persons and non-persons comprising one's world. The way of relating whereby one's identity is established may be called the *nature* of the relation one makes.

The nature of a person's relationship is the pattern of relating which defines the particular person one is in the relation. The nature is included in the form, and so in a personal relationship form and nature are always present.

In relating personally, therefore, a person is formed, and in becoming formed a particular person is constituted. The form (and nature) of personal relating defines for one who and what one is.

Since a personal relation is simply the form of relation made by a person, personal relations are made with non-persons too. However, a non-personal object or event cannot reciprocate the relation in the personal form. If it could, it would be a person. While a person relating to a person must reciprocate personally, even when he appears not to. Thus, an interpersonal relation necessarily differs formally from a person–non-person relation.

Paradoxically, though, a relation between persons need not necessarily be formally fully interpersonal. If I relate to an object under the impression that it is, for instance, a tailor's dummy when it is in fact a person masquerading as a dummy, the relation is not interpersonal from my viewpoint, though it is from the viewpoint of the other.

A relationship is formally fully interpersonal when two or more persons relating to one another implicitly recognize each other as persons. And they do this when each implicitly experiences the entity to which he relates to be relating to him in a form similar to the form in which he is relating to it.

Therefore an interpersonal relationship is one in which each, while relating to each, implicitly experiences each as experiencing himself relating to the other, and as experiencing the possibility of so relating, and as experiencing the possibility of knowing the form and nature of the relation they are each making with each other.[1] This is a relation of personal reciprocity. In this form of relating, each implicitly defines himself as a person and as this person, and each acts to confirm the other as such.[2]

Thus, in relating to you, I experience myself so, I experience the possibility of so relating, and experience the possibility of knowing the form and nature of our relation. At the same time, I experience you as experiencing yourself relating to me, as experiencing the possibility of so relating, and as experiencing the possibility of knowing the form and nature of the relation we make.

Similarly, in relating to me, you experience yourself relating so, you experience the possibility of so relating, and experience the possibility of knowing the form and nature of the relation we make. At the same time, you experience me as experiencing myself relating to you, as experiencing the possibility of so relating, and as experiencing the possibility of knowing the form and nature of our relation.

In this relation, each implicitly constitutes himself a person, confirming and confirmed by the other.

Also, each defines himself and the other more particularly. For I, in relating to you, allocate myself and you an identity. The pattern of interrelating establishing our identities is the nature of our (interpersonal) relationship.

William and Mary as persons see themselves as man and wife.

---

[1] Note that they are experiencing each other *as* experiencing. They are not experiencing each other's experience. One cannot experience the other's experience. One can only infer it, explicitly or implicitly though one may have a phantasy of experiencing the other's experience as we shall see in the case study. For a discussion on inferring the other's experience, see Chapter 3. For a discussion on experience, see Laing, R. D., *The Politics of Experience and The Bird of Paradise*, Chapter 1.

[2] In science fiction, a great deal of the anxiety evoked by the manlike robot is due to failure to experience oneself reciprocally confirmed at the level of personal self-experiencing and personal definition, when one is explicitly expecting such confirmation. While a great deal of the horror is due to the unexpected perception of the total absence of the experience of possibility in an entity that one had hitherto been experiencing as another.

William sees himself as a man, and as Mary's man, and Mary sees him similarly. While Mary sees herself as a woman, and as William's woman, and William sees her similarly.

In any relation between persons, form and nature are both present. An interpersonal relation is one in which each term of the relationship is reciprocally constituted a person, and simultaneously reciprocally allocated an identity that defines him more particularly.

A person may, of course, be implicitly allocated an identity as a non-person – a highly mystifying state of affairs – since to disconfirm him like this, he must be related to implicitly as a person. Either or both of the levels of personal experience, that of personal being and the level at which one is allocated an identity, may be implicated when a person is invalidated. Invalidation of the labelled person at both levels seems the rule in the families of 'schizophrenics'. And the practice of clinical diagnosis compounds the confusion.

Since persons are always in relation, one cannot study persons without studying the relations they make with others and with non-personal entities, particularly the others and entities of their usual social context. And the method used to observe must be one that allows us to study the personal form of relating. This form, as we have seen, includes both the person's pattern of acting towards the persons and natural events to which he is relating, and his pattern of experiencing the relationship.

The setting in which an observer can best study a person's mode of relating is an interpersonal relationship, one in which he is reciprocally open to being affected in his way of experiencing and being with the other. For only if he is personally open, i.e. open in his way of being a person, will he be able to experience reflectively how the other defines himself, others, and the relations between.

But the way a person relates is not simply a function of himself; it is a function, too, of the way the others, for instance the observer, relates to him. And so, the observer must be aware of his own pattern of response if he is to evaluate the behaviour and experience of the person he is studying. The investigator must become himself a person for study. Thus, I make sense of your behaviour and experience in and through making sense of myself, and I make sense of myself in and through making sense of you.

This way of studying is the way of understanding. To understand a person, the observer must relate to him fully reciprocally, while simultaneously observing their joint relationship. Or to put it slightly differently, the observer, with the cooperation of the other, constitutes himself as part of the field of study, while studying the field he and the other constitute.

Observing in this way, he requires an appropriate form of rationality. Since the field he studies is composed of himself and the other(s), by himself and the other(s), he must be able to reflect upon, and reason about, a reciprocity that includes himself as one of the reciprocating terms. He must study from a position within the situation he is reasoning about. This requires a rationality that is dialectical in form. Such a form is not embodied in the method of natural science.

The natural scientific method is designed to study events that do not reciprocate personally, but which, historically, were once experienced as so doing.

Formally, persons relate personally to things and organisms. But relating in this way is not synonymous with personalizing these entities. *Personalizing* means experiencing and relating as if the thing, for instance, is a person, i.e. capable of reciprocating the personal relation. It thus means failing to tell person from thing. There was a period in the history of experiencing in Europe when persons personalized the natural world. They experienced non-human events as animate, intelligent, and self-experiencing, relating fully reciprocally to and with persons. In the Western world the natural scientific method was developed to help preclude such an experience. The development of Western science and technology since the Renaissance is significantly the result of taking precautions against attributing personal experience, agency, and intention to natural events. The task of the natural scientist is, precisely, to establish the relationships between such events, on the assumption that things and organisms do not experience or establish for themselves the form and nature of their relationships. This includes the assumption that they do not experience themselves being studied, and so do not respond to such knowledge.

This does not preclude the possibility that natural entities in some sense experience the observer. It means they do not experience him as studying them, nor experience the form and nature of the relationship.

Since natural science assumes that the objects of its study form no relations in the personal sense, its method based on this assumption cannot be used to receive a reciprocal contribution from the object to studying itself, the observer, or the relation between. Its object cannot be a reciprocating subject, one who experiences himself relating to the observer as the observer is relating to him. Its object cannot validly be a person, though it can be the body of a person.

A person may, however, be treated invalidly as an organism or a thing. This might involve mystifying him in the way I described earlier, and might result in the person experiencing himself as a non-person. The clinical diagnosis of 'schizophrenics' is an invalidation of this kind. The human race is more likely than not to destroy itself because major sections experience other sections as non-persons, for instance the Reds ('The Russians, are they human?'), the Jews ('sub-humans'), the Niggers ('Go back to the trees in the jungle'), and so on.

Now, a reciprocity of a kind may be validly seen by the natural scientist to exist in the system he is studying, or between the system and himself, but this cannot be seen to include reciprocal understanding of the relation with the observer, or of the relations within the field by the events or entities comprising it. The natural scientist, because of his assumptions, may neither expect nor enter into full reciprocity with what he studies.

If he does, he is either personalizing a natural object, or he has found the object to be a person or group of persons, and has switched from the natural scientific way of relating to another.

Making the switch may be difficult, however, if he has been

habitually relating to the other or others as non-persons. For some time now psychiatrists have been urging that 'schizophrenics' be treated as persons. This seems an implicit attempt to break out of the natural scientific way of seeing them, which involves studying them as if they were things or organisms. The attempt is dialectically naïve, however, and unlikely to succeed if the psychiatrist is unwilling to become reflectively aware of how he contributes to the other's suffering through his clinical way of relating. He must see how he participates in, and contributes to, the social situation that induces and evokes the behaviour and experience he calls 'schizophrenic'. He must see himself and his clinical relation as part of the field for study.

But he cannot do this by the natural scientific method. For it is precisely his way of relating by this method he has to study. And its assumptions preclude him from experiencing himself as a primary aspect of the field.

This method renders the scientist's presence secondary. For even where he recognizes that he occasions disturbance in the system, and studies his technique of observing, as in microphysics, he does so primarily to minimize its effects on what he considers to be the primary field, which he experiences neither as himself, nor as the relation between himself and the system. In effect, the natural scientist relates to the field primarily from a position outside it, as the psychiatrist does when he studies the 'schizophrenic' clinically.

This method of relating embodies and expresses a particular form of reasoning. This form has been termed *analytic*.[1] The observer, positioned outside the system, registers events within the field, relating to them primarily as serial data and information to be processed, conceptualized, and manipulated, in contrast to participant observation in an interpersonal system, where the observer is open to being directly affected in the totality of his being by what is going on. And though a participant observer, too, must conceptualize, he does so to understand what is happening

---

[1] The term *analytic* is used throughout epistemologically. It is never used as a synonym for *psychoanalytic* unless the context makes it clear it is used in this way.

to himself and the other. It follows on what happens to him. It does not precede it.

Of course, a natural scientist may be affected too, but this is usually a result of his conclusions. Or, if events in the field do affect him directly, for instance, physically or emotionally, before his conclusions are reached, he must allow for this in a way that enables him to relate once more serially and conceptually. This relation of serial conceptualizing by an existentially detached observer is the form of analytic reasoning. It is a form inappropriate to a science of persons.

THE SCIENCE OF EXPERIENCE, A SCIENCE OF PERSONS AND SOCIAL SITUATIONS

The rationality required to study persons is embodied in *dialectical* science. This is a science of persons and groups of persons. It is a science of social situations. Social phenomenology is a dialectical science.

Persons experience. The way people relate to each other and to the natural world, is an expression of how they experience those others and that world. Phenomenology is the science of experience.

Behaviour is a function of experience. The pattern of a person's relationships makes sense through elucidating the experience his behaviour expresses. Existential phenomenology studies the experience of persons in relation to their way of being in the world with others and with nature. It studies the reciprocity between experiencing and acting.

Persons relate to other persons. They respond, and their responses are a function of how they experience those others. Their experience of the others is a function of how the others act towards them. John's experience of James is a function of how James acts towards John. Thus, to understand a person's experience of others, the actions of the others towards him must be examined. This experience is, however, a *function* of the actions of others. It is not necessarily an exact reflection. It may be an accurate perception, or it may be significantly a function of an experience in phantasy unrecognized as such.[1]

Only observation of the actions of the others will reveal how much it is a function of those acts. Direct observation of the relationship is therefore required.

For instance, John may respond with terror to a frown by James. This response may be excessive, or it may be justified. For James being the person he is, a frown by him may express a deadly intent towards John. But only direct observation of James and his relationship to John will allow us to decide whether or not John's response is excessive; whether it expresses an accurate perception, or whether, for instance, it is significantly determined by phantasy.

John's behaviour is thus a function of his experience of James, and his experience of James a function of James's behaviour towards him.

But the experience of persons interacting is always an inter-experience. For instance, in the matter of James and John we must also consider James's experience of the relationship. His frown may indeed indicate deadly hatred, but it may be a function of his perceiving John to have a treacherous intent towards him, which John, however, does not experience himself to have. Further, John may not realize that James sees him as having this intent. While James may or may not know that John does not experience himself as intending treachery, and may or may not know that John does not see James seeing him in this way. Unless the experience of each of the other is clarified, a spiral of reciprocal terror, mistrust, and misunderstanding will build up. Such clarification again requires direct study of the relationship.[2] This is the province of social phenomenology.

Social phenomenology studies relationships directly. It examines

---

[1] The problem of elucidating the phantasy component of experience is discussed in Chapter 17.

[2] For a detailed examination of the structure of a two-person relationship in the terms just discussed, see the chapter 'Interaction and Interexperience in Dyads' in Laing, R. D., Phillipson, H. and Lee, A. R., *Interpersonal Perception*.

the behaviour and experience of multiplicities of persons in relation to themselves, each other, and to the groups they comprise. It studies persons in their appropriate social contexts, and is concerned with the sense of their praxis, and that of their groups. It elucidates the reciprocities between persons, among persons, between persons and groups, and among groups. It is a science of the social and historical.

Such study by direct observation requires personal participation in the system by the observer. This may engender reciprocal changes in himself, the other or others, and in the relations between – a situation requiring, as we saw earlier, a form of rationality that allows the observer to reason as one of the reciprocating terms from a position within the field. For he must be able to distinguish changes in the group consequent on interaction with him, from changes due to the interaction of the others alone.

Dialectical reasoning helps him do this. Unlike analytic rationality, it is a way of reasoning about events or systems wherein the scientist is a fully reciprocating term comprising with others the field he studies. It is a form of reasoning about personal and group reciprocities, reflecting a double dialectic, the reciprocity of interpersonal action, and the reciprocity between behaviour and experience or between being and knowing, and should inform a valid social phenomenological study. It helps the observer discriminate between changes in himself and changes in the social field, and tell movements in the field engendered by him from effects engendered by others. It helps distinguish self from other.

Thus, simultaneously directed towards the observer and towards the system observed, it is a social and personal praxis facilitating a double clarification – personal, and of the system. The scientist makes sense of himself in and through making sense of the system, and makes sense of the system in and through making sense of himself.

Schematically, its pattern comprises three movements. First, a reciprocity between observer and the rest of the social field. In this movement the observer is aware he participates in the system, contributing to it, while being affected by it. But his knowledge of the social pattern, and the effects of the reciprocity are imperfect. Its effect on him is experienced on his freedom. He is liable to feel himself personally negated, determined by, and caught up in the system.

Next, a temporary nihilating[1] withdrawal from active participation. Here the observer, negating the system's negation of himself, relates primarily to himself, comparing and discriminating between his experience of himself and his experience of the system, between events in the system, and events within himself. Successful discrimination is followed by change in the observer's experience of himself, reflecting an inner movement. This change may be called self-realization. It is a shift in the totality of his being, resulting in an experience of personal affirmation. This movement of affirming in and through negating the negation is integral to the dialectic. In this second movement the social system as an object for action is held peripherally, ground rather than figure in the *gestalt* of his experience.

Third, a negation of the withdrawal and a return to the reciprocity with the rest of the social field. Self-realization, allowing the observer to see clearly what is outside him, allows him to clarify the working of the system and to relate to it with greater awareness of the options available, his relation to himself now being held peripherally. In this movement he affirms his relation to the system in and through negating his negation of it, though his affirmation is at a higher level of personal development.

In reasoning dialectically, two poles mark the limits of the movement of attention – self, and self and system. The emphasis moves reciprocally between them – from self and system to self, and from self to self and system, the poles marking three movements or moments, which are phases of a progressively

---

[1] The term is derived from Sartre, J.-P., *Being and Nothingness*. It is used for the praxis whereby consciousness distinguishes between itself and the object of which it is aware in and through the experience of a separating nothingness. In this way, consciousness becomes aware of itself as distinct from the object, and of the object as distinct from it. The relationship of consciousness with object will be discussed in Chapter 16.

196

developing spiral, the third being a return to the first at a higher level of personal and social development.

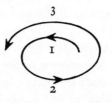

self   self ⇌ system

<u>movement of attention</u>

Thus, the dialectical movement is a way of observing, and a way to bring change, which the observer experiences as a movement in himself and in the system observed. This change is integral to the method. Dialectical understanding is understanding of the dialectic in and through the experience of reciprocal change wrought in oneself and in the system observed.

In the field of the sciences of persons much confusion exists because natural scientific, rather than dialectical, principles have been applied. Since reciprocity between persons, groups, and between persons and groups constitutes the basis of the events studied by those sciences, analytic rationality, by its non-reciprocal nature, cannot elucidate them.

The natural scientific method, when applied to studying a person, simply extrapolates him from his appropriate social context and system of relationships, and the effectively detached observer, applying the principles of analytic reasoning, perceives him as if he were a simple totality with qualities, and characteristics to be typed, classified, and treated *serially*, i.e. as a unit in a series of similar units. It fails to clarify the constantly shifting interplay of experience and action between the person and his significant others.

When applied to the study of a group, natural science functions to treat it as a unitary entity obeying mechanically determined laws. It fails to perceive it as interplay of persons relating to one another, each in terms of his experience of the others. The position with a group is further complicated by the fact that an inertia often creeps into its praxis, whereby events occur of which no person, group, or sub-group is the author – *group process*. These events often function to frustrate the express aims of the group – *group contradiction*. Group process gives the appearance of mechanical fatality, but it is the outcome of the pattern of interpersonal action, and cannot be clarified except by elucidating the details of how the members relate to one another.[1] And this can be done only in and through participant observation, i.e. by applying dialectical reasoning.

Thus, in the field of the study of persons, the natural scientific technique, originally developed to preclude personalizing organisms and things, functions to reify persons.

It was said the Danzig family praxis was to be rendered intelligible in and through a new totalization. The praxis of totalizing is integral to the dialectic.

Social situations constantly change. No two systems are exactly alike, and the same situation never recurs exactly, even with the same participants. The dialectical principle allows for this. It allows that in human affairs the unexpected will always happen even if it does not. It recognizes the inevitability of the occurrence of the unexpected as such.[2] Though it does so, not by the natural scientific method of calculating probability and working out averages,[3] but by according to the unexpected event its full value

---

[1] *Sanity, Madness, and the Family* is devoted to describing how this was done in the case of eleven families of diagnosed patients.

[2] The experience of the world as contradiction, and the inevitability of the disrupting intervention of the unexpected seems to be the original experience expressed in the tradition of Satan as Lord of this World. The relationship of Satan to the experience of contradiction is discussed in the Appendix on the Azazel.

[3] Dialectical science is concerned with making generalizations and comparisons, but these must be approached in their proper order, because the relationship of the general to the specific in a dialectical enterprise is paradoxical. Valid praxis requires questions relating general to specific to be part of a concrete project in respect of the particular general social situation too. This means that they should be part of an enterprise directed to resolving contradictions of that

in the scheme of things. The observer radically restructures his view of the situation, reconciling the events that contradict him in a new, more comprehensive synthesis. And this he repeats when further contradictions appear in conflict with his new *gestalt*. This comprehensive synthesis is a *totalization*.

By such acts of comprehending, dialectical reasoning progresses. Each totalizing unification is a synthesizing act of consciousness, reconciling the elements of experience in a new whole that transcends the observer's existing *gestalt*, which is dissolved into, and preserved in, the wider synthesis.

The progression depends on recognizing the principle of contradiction, the principle of the inseparability of the experience of contradiction from all human experience in whatever mode this experience occurs.[1] And this understanding may occur only dialectically – through personal experience and action. The progressive reconciliation of the contradictions of experience in successively more comprehensive syntheses is the principle of recognizing the contradictory nature of reality, and of the validity of contradiction as such.

This movement of progressive reconciliation may be summed up as a movement of totalizing, detotalizing and retotalizing the disparate elements of experience. It occurs in three moments, corresponding to the reciprocal movement described earlier. In the first moment, the observer's pattern of experiencing himself and the system is disrupted, in and through his becoming aware of elements in the situation not congruent with his existing totalization of the system and of his relation to it. In the second he negates this synthesis. In the third, he retotalizes the situation, reconciling the former *gestalt* with the contradicting elements in a wider view.

situation, in and through identifying and facilitating supersession of the relevant general principal contradiction. In this way, the general becomes specific and general. Supersession of the principal contradiction is discussed in Chapter 15.

---

[1] Perception, phantasy, transcendental, memory, imagination, dream. The modes of experiencing are discussed in Chapter 17.

These moments comprise a movement regressive-progressive in form. Regression-progression constitutes the method of totalizing.[1] In the first moment the observer registers phenomenologically the situation and its contradictions, those of the rest of the system and those in which he experiences himself caught in participating. In the second a regressive-analytic moment, he analyses both sets of issues historically, one set in terms of the history of the system, and the other in terms of the history of his relation to it. In the third, a progressive-synthetic movement, the historical findings are, by means of a hypothesis, related synthetically to the phenomenologically observed events in a wider totalization in which he makes sense of the system and of his participation.

The emergence of the hypothesis appears itself to be a function of a reciprocity. For it often presents itself to consciousness, if it does present itself, as an intuition or flash of insight which cannot be produced at will, which must be awaited, and yet, which does not come unless one has been thinking hard on the situation. It thus appears a function of a dialectic between periods of active reflection and periods of rest during which the intuition or flash of insight happens. This emergence of the new as unpredictable and non-contrivable is the appearance of the unexpected at the heart of the dialectical rationality itself, and is constitutive of that rationality.

The appearance of the happening is paradoxical, however. For, while it is experienced as process, i.e. it happens, it may also be experienced as praxis, specifically as the praxis of an intelligence that is other than that of the person experiencing. When this occurs the reciprocity of which the intuition appears a function can be described as an *interpraxis* between the person and a non-personal presence. While the experience of the intuition's emergence can be termed an experience of *revelation*. Revelation

[1] For an extended exposition of the regressive-progressive method, see Sartre, J.-P., *The Problem of Method*. For a short exposition of Sartre's statement, see Laing, R. D. and Cooper, D., *Reason and Violence*. I shall be referring again to this method in Chapter 17.

in this sense is an intervention, constitutive of a moment of the dialectic, whereby the participant makes sense of himself and his social situation.

Now, in relating to the system, the observer is acting, for acting involves relating in the form of the personal. By *acting* I mean: to do in respect of, to know that I do, and to know in some measure what I do if I am doing it.[1] To do is to seek knowingly to modify the shared world of social reality. Even when I act on my experience, for instance stifle my feelings, I do so in the context of a relationship with another or others in order to modify the relation. One cannot relate without seeking, implicitly at least, to modify the relation, even if this comprises withdrawing from it.

The dialectical observer thus makes sense of his situation in order to act on the sense made. There is for him a necessary reciprocity between thinking on a situation and acting in respect of it. This necessity and the awareness of it is integral to his enterprise, which can be described as a praxis facilitating existential realization. The realization is twofold: emotional and practical. The observer, in and through realizing emotionally the truth of himself and of the system with which he is involved, may be freed to actualize this truth in practice in respect of the social field.

Dialectical reasoning is thus a rationality of action, and as rationality it is the *differentia* of the human. It is the principle distinguishing persons from non-persons. Its logic is that of social truth in action. It is a rationality requiring action, and one attained through acting. It is reasoning in, through, and for action in the field it is reasoning about; an action research. As reciprocity between being and knowing, it is knowing for social being. This may involve deliberately not acting.

Rational social praxis is action based on reflective awareness attained through a totalization arrived at dialectically. This is the logic of the enterprise – reflective knowledge of social and historical praxis and process in, through, and for social and historical action.

[1] For a discussion on the form of action, see Macmurray, J., *The Form of the Personal*, Vol. I, *The Self as Agent*.

CHAPTER 15

Dialectical truth

How may the truth of a dialectical relationship be tested?

As reciprocity between observer and system, and as reciprocity between knowing and acting, dialectical truth has a fourfold aspect: the truth of one's knowledge and the truth of one's acts, in respect of oneself and regarding the system.

What one sees and does in respect of oneself may be termed its *personal* aspect, involving self-knowledge and self-realization; in respect of the system, its *societal*. I shall discuss principally the societal, the truth of one's view of the system and its relation to oneself, and the truth of one's acts in respect of the system.

But the truth of one's view of the field and its relation to oneself depends on the truth of one's view of oneself and one's relation to it. Error in one reflects error in the other. For I make sense of the system and its relation to me in making sense of myself and my relation to it. And I make sense of myself and my relation to it in making sense of it and its relation to me. These are the reciprocal components comprising my totalization.

And so, testing my view of the field and its relation to me involves my relation to me and my relation to it. In discussing the societal aspect of dialectical truth, I shall discuss the personal when relevant.

Since the observer's relation to the system involves knowing and acting, his view of it may be tested in two stages: theoretical and practical. The theoretical may be termed the stage of *reconciliation*, the practical the stage of *effective action*, or of confirmation through practical realization.

In the theoretical the participant, confronted with multifarious

202

contradictions in the system, and between it and himself, requires a guiding thread. This thread is the possible principal contradiction. It is the theme that reveals the order in apparent social disorder. It makes sense of the system and of its relation to him.

The observer formulates the contradiction. The formulation is a guiding hypothesis tested in and through a unifying organization of the data in which all contradictions relevant to the praxis studied are reconciled.

Ambivalence, for instance, is a unifying concept denoting the experience of certain conflicting feelings that are expressed in the simultaneous display of certain contrary attitudes. In a psychoanalytic session viewed dialectically, i.e. as a relation between two persons, the principal contradiction expressed in the analysand's way of experiencing and acting in respect of the analyst is the theme common to the various conflicting aspects of what the analysand says he says and does, and what he is perceived to say and do in the relationship and includes the conflict between becoming aware and remaining unaware of the theme itself.

With the totalization, the observer enters the practical stage. By synthesizing the contradictions of action and experience in the system into a more comprehensive view, the problematic praxis is rendered intelligible. But a *gestalt* that makes contradictory behaviour intelligible is not, by that token, necessarily correct. It imparts clarity. Clarity is experienced as self-validating, and yet a form of clarity may be experienced over a false resolution. Indeed, the most effective form of mystification is where the mystifier induces the other to experience himself as clearly understanding the issue over which he is being mystified. How, then, may the clarity of the totalization be tested? How may one verify intelligibility?

Since the totalization is for action, it constitutes a type of working hypothesis. And its validity, which is also the truth of the intelligibility it imparts to the system, may be tested by the criterion of practical realization. A valid totalization should enable the observer to act effectively in relation to the field. Realization in practice confirms the truth of the working hypothesis, validating simultaneously the participant's view of the system, himself, and the relation between.

But what is effective action?

Effectiveness is effectiveness towards a specific end, and the test of effectiveness of action is whether the end, already specified, is attained. For instance, the validity of Lenin's view of the Tsarist social system may be gauged by the extent to which he successfully led a successful social revolution, the necessity for which, and the praxis of which, he claimed to understand better than any opponent or rival.

In the practice of psychoanalysis, which has dialectical elements, the test of effectiveness of action may be similarly applied to the analyst's interpretations. The intervention has three components: making an attribution, based on a theoretical formulation, about the other's experience – 'interpretation', in a particular way, at a particular time. Intervention is effective if it facilitates the analysand's realization of the experience to which the analyst refers. Increased awareness confirms reciprocally the analyst's view of the other's experience contained in the formulation.

It confirms, too, his timing and manner of making the interpretation. Practically speaking, manner and timing are as important as the formulation. They, too, are functions of the analyst's totalization, particularly of his view of the relation between himself and the other.

The question of testing the validity of interpretations is the subject of much discussion among psychoanalysts. The problem, however, is as much one of how and when one says, as of what one says.

The practical test, however, does not distinguish between the observer's view of the system (or other), and his view of the relation between the system and himself. If one view is correct, so is the other. And so, in practice an interpretation cannot be tested apart from the timing and manner of making it. It can only be tested separately in theory, i.e. by the test of reconciliation. Increased awareness validates what the analyst said *and* how and when he said it. It validates his relationship. It tests whether the relationship is therapeutically successful.

Theoretical in the sense used here is, of course, consonant with the Greek θεορια, meaning 'contemplation of one's acts', in this case the relation between oneself and the other.

If it is understood in this way, the theoretical will be seen to be a necessary moment in the dialectic between experience and action, and the objection often made that psychoanalytic interpretations are theoretical will be seen to be invalid, since that objection can be seen to be based on a non-dialectical stance. From a dialectical viewpoint, the questions to be asked are: (*a*) Has this interpretation met the test of reconciliation, or is it mere speculation? (*b*) Is the relationship therapeutic by the test of practical realization?

On the macrosocial scale, too, realization in practice does not distinguish between the observer's view of the system and the timing and method of intervening. Only in theory can his view be judged separately. In practice, it is his relation to the system that is tested. In acting effectively, his relation is justified.

And so, for instance, though Che Guevara's view of the system in Bolivia might have been correct in theory – I am not saying that it was – by the practical test his failure disconfirmed his totalization and invalidated his relation to the situation and to those comprised in it.

His failure was not his death, of course. It was that he led a group praxis claiming to be social revolutionary, which seems to have been physically annihilated. A social revolutionary group praxis cannot be so annihilated except by genocide. For the social revolution is the praxis of a revolutionary people reflectively constituting and participating in a functional hierarchy of interdepending revolutionary groups, each level comprising a system of interacting and interdepending groups of peers concerned to act and clarify their praxis.

The functional leader of the topmost group is one of a group of peers too. If he is killed or fails, another takes his place. If all are killed or fail, others arise from below. For the revolutionary struggle goes on indefinitely until it is consummated, since it is the praxis of an awakened people, and it seems not enough members of the local Bolivian peasantry were awake or had been awakened by Guevara to sustain the group of activists in their midst. He failed in revolutionary leadership.

This type of leadership is not romantic. It functions to help crystallize the energies of the awakening people, helping it find its true direction. But the traffic is two-way, for the leadership is sustained by the people it leads. True dialectical leadership realizes the reciprocity, acknowledging that it needs the people as the people need it. Otherwise it will fall into a romantic mystification in which it sees itself as a privileged elite bringing liberation to others. A revolutionary leader, therefore, who is not one of his people is no revolutionary. Of course, he may be adopted into his people.

In a revolutionizing praxis, therefore, there is no place for charismatic leadership in the romantic sense. If the leading group is romantic, it will fall into the cult of the personality, and betray the others. It will elect its own charismatic leader, who will fall into omnipotence, while the rest of the group, and the groups of others become serialized and infantilized, no longer reasoning dialectically, but seduced and terrorized into internalizing, and identifying with, the leader's view of the situation.[1]

Now, the examples given of effective action illustrate a certain principle, which may be called the principle of *dialectical realization*.

The aim of action on a macrosocial scale[2] is to change radically the relevant social situation. A social system is radically changed when the current principal social contradiction has been abolished. This happens when it is transcended in and through a new social praxis, which comprehends the old in a wider practical synthesis.

Lenin sought to abolish the social contradiction of the existence of a small class, which owned the means of social production of

---

[1] For a discussion on omnipotence and ego-centredness, see Appendix on Reversion.

[2] *Macrosocial* refers to the wider society and its sub-groups; *microsocial* refers to a group of which all the members are in reciprocal face-to-face contact. I am using examples from macrosocial praxis, because, among other reasons, it is probably in this sphere that attempts to apply dialectical reasoning are best known.

the means of subsistence, and a large class, which had to work for the smaller group and was mystified into not seeing this state of affairs. This opposition he saw as the principal contradiction, though the classes concerned constituted a minority of the population of Tsarist Russia.

On the microsocial scale, say in psychoanalysis, one view of the aim of therapy is to facilitate the resolution of unconscious intrapersonal conflict.[1] The conflict may be seen to result from incompletely experiencing a forbidden desire to relate in a certain way to oneself and others, and to parts of oneself and others. It is seen expressed in a derivative form of experience and behaviour. This derivative form is a compromise pattern of relating to others, symbolizing the original desired relation and the taboo on experiencing it. The compromise form is carried over into different interpersonal situations in which the person relates to the other to a significant extent unconsciously in phantasy. By this, I mean he is either unaware of the phantasy content of his experience or, if he is aware, he is unaware the content is an experience in phantasy.

The compromise form appears in relation to the analyst as a pattern of experience and behaviour which, empirically speaking, is inappropriate (*transference*). Thus, in the psychoanalytic situation unconscious intrapersonal conflict may be seen to express itself in the experience by the analyst of an interpersonal disjunction or contradiction.[2]

---

[1] I am retaining the use of such terms as 'unconscious conflict', 'unconscious phantasy', and the like, because they are in such general use. But, phenomenologically, they are misleading, since it is we who are unconscious of the conflict, or of the object or of the experience of phantasy, not they of us. 'Unrecognized conflict' or 'phantasy' would be better terms.

Much confusion, recognized and unrecognized, exists in psychoanalytic writing and discussion because this distinction is not clearly made. The failure to do so is a function of reifying the unknown regions of oneself by calling what is unknown the 'Unconscious'. We are unconscious of it, not it of us. In my view 'Unknown' is a more accurate term than 'Unconscious'.

[2] We are not discussing at this point the analyst's possible contribution to the disjunction, stemming, say, from unconscious intrapersonal conflict of his own – *counter-transference*.

An analysand may of course, be in conflict over a number of issues without realizing it. There is, however, at any one developmental moment a principal conflict. The analyst's task is to facilitate its resolution by helping the other become aware of it and its nature. But it must first be identified.

This may be done by identifying the principal contradiction in the relation between himself and the other, and then inferring the nature of the intrapersonal issue and phantasy relation the contradiction expresses.[1] The analyst may be described as aiming to help abolish the interpersonal disjunction by facilitating resolution of the intrapersonal conflict. From a dialectical viewpoint, therefore, a test of the successful analysis of the unconscious intrapersonal conflict would be the abolition, through supersession, of the interpersonal contradiction that expresses it.

However, this cannot happen if the analysand is unaware or incompletely aware of the disjunction. And so the analyst's comments must have two components: interpersonal and intrapersonal. The latter may be called the interpretation proper. The interpersonal comment has itself two components. The other's attention is drawn to his pattern of interpersonal experience and behaviour in the relationship. Then, that aspect of his interpersonal praxis which, empirically speaking, is inappropriate is pointed up. When this is grasped the emphasis moves to elucidating the intrapersonal experience that the inappropriate interpersonal praxis expresses, relating the experience to his way of behaving. In the term elucidating, I include helping him experience and work through the relevant emotional issues and unconscious phantasy relations permeating his relations with others.[2]

In and through experiencing, working through, and comprehending in a wider personal synthesis the negated issues and

---

[1] The problem of a logic of inference, and how to apply it, is discussed in Chapter 17.

[2] A similar schema is applicable in family and group analysis. Firstly, the pattern of intragroup communication is analysed. When this has been grasped, the focus is moved to that aspect of the pattern which is persistently inappropriate, for instance mystifying in different ways. When this has been recognized, and the participants see they persist in reproducing it despite themselves, the emphasis

relations occasioning conflict, the analysand may develop existentially and, in developing, outgrow and integrate the issues and relations he comprehends. Thus, the conflict may be resolved, and the interpersonal contradiction superseded. Removal of the disjunction marks the practical realization of the analyst's totalization of the social situation comprising himself and the analysand. The realization is expressed in a moment of true meeting between them.

This moment is, however, the criterion of resolution, not the aim of analysis.[1] This aim may be restated as an attempt to facilitate the analysand's being fully open to the significant others in his world, which in the last analysis means to all persons to whom he relates, irrespective of whether they are relating openly to him. Though naturally it does not mean he must tell everyone he meets all about himself.

And, by the same token, genital maturity may be defined as the realization, in practice, of the possibility of reciprocal openness in and through sexual love between a man and woman.

In the moment of meeting, the interpersonal disjunction is resolved. And this resolution is the touchstone of resolution of the analysand's relevant intrapersonal conflict, and of that of the analyst, if any, i.e. of his 'counter-transference'.

The criterion of effective action in a social situation is supersession of the principal social contradiction. Supersession confirms definitively and in retrospect the truth of the totalization in terms of which the observer acts.

However, abolition of the principal contradiction does not mean that all contradiction is abolished. On the contrary, successful praxis may be expected to bring forth a new principal contradiction, though this will be based on a different principle of

moves to elucidating the possible pattern of phantasy experience the interactional pattern expresses.

It would, of course, be pointless to draw their attention *first* to their pattern of phantasy experience. For if they cannot see a pattern of interaction they wish to clarify and cease to reproduce, they can make no proper use of the interpretation.

The schema is based on the axiom that behaviour is a function of experience.

[1] There are psychotherapists who now talk as if this is the aim of psychotherapy.

praxis. The perceived principal social contradiction of capitalism in Russia seems now to be replaced by a new contradiction comprising a new class of privileged bureaucrats and technocrats, on the one hand, and the less privileged mass of the people, on the other. The privileges of the new class seem a function of their control of the means of social production. But, unlike the old, their control is not based on private ownership of those means.

And in China after 1949 a similar state of affairs seems to have arisen. The cultural revolution that started in 1966 has been described as an attempt to depass this situation, and move into the next phase of social development.[1]

In a psychoanalytic situation, successful resolution of the principal intrapersonal conflict is followed by the experience of fresh conflict and further contradictions. These are the expression of new existential issues which have now become relevant.

A dialectical praxis is definitely successful when the existing social or interpersonal situation is transcended in such a way that the current principal contradiction is depassed in a wider practical synthesis, and a new principal contradiction, based on a different principle of praxis, brought into being.

The presence of contradiction is not, of course, necessarily destructive. On the contrary, the experience of its presence seems required to stimulate personal growth and social development. It is destructive only if the particular contradiction is no longer historically necessary, and there is a taboo on recognizing either that a contradiction exists, or that it is historically redundant. That is, it is destructive if it has brought the person or group to the point where they are ready to develop beyond it, and they are forbidden to realize this. If the taboo persists, then the struggle to recognize it and the relevant contradiction, and then to transcend them both, is liable to be painful and violent. There is, in fact, a double contradiction, the original social or interpersonal contradiction, and the contradiction of the taboo itself.

The two stages of testing a dialectical praxis may be seen to

---

[1] For a discussion on the new social contradiction in Marxist countries, see Djilas, M., *The New Class.*

correspond to different degrees of truth. These are the degree of *probability*, and the degree of *certain practicality*. Meeting the test of reconciliation validates provisionally the formulation of the principal contradiction, and makes the totalization probably true. While meeting the test of effectiveness of action validates definitively the formulation and makes the totalization true for certain practical purposes. Thus, the dialectical scientist must carry his experience into action if a probable conclusion is to be transformed into practical knowledge, or knowledge for practical ends.

The degree of probability in the first stage can be increased by progressively reconciling further contradictions until the totalization may be judged highly probably true. The degrees of high probability and certain practicality can be seen as the highest degrees of truth of a totalization. They appear to be reached in a particular order. For a praxis that has not met the test of reconciliation cannot be said to be ready for the test of practical realization. For instance, from a dialectical viewpoint a psychoanalyst who has not reconciled the contradictions appearing so far in a session is, in a sense, not in a position to make a correct interpretation. Though he may be in a position to make other kinds of valid response, verbal and non-verbal.

If, in the course of acting, for instance after interpreting, the observer is confronted with fresh contradictions, he must reconcile these with his existing synthesis. Each retotalization is a new test of the truth of the principal contradiction. And each successful reconciliation of opposites renders the relevant totalizing unity highly probably true for the next stage of action.

Thus, the dialectical relationship as a continuing totalizing, detotalizing, and retotalizing reconciles all fresh dualities and allows the scientist to continue to work effectively in a changing social situation towards superseding the principal contradiction.

From this praxis of testing and retesting it is clear that the truth of a totalization is strictly relative to the data perceived. Fresh experience in and of the situation requires a new totalization, the truth of which becomes definitively established when it is no longer historically relevant, i.e. when the concrete situation it was formulated to meet has been totally depassed with its aid. Then it becomes simply a totality, historically complete and out-of-date. But even now its definitive validation renders it only practically true.

The totalization, as a prescription for social and historical action, is a prescription for an ongoing praxis aimed at relegating itself to the past, as a view that was once definitely true for certain practical purposes. Thus, the abolition of what he perceived as the principal social contradiction of pre-revolutionary Russia, does not mean that Lenin's formulation was absolutely correct. It means it was correct enough for his purposes, and more correct than those of his opponents for theirs.

No totalization is absolutely true, for this reflects absolute being and knowing. Such being and knowing, if it can in some sense be, would have transcended the dialectic itself with its distinction between experience and action and self and other. It would seem not humanly livable or knowable.[1]

Since a totalization is only definitively validated in retrospect, passing from experience to experience in action always involves a degree of uncertainty. In reasoning dialectically, the observer is required to act on the basis of an evaluation he knows is no more than probable or highly probable, and only so on the evidence of the data known.

Since no two contemporary social situations are quite the same,

[1] Many traditions seem to indicate that such transcendence is incompatible with human being-in-the-world; for instance, the Buddhist tradition of holy men who reach such a degree of unification of experience and being that they become finally freed of their bodies and from the *materia* of the world, in and through becoming one with the utter void of pure transcendence.

The tradition of the Buddha as the compassionate one who could have achieved final liberation, but who refrained, perhaps refers to one who refrained from a final act of unifying transcendence in order to remain in the world to teach. The tradition of enlightened men, who, after a period of trial and temptation, descend from the holy mountain to teach, perhaps refers to similar acts of refraining, the holy mountain symbolizing the peak of the dialectical enterprise of possible unifying transcendence in the world. For, no matter how high the mountain, it is solidly part of the earth.

And see the Appendix on the Azazel for a discussion on the relation of temptation to the transcending of contradiction.

and none recur exactly, he is required to be constantly ready for events that contradict his appraisal of the position. He must approach each encounter without preconceptions, or at least knowing what they are, and be prepared at any time to revise his view radically. He should not transfer findings from one social situation to another, no matter how similar, without retesting his findings. In each situation he is required to reformulate the principal contradiction and test it again.

For instance, in the course of a psychoanalysis the same inter-personal situation appears to recur repeatedly. Discovering and rediscovering in each session the relevant unifying theme, in-volves retesting the analyst's formulation of the principal contra-diction. Failure to do so is liable to lead him into a trap similar to that in which the analysand is caught – the trap of enacting transference. *Transference enactment*, the carrying over of behaviour and experience from one social situation into another, is a function of failure to appraise adequately the relationship with the other, dialectically.[1] However, the formulation can be no more than probably true on each occasion for action, and only so on the basis of the data perceived.

Thus, the scientist acting correctly, always acts to some extent in the dark. This is inevitable. A praxis that is completely certain of the truth of its totalization is not dialectical. Neither a fanatic nor a dogmatist acts dialectically.

How may the scientist work towards superseding the principal social contradiction of the system in which he is participating?

A social system is simply the pattern of interaction and inter-experience of the persons comprising it. This applies even to a reified system that appears to impose its stereotyped or institu-tional patterns on its members. For the perpetuation of the system depends on the persons accepting the institutional patterns for whatever reasons, and reproducing them. Each member remains at all times free to refuse to reproduce the pattern. He may have to risk unpleasant consequences, but he remains free to choose.

[1] Note that I am not talking of *transference*, which is a carry-over of experience. I am talking of *transference enactment*.

Even when he has been conditioned in childhood to reproduce the pattern, the reproducing represents an original existential choice, which is maintained as a component of his current identity. He can become free of the conditioning in and through rediscovering the original choice, and re-experiencing the original social situation as he lived it, and the factors that weighed with him in choosing.[1]

Consequently, contradictions of the system are the outcome of the intragroup praxis. This is true even when contradictions function to negate the explicit intentions of the members. Supersession of the principal contradiction can, therefore, be brought about only by the action of the group members themselves. It cannot be brought about by the scientist alone. He requires the cooperation of the relevant members of the system if his intervention is to be effective.

The observer, therefore, cannot be accurately described as *causing* supersession of the principal contradiction, as if he were a natural scientist manipulating a system of things through setting in motion a mechanically determined sequence of events. He is most accurately described as *facilitating* its supersession in the system.

And he may do so in and through mediating to the relevant other or others his experience of the pattern of interpersonal or intragroup action of which the contradiction is an outcome; an experience that he should mediate as his, which may not be theirs, thus implicitly inviting them to examine and compare theirs with his. In this way each may be helped to discover for himself the intelligibility of his praxis, the observer's and that of the others.

And in mediating his experience as his, the scientist implicitly mediates to each his view of how to reason and act dialectically. For each is implicitly invited to discover for himself how he comes to make sense of the group and of his participation in it, comparing his experience with the observer's. Thus, the scientist may facilitate supersession of the principal contradiction.

[1] The Danzig family is an example of a reified system.

The enterprise of mediating is thus a project of teaching in, through, and for social and historical action. It is also an enterprise of learning by the observer. For he must be reciprocally open to others, elucidating the nature of the dialectic in and through elucidating the system, including himself. Correct social and historical reasoning requires the scientist to study with others, his and their shared praxis in and through action directed towards the system he and they comprise. In this way supersession of the principal contradiction is facilitated.

And the relevant members with whom an observer studies are those who are ready to understand and learn dialectically; those who explicitly wish to change their pattern of relationships radically, in and through understanding themselves and their social context.

This does not mean they already require to know reflectively the nature of the issues involved, or the nature of dialectical reasoning. It means simply they are persons who are struggling to make sense of themselves and their social situation in order to do something about it. With such persons and groups it is appropriate to study the shared praxis and its contradictions.

This holds because the dialectic may be understood only through reference to one's own experience and actions. Its nature is such, it is revealed only implicitly, only to an observer who is already trying to make sense of, and to act in a social situation in which he is participating, and in which he recognizes he is participating. It is not revealed to observation from without the system. It cannot be understood analytically. The principle of contradiction and transcending reconciliation may be discovered only from within.

The dialectic is not hidden, however. On the contrary, it is perfectly open, for, in a sense, it is the rationality used by every person all the time. But this is true only in a sense. For to reason dialectically means to reason aware of the pattern of reasoning. And its very openness causes it to be overlooked. In so far as it is a mystery, it is hidden in a clear light, for its pattern is to be found in the clarity that reveals and conceals it.

Since the observer tries to make sense of himself in and through making sense of the system, persons and groups attempting to reason in this way may be seen as striving to develop existentially. This form of personal and group change appears as a function and a result of dialectical rationality, and happens in and through transcending the contradictions of personal and group experience and action in a wider practical and experiential synthesis. In relating to another, or in participating in a group struggling implicitly to effect such change, an observer is facilitating a development already implicit in the situation. This is the aim of his dialectical enterprise. It is to participate in and to facilitate social and personal developmental change already implicitly present in the group and in himself. Supersession of the principal contradiction as the observer formulates or reformulates it validates definitively his totalization, and confirms the change realized in him.

And so, if during psychoanalysis the analysand's totalization of the relationship and contradictions is facilitated by the analyst's interpretations, and the totalizing is accompanied by increased awareness of the issues to which the analyst is pointing, then the analysand's view cross-validates the analyst's.

If the disjunction between them is resolved, and the old pattern of interaction dissolved and preserved in a new, more comprehensive praxis, the joint supersession definitively validates the view of each, and in the moment of meeting each is confirmed personally. Successful psychoanalysis is, thus, a therapy for the analyst too.

Similarly with a group, dialectical supersession as a shared group praxis requires each to make his own totalization and contribute his own view. Each becomes a participant observer along with any original observer. If the principal contradiction is to be transcended, each must arrive at a formulation for himself of the nature of the contradiction, and each totalization must cross-validate, and be cross-validated by the others. Supersession of the contradiction validates definitively the shared views of all, and confirms them severally in their meeting.

Now, paradoxically, action may take the form of non-action. If the observer cannot help, he should not hinder. If the situation is unripe, he facilitates change by refraining. If it becomes closed, he facilitates by desisting.

In family-oriented therapy, for instance, it is correct to form a therapeutic relationship only with the member who is ready for change, by arranging individual therapy in a setting other than the family. On the macrosocial scale, correct praxis requires the social movement to concentrate first on the dialectical training of movement workers before attempting wider participant action and learning. Wider participant action should be a function of the desire of members and groups of the wider society to revolutionize their relationships.

The Chinese cultural revolution as an attempted dialectical praxis on a mass scale was the culmination of a campaign by trained cadres to teach through participation what the Chinese term the 'Thought of Mao Tse-tung'. The campaign appeared to be an attempt to teach widely the elements of dialectical reasoning, and functioned as a preliminary to mass social action, Mao presenting himself apparently as an exemplar of the dialectic. Whether he has been successful remains an open question.

The dialectical scientist acting correctly should thus not try to force on a situation change for which it is not yet ready. Since change cannot take place without the reasoning cooperation of sufficient of the members of the group, an observer who attempts to force change has by that token fallen away from reasoning dialectically.

Paradoxically, however, correct praxis invariably involves failures. Indeed, failure seems a necessary aspect of the experience, though naturally it should not be deliberately courted. As a praxis of totalizing, detotalizing, and retotalizing, the dialectic is, in effect, an ongoing existential project of trial and error. Any judgement that the situation is ripe involves the risk it is not. But in the long run this does not matter, in a sense, if the failure is approached dialectically. For it may make available new data about the situation, the totalization, or the observer himself.

Thus, it has been said that the success of the Russian Revolution of 1917 was made possible by the failed attempt of 1905. And Mao implies a similar view when he insists that a correct approach can turn tactical defeat into strategic success – the thesis of the 'paper tiger'.

For correct praxis, failure is a signal for retotalizing the situation, which now includes the fact of the failure.

And this applies to a microsocial situation, too, say in psychoanalysis. Failure to facilitate therapeutic change should indicate to the analyst the need to review his perception of the other's pattern of experience and relating, and his own, too, particularly in respect of the other. Failure, if correctly approached, may bring the analyst new understanding of himself, and better understanding of the other.

The psychoanalytic experience has, of course, elements of a more radical dialectical approach to defeat. The experience of failure in his personal relations brings the other to the analyst in the first place. And the method of therapeutic regression, intended to help free the person from carry-overs bedevilling his relations, requires him to accept what is in effect an experience of radical personal defeat. He must let himself fail in his experience of himself as rational, integrated, and autonomous in the presence of the analyst, discovering, reliving, and working through the relevant childhood phantasy relations, finding in weakness strength, in defeat a moment of healing. Said William Blake, '*A fool, if he persists in his foolishness, may become wise.*'

Nor should a dialectical scientist set a time limit for resolving the relevant social and existential issues. On the macrosocial level, this appears to be the position of Mao, for instance, when he says that the revolutionary struggle must be seen as a series of battles of quick decision in a protracted war for which he implies no time limit should be set. The Chinese revolutionary struggle lasted twenty-seven years.

And on the microsocial scale, in the psychoanalytic situation, any attempt by analyst or analysand to set a timetable usually tends to hinder resolution. The role of a dialectical scientist is that of a midwife patiently easing the birth of a new existential order ready to be born.

Since his aim is to facilitate existential change already implicitly present, it follows that the scientist should not try to impose on the emerging pattern his conceptions or preconceptions. He must allow it to unfold according to the laws proper to itself. A psychoanalyst, for instance, must not seek to impose on the analysand his idea of what the other should or should not be. There is no question of seeing it as his task to teach the other to conform to society or to any particular morality. He is there to learn from and to help the other discover and actualize his own existential possibilities, whatever they may be, and wherever they may take him, whether they are specific talents or general human possibilities like the capacity to make heterosexual love.

And as a corollary, the analysand must learn to refrain from imposing on himself his own preconceptions about who he should be. He must learn to let his pattern of experience unfold without hindrance. He is in effect a dialectical scientist in training.

This enterprise of self-discovery is, of course, an expression of the analyst's own morality. For he, too, must be engaged on a similar ongoing project. But there is no question of imposing it on the other. It is a decision he must have made for himself, implicitly at least, before the analysis is embarked upon. Otherwise there is no valid basis for starting. And this decision the other must discover and rediscover for himself, explicitly and repeatedly in the course of the relationship. While the analyst, too, must rediscover his project. Only thus can he remain constantly open to the other, effectively encouraging and supporting him in his trials.

The only principle a dialectical scientist may require of a person or group is one he must practise himself: that of discovering and actualizing his true self in relation to himself and others in whatever way his social and historical situation requires. Though even this he may mediate explicitly only if the person or group is ready to receive it. Otherwise, he refrains. He must know how and when to let be. He must know when to teach by example and when by precept.

Now, though the dialectic is a rationality of persons and groups, it functions to determine one's relations to the natural world, too. It brings the natural under the hegemony of the personal, so that an observer's natural scientific project is related to his social and historical situation in a way that facilitates supersession of what he sees to be the relevant principal contradiction.

It thus precludes research simply for the sake of technique, and would preclude making a hydrogen bomb, for instance, because the scheme is 'technically sweet'.[1]

It helps the participant test the existential validity of his natural scientific project in and through subordinating it to his enterprise of actualizing himself truly in relation to himself and others.

To actualize himself truly in respect of himself implies actualizing himself truly in respect of others. For it means seeking to clarify how he contributes to the failure of his personal relations, in a way that allows him to relate more authentically. This is the justification of dialectical reason. The moment of meeting is the test of its truth. The dialectic as social and historical praxis is knowledge for the sake of action, and action for the sake of friendship. History culminates in the celebration of community.

[1] The reason given by Robert Oppenheimer, late doyen of American atomic scientists.

CHAPTER 16

*Analytic reason and the experience
of contradiction*

If the dialectic can test the validity of a natural scientific project, what is its relation to analytic rationality? It contains the analytic as a moment or component. What does this mean?

We must consider in more detail the experience of contradiction.

Contradiction in a social system may be defined as the experience of simultaneous affirmation and negation within the system in respect of an issue. The major contradiction in British society during most of the nineteenth century was the experience of the contrast between the increasing wealth of a few and the increasing poverty of the many in a context in which the national wealth was steadily rising. The experience of increasing national wealth was thus simultaneously affirmed and negated. National wealth was the issue.

Contradiction as the experience of opposition should be distinguished from the terms that oppose one another. The contradicting terms in the example just given are increasing wealth and increasing poverty. The experience of increasing mass poverty contradicted the experience of increasing national wealth. The increasing wealth of certain persons affirmed this experience.

Contradictions have different forms. By *form*, I mean structure. The contradiction in the example may be called simple. A simple contradiction is one in which the opposing terms are generally evident to those participants who wish to see whether the facts support a proposition about an issue. In the example, the proposition is: 'Britain is getting richer.' And in the nineteenth century the negating term was generally evident.

In some contradictions, however, one or both terms of the opposition are masked. Such contradictions may be called *paradoxes*.

For instance, in Britain the national income has risen over the past seventy to eighty years. And unlike the position during most of the nineteenth century the income of the mass of the people has increased too. Both rich and poor have become richer. But the rise in working-class income masks a contradiction, for the increase is absolute, not relative. The proportion of the national wealth this class receives is the same as in the 1880's. An absolute increase in national wealth has resulted in a richer working-class, but one that is as economically exploited as eighty years ago, and no longer realizes it. One term of the contradiction over the proposition, 'The British generally have grown richer in the past eighty years', is thus masked.

Both terms of the contradiction, and the contradiction itself, would be masked if no reference were made to the national wealth and the rich did not make their affluence evident; or if it were proclaimed that the country was getting poorer and was unable to pay its way.

This form of mystification based on double masking is currently being perpetrated in Britain, and has met with some success with some members of the working-class who are joining the 'Back Britain' campaign. They are proposing to work for varying periods for nothing, although it should be evident that whoever is suffering in this capitalist crisis it is not the rich.

Paradoxical social patterns may exist on a microsocial scale, too, as, when one or more participants in an interpersonal relationship implicitly negate what they explicitly affirm. For instance, when William tells Mary he loves her in an indifferent tone.

This paradoxical communication becomes a double paradox if William implicitly negates his implicit negation, thus apparently affirming his explicit communication. For instance, if he says he loves her in an uncertain tone that conveys uncertainty about his declaration and about his uncertainty.

The paradox becomes multiple if he makes the declaration ironically in a way that conveys there is a catch, but which leaves it unclear whether he is being ironical about his declaration, or about his irony, or about her, or any combination.

The double-bind communication described by Bateson and his colleagues[1] is a classic example of a multiple paradox.

If one or both terms of a social contradiction are masked, the person or group is liable to be mystified about what is going on, or even doubt if anything is going on at all.

If one term only is significantly masked, contradiction as such is experienced, but the person cannot at the time put his finger on what is wrong in the relationship of the other to him.

For instance, under certain circumstances William's constant protestations of love for Mary might begin to cause in her a feeling of doubt, which only later crystallizes into the question: 'Is he protesting too much?'

If both terms are in varying degrees significantly masked, the person (or group) may be unsure whether there is a catch over an issue. Or if he feels there is, he may be unsure whether he is perceiving or imagining it, or whether it is due to him or to the other. Many poor people in capitalist Britain are ashamed of their poverty and feel it is their own fault, not that of the competitive system which ensures that the few with marketable advantages always win.

Paradoxical communications are mystifying in that they tend to engender confusion over an issue, rather than conflict.[2] A person subjected to prolonged and intense mystification may be driven crazy or frantic as if crazy if he is placed in a position in which he can no longer maintain a feasible identity. This happened

Bateson, G., Jackson, D. D., Haley, J., and Weakland, J., 'Towards a theory of schizophrenia', *Behavioural Science*, 1956, I, pp. 251-64.

[2] For a detailed analysis and discussion on different kinds of interpersonal paradoxes, and on the relationship between paradox and the experience of confusion, see Watzlawick, P., Beavin, J. H., and Jackson, D. D., *Pragmatics of Human Communication*.

in the case of Sarah Danzig and the others labelled schizophrenic described in *Sanity, Madness, and the Family*. Techniques of brainwashing, too, depend on making ambiguous and paradoxical communications to a person placed in an ambiguous situation.

Paradoxically, however, the perfect mystification occurs where the double masking is so good that the person does not feel any problem or issue exists at all.

Contradictions may be classed, too, according to their relationship to the social system that produces them. This relationship defines what may be termed the *nature* of the contradiction.

For instance, a contradiction may be governed by the rules of the system in which it occurs, and is thus no threat to the system. The opposition between the Labour and Conservative parties in Britain, or between parliamentary parties in a liberal democracy, is of this kind. It is a contradiction in which each term of the opposition shares the same basic principle of praxis. This kind of contradiction may be called *regulated*. The Labour-Conservative duality is also simple in form, since the terms of the opposition are generally evident.

On a microsocial scale, a simple regulated contradiction would exist in the case of a constantly bickering married couple whose marriage continues even when the quarrels are bitter. The relationship between Mr and Mrs Danzig embodied a contradiction of this kind.

However, some contradictions do threaten the social order in which they occur. This happens when the negating term of the opposition is based on a significantly different principle of praxis to the affirming term. A case in point is the opposition in Vietnam between the NLF and the Saigon Government, where the NLF is the negating praxis.

Such a contradiction may be termed *radical*, because the terms of the opposition embody different principles in their basic group praxis.

A contradiction can be radical on one level and regulated on another. For instance, an opposition between fascists and liberal democrats in a liberal democracy is radical on the political level, but regulated on the economic. For, while fascism is incompatible with liberal democracy, it is compatible with capitalism. And so, conflict with liberalism does not threaten the capitalist economic infrastructure of the liberal democratic state. Hence Krupps's continuing survival and prosperity in Western Germany.

On the other hand, Marxist economic praxis has so far failed to evolve a liberal political system of regulated Marxist opposition, though there appears to be some move now in this direction in Eastern Europe.[1] Any mass political opposition seems to be seen by the party leaders in the various Marxist countries as constituting a radical opposition on the economic level. Since there is nothing in socialist economic principles that need preclude a regulated political opposition, the absence of such oppositions would seem to indicate lack of general agreement among Marxists about what constitutes the basic principle of socialist economic praxis. The ideological splits within and among the Marxist countries indicate this too.

To complicate matters further, a simple contradiction may mask a paradox, while a regulated may mask a radical.

The fact that there has been no significant redistribution of wealth in Britain over the past eighty years is, as I have shown, a masked term of a paradox. This paradox is a radical contradiction, since any attempt to put it right would involve a fundamental change in basic economic praxis. This masked radical economic contradiction is further masked by a simple regulated contradiction on a political level, namely the Labour-Conservative opposition, which negates the masked negation of the economic proposition: 'British capitalism no longer exploits economically the mass of the British people.' This simple regulated contradiction masquerades as a radical, masking the true radical.

If a regulated contradiction can appear in radical disguise, how may it be revealed for what it is?

One possible test of its existence is the persisting coexistence of conflicts and oppositions in an ongoing system, which they appear

[1] This was written before the Russian invasion of Czechoslovakia.

to threaten to destroy and yet never do. Such a threat must be more apparent than real.

Thus, the struggle between labour and capital, over what is in effect their shares in the profits of the capitalist system, can never in itself destroy the system, no matter how violent the clashes. Because the system is based on such an opposition, and on disguising it as necessary.

Of course, individual firms and corporations, and even nations, may be destroyed in such struggles. But this does not destroy the system, for the individual entities are simply taken over by their capitalist competitors, capitalism being an imperialism by its competitive nature.

No labour movement whose main aim is higher wages and better welfare benefits has ever brought about a social revolution in a capitalist economy. The system can only be revolutionized by a movement that is reflectively aware of the central principle of capitalist praxis, of which the opposition between wages and profits, *and the need to disguise it,* is a necessary expression.

This test of a regulated contradiction has been applied to the Danzigs, too, as we shall see.

To sum up, contradictions can be classed as follows:

Form	Nature
Simple	Regulated
Paradoxical	Radical

Neither the classifications nor the permutations are intended to be exhaustive.

Now, an event may be experienced as contradicting if it is seen by the observer to be of the same kind as those comprising the system he is studying, and which yet confounds his totalizing expectations of how the situation will develop, i.e. if it is experienced as negating what he affirms to be the case. It is in and through the experience of the negation of what his totalization affirms that he becomes aware of the existence of a contradiction.

Contradiction is not synonymous with the experience of conflict. If John attacks James and James counter-attacks, they are in conflict. But James's response is not experienced by John as contradicting unless he expected James not to resist. Nor does James experience John's attack as contradicting if he expected it as part of his totalization. The experience of contradiction is a function of the appearance of the unexpected, or the absence of the expected, in a system in a manner that defeats or threatens to defeat the ends of the praxis of persons and groups. It is not the same as an unexpected obstacle, therefore, if the obstacle is not seen as part of the system.

The definition of the parameters of a system may, of course, change, so that events experienced as purely contingent so far as the system is concerned, or as belonging to a different category to those comprising the system, may come to be seen to be a function of a principle that determines them and the original system. Such a change would involve a retotalization in which a more comprehensive synthesis is formed.

For instance, a natural event perceived as an act of God, so to speak, may be discovered to be a function of acts of men. The destructive floods of the great rivers of China appear to be significantly a consequence of deforestation, originally undertaken to increase food supply.

Schizophrenia, too, is an example of an event apparently principally natural, which now appears to be significantly a function of acts of men.

In a social situation contradiction is liable to appear as a function of a pattern of unpredicted behaviour, or as a function of the absence of a pattern expected. The patterns may be interpersonal, intragroup, or intergroup. *Intergroup* contradiction is a function of the experience of the unexpected by one group in relation to another, where the group experiences both belonging to the same system. An attacked nation may experience an unexpected attack as the expression of a contradiction if it experiences itself and the attacker as belonging to the same human community. The attacking nation will not experience the unexpected resistance of the other to be the expression of a contradiction if it sees itself as human, and the other as sub-human or non-human (niggers, wogs, Reds, etc.). For it sees the other as part of a different system. The unexpected resistance it will experience as an obstacle or some kind of foreign event. The incomprehension of many Americans of the unexpected continuing resistance of the NLF in South Vietnam is a function of this way of experiencing the situation. They see the NLF as foreign invaders, and not part of the same people whom they see themselves as defending. While they do not see that their way of defending – 'It was necessary to destroy the town [of Ben Tre] in order to save it[1] – strengthens their enemies. The British in a similar situation in Malaya perceived and acted much more truly and intelligently.

Intragroup contradiction is liable to be experienced through group process that defeats the ends of group members. A contradicting event need not be in itself contradictory. It may be quite self-consistent. To be a term of social contradiction, it need only function to defeat or tend to defeat unpredictably the ends of social and personal praxis.

An event later seen as a term of social contradiction is experienced initially as an unintelligible happening or absence of happening, an opacity in the expected scheme of things, a simple totality that is simply what it is. As soon as it becomes reconciled with a pattern of praxis of a person or group it loses its thinglike opaqueness and becomes intelligible socially. And if the observer infers the experience of the other or others that the contradiction expresses, then it may be described as comprehensible.

For instance, to make socially intelligible the floods of the great rivers of China, we would have to examine the praxis of the social system that failed to envisage the consequences of deforestation as a means of increasing food supply. To make comprehensible this praxis that failed to realize a dialectic exists between the balance of nature and the acts of men, we would have to clarify the institutional pattern of experiencing, and relate this to the pattern of social organization.[2]

[1] In the words of an American field commander.
[2] Similar studies could be made on deserts. The creation of dust bowls in the United States appears closely related to a pattern of farming that failed to envisage

Similarly in a microsocial situation, say in the family of a diagnosed schizophrenic, where the person's apparently unintelligible behaviour and experience can be made socially intelligible by studying the events in the context of the family pattern of interaction. This pattern can be made comprehensible by elucidating, and referring it to, the pattern of experience the interaction expresses. The study in this book is concerned to make comprehensible the Danzigs' intragroup action.

The first stage, then, in the observer's relationship to the contradicting event is an analytic-positivist stage. The event, experienced as a simple totality, is examined, and its immediate features defined. Secondly, it is related to and reconciled with an observed pattern of behaviour, interaction, or organization. Thirdly, the group's pattern of experience is elucidated. And lastly, the pattern of behaviour, interaction, or organization is related to the pattern of experience. Unless the characteristics of the event are accurately defined it cannot be clearly related to the observed pattern of praxis. For the purposes of definition, therefore, the event must be treated initially as a thing. This requires the dialectical observer to

---

adequately the consequences of that pattern. A question to ask is: To what extent is the pattern of farming, and the failure to envisage its consequences, a function of a particular type of social organization? The problem of dust bowls is, of course, an aspect of the wider problem of biospheric destruction and pollution.

Similar studies could be made, too, on storms, earthquakes, volcanic eruptions, rainfall, and so on. To what extent and in what way are they affected by the actions of men on the balance of nature? If it is found they are affected, it may then be asked why this dialectic was not recognized in principle before. In other words: What is the relationship between the relevant pattern of social organization which affected the balance of nature, and the failure to recognize this possibility adequately?

Because of biospheric pollution, these are life-or-death questions for the human race. Most counter-measures so far suggested presuppose and require the continuing existence of the same social and industrial system responsible for the damage in the first place.

In general, we know little about the dialectic between natural and social events. Nature, here, must include men's personal natures. For a social system that persistently acts adversely on the balance of nature without realizing it, must be one that also functions to act on the natures of the persons comprising it, so that they do not see the harm they are doing. The damage to the macrocosm reflects the damage to the microcosm.

relate to it analytically. Analytic reason is thus a necessary component of dialectical.

Consider, for instance, my relation to Sarah Danzig's acts towards the Sister of the ward and towards myself, the doctor-in-charge. Her acts were momentarily experienced simply as mad.[1] The Sister, she accused of withholding her letters and failing to pass on telephone messages. Me, she accused of detaining her maliciously. The accusations in this moment were registered positivistically as opacities, and labelled 'delusions'. They were experienced as serial entities or classifiable items existing outside my current totalization of my relationship with Sarah, and of my view of the relationship of the Sister to her.

Next, to make the accusations intelligible, I negated my positivist stance and, addressing the situation dialectically, I related to Sarah rather than to the accusations. I elucidated her experience of the relationship between her and the Sister, and between her and me. And her replies led me to study the situation in her family.

The study showed that, because of the way they related to her, her perception of the ward situation was not unreasonable. But, however accurately or inaccurately she saw this situation and the situation with her family, her accusations could no longer exist as opacities. For, in and through studying her experience and its current social context, the accusations became reconciled in a wider totalization that included a view of her view and, therefore, an understanding of why she spoke and acted in the way she did.

This does not mean there were no phantasy or 'transference' aspects to the way she related to the Sister and me. But the issue at this stage was whether, and to what extent, what she said and did was reasonable in the light of how the relevant others in her world were *currently* acting towards her. Only by first determining how they in fact acted was it possible to elucidate the nature and extent of any phantasy component to her experience of them. For we normally determine what is phantasy against the ground

[1] For a detailed clarification of her actions, see the early study.

of a decision or assumption, implicit or explicit, of what is reasonable. In Sarah's case, the ground had to be established through directly observing the family interaction.

When this was done her family was seen to be deceiving her. They told her they telephoned every day, and that they wrote frequently. In fact they did neither. They assured her they did not want her out of the way, that they wanted her in hospital for her own good. In fact her brother warned me not to be deceived by her amiability into letting her go. While her mother said she wanted her in hospital for the sake of Mr Danzig. The wider view made her experience of the Sister and me intelligible.

The finding that her family was deceiving her has, of course, important implications for treatment and psychotherapy. In relating to a person invalidated like Sarah, it is particularly important to confirm him initially in the accuracy of his perceptions when they are reasonably accurate. And only afterwards, when he trusts you not to invalidate him, should he be invited to question whether and in what way his experience is influenced by phantasy, if the issue of phantasy is relevant.

And if his perceptions are judged to be markedly inaccurate, this must be pointed out in a way that does not invalidate his right to them. That is, one must agree with him to disagree.

To interpret his experience as phantasy or imagination without establishing its degree of perceptual accuracy, and confirming him in it, is not only faulty practice, it is also destructive, since it tends to perpetuate the existing mystification and invalidation of his experience.

And even if his perceptions are so permeated by phantasy that one judges him mad, the question is: Has he been driven mad by others, albeit unwittingly?

There is, of course, considerable difference between being labelled mad, and being mad. Some labelled schizophrenics are mad by any criterion that I know. While some, in my experience, are not, but have been mystified into believing they are. And some have been driven frantic as if they were mad.

And even the mad ones are not necessarily mad in the way they are said to be by those who label them. People are often labelled mad for uttering what their families and/or the medical and nursing staff see as not to be uttered abroad. This happened in the case of Sarah, as we have seen. Very often what these persons utter and do is deliberately highly provocative, and is experienced by the others as scandalous, their sin being to wash other people's dirty linen in public. But the true scandal is that persons are formally labelled mad or ill because they are scandalizing others.[1]

But to return to our example. In the Danzig investigation the analytic stance occurred as a moment of the dialectic. The dialectic was not a moment of the analytic. The dialectic is never such a moment, since analytic reasoning does not progress in totalizing moments. Dialectical reason, as the reason of totalization, comprehends the analytic as one of its moments. The analytic never comprehends the dialectic. And because it never comprehends it, analytic reason cannot understand the dialectic.

However, the analytic moment can be split off and, in a sense, be used independently. The observer then has no perspective on himself as one reciprocating the other reciprocating him. Consequently, the other is not experienced as a person, and is even experienced positivistically as a non-person. This stance, the negation of personal reciprocity, may be described technically as the *non-dialectical negation of the dialectic*, in contrast to dialectical reasoning, which is the *dialectical negation of the analytic*.

To simple analytic reasoning, the dialectic is thus an unintelligible intrusion into the analytic reasoner's scientific scheme of things. And though by its nature it cannot comprehend the dialectic, the simple analytic reasoner cannot comprehend this, and tries to account for it. He classifies it. He treats dialectical reasoning as a thing, in accord with analytic reason's positivistic form. He relates to it from without, seeing it as something that some people have, or do, or make a fuss about, with the implication or explication that its presence is due to the operation of some

[1] For a report and discussion on medical labelling as a means of social control of those who depart from social convention, see Scheff, T., *Being Mentally Ill*. For a history of labelling the unconventional or scandalous as mad, see Foucault, M., *Madness and Civilization*.

natural law that makes such people different in essence from himself. He sees these others, implicitly, as being of another species.

For instance, the clinical diagnosis of schizophrenia (or splitting of the 'mind') as an illness, in the usual medical sense of something primarily wrong inside the person, is based on perceiving the behaviour and experience of certain others as opaque totalities, socially unintelligible events to be described, classified, explained, or interpreted, the mechanically determined result of some internal process – genetic, constitutional, endogenous, exogenous, organic, psychological, or any combination[1] – and not as their intelligible response to their experience of how others, including the examining psychiatrist, are currently acting towards them. That is there is a failure to see that the primary problem is not inside them, but is how others are relating to them.

This failure in perception is a function of the psychiatrist's falling into a simple analytic-positivist stance. By doing so, he precludes himself from relating to the other as a person, and precludes himself from attaining any perspective on himself, i.e. he precludes himself from seeing he is precluding himself. He is blind without realizing it.

Where, then, is the splitting? It is inside the psychiatrist. He has split off the analytic moment from the rest of the dialectical form and, maintaining himself divorced from his own dialectical possibilities, fails to reciprocate the other, who is trying to reciprocate him. When the patient tries to continue to relate dialectically by commenting, for instance, on how the psychiatrist is failing to relate, his remarks are seen as further manifestations of a disease process.[2]

This splitting means that psychiatrists have no reliable way of testing either the accuracy of a person's perceptions of others, or the realism of his acts – a state of affairs implicitly suspected by

[1] For a discussion on this issue, see Laing, R. D. and Esterson, A., *Sanity, Madness, and the Family*, 'Introduction'.
[2] For an excellent example of this state of affairs using the psychiatrist's own report, see Laing, R. D., *The Divided Self*, pp. 29-31.

lawyers in this country, and manifest in their scepticism about psychiatric evidence.

To judge if a person is deluded about the way his significant others relate to him, the psychiatrist has only his own phantasy about the person's relevant social context to go on, plus his phantasy of what a 'mentally healthy' person is like.

Even if he sees one or more members of the family, or goes on the family report of a psychiatric social worker, his judgement is not based on an interactional study. At the best, the social assessment consists of inspired guesses. At the worst, it is based on the unverified phantasy of the psychiatrist and his co-worker, who reflects essentially the same medical-type biases and preconceptions, for she is trained in effect as a medical auxiliary.

The matter is complicated further by an equivocation over the term 'normality', whereby it is equated with health. So that being healthy means, in effect, being like everyone else in one's society. A person is judged mentally well if he conforms to institutional norms.

And so, a white South African who sees a black African as his equal, is mentally unwell because he is not 'normal', while a white racist is healthy.

Psychiatrists are taught to measure human relations and human experience against simplistic institutional middle-class banalities like: a child should always love her mother, especially if her mother says she loves the child; or a person who is sad should look unhappy unless he is keeping a stiff upper lip; or pre- and extra-marital sexual relations are signs of lack of moral restraint.

And so, if a child shouts that her mother hates her, and her mother looks hurt, the child is suffering from 'paranoid tendencies'; or if someone giggles when speaking of an event that frightened her she is showing a disease symptom called 'incongruity of thought and effect'; or if she has pre- or extra-marital sexual relations this is a sign of a defect in the social conscience called 'psychopathic tendencies', particularly in suburbia.

Once he is diagnosed, the person has to be treated for his own good. He must be 'helped' to have the 'right' thoughts and the 'right' feelings, and 'helped' to do the 'right' things. He must be 'treated' in order to make what is delicately termed 'a proper social adjustment'. He must learn to adjust to what is called 'reality' – this being equated with current institutional norms of experiencing and acting. By the criterion of social normality, Jesus Christ or any social or other reformer becomes a candidate for treatment.

It has long been known that psychiatry cannot distinguish between cranks and saints, between eccentricity and genius. We can now begin to see why.

This simple positivist way of seeing and relating to persons is inculcated or confirmed in the psychiatrist during his training. He is taught to detect – 'diagnose' – people whose thoughts and acts do not conform to the institutional norm, in much the same way as priests were once taught to ferret out witches, and Nazis and South Africans to detect the racially inferior. Although, unlike Nazis and South Africans, but like priests, the psychiatrist sees himself as having the good of the persons concerned at heart.

The similarity with priests is exact, because priests saw themselves as burning the bodies of witches to save their immortal souls, while psychiatry treats the person as an organism to save his 'mind'.

In recent years there has been an increase in the numbers of persons diagnosed as mentally ill. There has been an increase, too, in the numbers of psychiatrists. Psychiatrists say they are simply detecting signs of mental disease in people.

The position is again analogous to witch-hunting. An increase in the number of witches in the past correlated positively with an increase in the number of witch-hunters. Only after much fear and suffering did Europe and North America realize to what extent witches are made by witch-hunters. Motivated by socially unverified phantasy, the hunters found witches as McCarthyism later found Reds – under every bed. The only people safe were the witch-hunters themselves.

Unless we are careful we may find a similar position arising over so-called mental illness, where the only people above suspicion of having the wrong thoughts and the wrong feelings will be those trained and licensed to practise the psychiatric way of seeing others. Could anything be more dangerous to our social well-being?

This is not an argument, of course, against recognizing that some people are mad. It is an argument for recognizing who the mad ones are, and an argument against the assumption that psychiatric training fits psychiatrists to do the recognizing.

Nor is it an argument against all forms of classifying mad persons. Classification is necessary as the analytic moment of the dialectic, but it should be on the basis of understanding their existential problems, not on the basis of assuming they are suffering from a clinical one.

Nor does the argument mean that persons currently labelled schizophrenic do not experience themselves split or fragmented in different ways. They may do, but these ways are not the point of this discussion. The point is a particular type of split, which is in a sense the most crucial of all. For on a measure of healing of this split depends the possibility of the healing of all other splits, intra- and interpersonal. The psychiatrist's madness is, in a sense, the most dreadful of all. Since, in acting on his experience to bring about this split, he is attacking the very heart of his own humanity.

To sum up, dialectical reasoning is the dialectical negation of the analytic. It comprehends it in a wider synthesis. *Sanity, Madness, and the Family* contains a number of descriptions of dialectical negation. Each case presented is prefaced by a description of the diagnosed schizophrenic from the clinical or analytic-positivist viewpoint, which sees the person as manifesting a pattern of mechanically determined events called 'symptoms'. This view is negated when the study moves into its dialectical phase. In this, the person's experience of his social context is elucidated, and related to the observed actions of the others. A totalization is made rendering intelligible the hitherto unintelligible events used to justify the diagnosis. The dialectical moment thus makes the analytic intelligible, in and through comprehending it in a wider synthesis.

The nature of dialectical reasoning, and the possibility of recognizing it, is a function of the dialectical nature of human consciousness. It must be assumed that the possibility of understanding the dialectic through relating dialectically remains even in a consciousness most estranged from it.

The dialectical pattern of relating is paradoxical. The participant experiences himself apart from the system yet a part of it, affected yet affecting, detached from the object to which he belongs, yet belonging to the object from which he is detached. Human consciousness shows an analogous paradoxical form.

Human consciousness is always consciousness of an object. This may be an object of the world experienced as inner, or of the world experienced as outer, of the world of shared reality, or private, of the world of self, or self and others. It may be an object of perception, imagination, phantasy, memory, dream, or transcendental experience. There is always an object present to human consciousness. Phenomenologically speaking, there is no human consciousness without an object of which it is aware. There is no absolutely free consciousness that is human. There is no human consciousness that is simply aware.

A consciousness that is always aware of an object may be termed a *positional* consciousness.[1] It may be termed positional because it is a consciousness that posits or positions before it in space in a world,[2] an object, which it sets forth, so to speak. This positional form of consciousness is of the pattern of human consciousness. Human consciousness, as a consciousness that always knows, or is aware of, an object, is by that token, always positional.

If positional consciousness is consciousness always aware of an

---

[1] The terms *positional* and *non-positional*, and the equivalent terms *thetic* (set forth) and *non-thetic*, are derived from Sartre, J.-P., *Being and Nothingness*.

[2] The terms *space* and *world* are used synonymously unless otherwise stated. They denote regions of experience. Phenomenal space or world may be perceptual, imaginary, dream, phantasy, memory, or transcendental. The structure of these worlds and forms of space, and their relations to one another has yet to be defined. For human positional consciousness at this historical juncture, perceptual space and the world of perception appear to have primacy over the others.

object positioned or posited in a world, non-awareness of a present world of objects means non-presence of positional consciousness. Therefore, a being unaware of a present world of objects is not positionally aware. As a corollary, with no world of objects of which a possible positional consciousness could become aware, there would be no positional consciousness either, because, phenomenologically speaking, the presence of consciousness depends on being aware. And since human consciousness is always positional, with no world there would be no human consciousness. The presence of human awareness depends, therefore, on there being a world of which it can be aware.

Conversely, without positional awareness there can be no consciousness of a world of objects. Phenomenologically speaking, human consciousness constitutes the world of which it is aware.[1] We may say, therefore, that positional consciousness depends on the world, and the existence of the world depends on positional consciousness. Positional consciousness and the world are thus two terms of a dialectic. Neither is reducible to the other. Each is inescapably related to the other. They form a reciprocal unity, separate and related. This is the explicit dialectic of human consciousness.

There is also an implicit dialectic. The object of positional consciousness is always other than the consciousness that knows it. I am aware of my pen as I write. The awareness I am is not the pen of which I am aware. The pen is an object positioned in the perceptual world by myself aware. It is not the awareness aware of it.

But I am also aware of being aware of the pen. This awareness is direct and immediate. It is a direct, immediate awareness of awareness. It is not an awareness of an object. It is simple self-awareness – awareness aware of itself in and through its consciousness of an object in the world.

It is not an awareness of an object, since consciousness is not an object. It is the condition of the possibility of experiencing

[1] This does not preclude the presence of an absolute, creative consciousness, that creates the reciprocity positional consciousness and world.

objects. In (positionally) knowing the object, human consciousness knows it knows it. It is thus always a self-consciousness. This self-consciousness is direct, immediate, integral, and translucid. It is not positional, for it knows not an object but itself. It is consciousness non-positionally aware of its positional self. The awareness I have of being aware of the pen is a *non-thetic* awareness of the consciousness positing it.

This non-thetic self-consciousness must be distinguished from the awareness of consciousness achieved by introspection. The introspecting consciousness is positional. For even when the observer has placed in parenthesis, so to speak, the world outside, the consciousness he is examining is not the consciousness examining it. The examined consciousness is always past, even if only immediately past. It is a state of consciousness, a congealed experience. It is never the examining consciousness, which is continually present consciousness presently experiencing – an immediate self-consciousness simply self-aware. It is never I.

Consciousness appears present, however, in a twofold implicit dialectic with itself. It appears a double self-consciousness.

Thetic consciousness, as consciousness of an object, is other than the object it knows. *Non-thetic* consciousness is not other than what it knows, for it knows itself. Yet it is not simply what it knows. Non-thetic consciousness knows more than its positional self. It also knows its non-positional self. I know I know, and I know I know I know. That is, while I know directly and immediately that I know the object, I know directly and immediately that I know directly and immediately.

Knowing I know, or knowing knowing, may be called *secondary non-positional self-consciousness*, or secondary clarity. Knowing I know knowing may be called *primary non-positional consciousness*, or utter or primary clarity.[1]

---

[1] Utter and secondary clarity appear to correspond to the primary and secondary clear light of the Tibetan Buddhist tradition, and to *En Sof* (Infinite, Boundless, Without Beginning or End) and *Kether* (Crown or Primordial Nothing) in one version of the tradition of the Kabbalist Tree of Life or Sephirotic Tree.

Kether is the highest level or sephirah of the tree, and of it nothing can be

Human awareness thus appears a thetic consciousness of the world, and a primary and secondary non-positional self-consciousness.

This twofold self-knowledge is the implicit clarification of itself by human consciousness. It is the experience of experience, a clarification of clarification, the implicit discovery by consciousness of itself on the permanent brink of utter translucidity.

Oriented to knowing simultaneously the world, which is other than itself, and itself,[1] human consciousness is an explicit consciousness of the world, and a twofold implicit self-consciousness. And its clarifying non-positional self-discovery is a function of this pattern. For in and through the repeated experience of the reciprocity between the implicit dialectic (consciousness with, or rather of, itself) and the explicit dialectic (consciousness and world) the possibility of the clarification of experience arises. The participant observer realizing himself in, through, and for acting in the world may come to know himself as consciousness experiencing, realizing the permanent possibility of the experience of experience and the permanent impossibility of grasping it.

Valid dialectical praxis refers ultimately to the ground of all relations in and through the relation of ground with world. Dialectical rationality, a praxis of reconciliation and dynamic unity, is an enterprise of continual and continuing reappraisal and renewal, constantly bringing forth new experience[2] with deepening understanding and wholeness.

---

said, nor can it be grasped. While En Sof is beyond Kether and not part of the tree at all. The Creation, i.e. the world, is said to proceed from the level of Kether, which may thus be seen as corresponding to non-positional consciousness of itself as positional. While En Sof is an undifferentiated unity pre-existing and yet totally transcending all syntheses, which may be experienced only from the level of experience of Kether as Void, and only fleetingly.

---

[1] A consciousness not oriented in this way would not be a human consciousness.
[2] The Greek term *metanoia* in the New Testament, commonly translated as 'repentance', seems to carry this connotation among others. The relationship between repentance and dialectical praxis is referred to again later, particularly in the Appendix on the Azazel.

CHAPTER 17

Examination of data: method

We can now return to the question of making intelligible the Danzig family praxis. And I propose to discuss a possible way of organizing the raw data gathered in the manner described in the Introduction.

That method of observing and recording made it possible to study simultaneously: (1) each person in the family; (2) the relations between those persons; (3) the family itself as a system. Specifically, family members were seen singly, in pairs, and in all possible combinations.[1] The sessions were tape-recorded or written up immediately afterwards. All tape-recordings were transcribed, and a concordance-index, based in the observer's totalization of the family interaction, compiled. The transcriptions, the sound records, and the written records constituted the data.

The index was a certain organization of this data. It related the different viewpoints to one another and to the pattern of interaction, and revealed that the diagnosis of schizophrenia was socially intelligible. The published descriptions were written on the basis of this index and its findings.

In totalizing the interaction, organizing the data, and describing the families, the dialectical principle was applied. A method embodying the same principle has been used in the present study.

Behaviour is a function of experience, and common praxis a function of shared experience. Just as the words and actions of

---

[1] This is an ideal. It is not always possible to carry out all possible combinations. For the structure of the investigation of the Danzigs, see Introduction.

the diagnosed schizophrenic become intelligible when seen in the context of his or her family praxis, family praxis becomes intelligible when interexperience is related to interaction.

How may this be done? By a method following the four-stage schema outlined in Chapter 15:

(1) The event we are trying to understand is examined and defined.

(2) The pattern of intragroup action is clarified.

(3) The pattern of experience is elucidated.

(4) Experience is related to action, or rather interexperience to interaction.

INTERACTION

We start with the pattern of interaction.

Any multiplicity of persons constituting and maintaining themselves as a group, do so on the basis of a shared principle of praxis. All ongoing social systems are based on a shared central principle. A family is such a system.

Some patterns of relating are necessary to maintain the group, while others are not. All necessary relations are expressions of what may be termed the *basic* or *main group praxis*. This praxis is the pattern of relating which constitutes and maintains the group in being as the group it is. The central principle of the group is the principle of this praxis.

The existence of an ongoing group depends on being the group it is. There is no pure group being, no group that exists independently of being a particular pattern of praxis and process. If a group changes its central principle it becomes reconstituted. It becomes a different group, even if it comprises the same persons.

Adequate study of the praxis and process of a social system requires knowledge of the central principle of its praxis.

How might this be discovered? Perhaps by asking the group members? But what if they are misinformed or mystified? Then by observing the group praxis, for this embodies the central principle? But adequate study of the system requires prior

knowledge of the principle of the basic praxis. How do we proceed? How resolve the contradiction?

It may be resolved by a dialectical method. The principle of
dialectical inquiry is the principle of identifying contradictions,
and stating, examining, and resolving the paradoxes of experience
and action. By applying this principle, we may systematically
study in developing stages the pattern of group praxis. Each
stage is a totalization that arises from the preceding and progressively deepens the understanding of the working of the
system.

THE INITIAL TOTALIZATION

The first study of the Danzigs was the first stage of the procedure
of totalizing, detotalizing and retotalizing, and we must consider
how and why it was done.

It sprang from a doubt about the clinical method of approaching the problem of persons who came to be called 'schizophrenic';
the doubt being the expression of a contradiction in which I
found myself when confronted with members of the families of
these people.

The relatives invariably represented the issue as primarily
medical. That was why they came to a doctor. And I had been
trained to see persons behaving and experiencing like Sarah: (*a*)
to be suffering from something wrong inside them; and (*b*) to
see the something as a medical-type process called 'schizophrenia'.
But my experience with such persons was that I found them
accessible when, according to their families and to the psychiatric
experts concerned, they were not supposed to be. When I spoke
to them about their home lives they usually described acts by
their relatives that seemed very crazy indeed, and which, if true,
appeared to justify to a considerable extent the apparently crazy
things these persons were saying and doing.

It seemed, therefore, my medical and psychiatric training was
possibly leading me to prejudge the issue in two ways: by
assuming there was something wrong inside these persons; and

by assuming that if there was something wrong it was some kind of medical illness or medical-type process. If either of these assumptions was wrong it meant that the diagnosing psychiatrist was, in each case, sharing a misperception and a preconception with the members of the person's family, the diagnosis simply reflecting and confirming the family's prior assumptions.

I therefore decided to question the clinical view by an appropriate method, and to attempt to resolve the contradiction in my experience. This required me to switch my focus from the person whom the family was calling mentally ill, to the family itself. But what question was I to ask?

Now, the Danzigs in presenting themselves defined their daughter Sarah in a particular way. But in defining her they defined themselves. For they defined her in terms of their perception of her relationship to the group, and this involved defining the group too. It was in respect of the group's definition of itself therefore, that the question was asked.

The group's self-definition is equivalent to the member's group identity for themselves. It is how the members recognize themselves collectively, and may be derived from their description of themselves. I define it as the attribution by which the senior members characterize the group at the time of study. The senior members are the persons who are seen by themselves and others as the guardians of the group's tradition and ideology. In the modern British family[1] they are usually, though not necessarily, the parents. With the Danzigs it was the parents. In questioning the group's self-definition, I was questioning the group members' collective identity for themselves.

The Danzigs defined Sarah as one whose experience was not socially intelligible in terms of what was happening in the family. By this they implicitly defined their family praxis as not a

---

[1] By *family*, I mean that nexus of persons, usually, though not necessarily, of the same kin, who see each other as constituting the group. A *nexus* is a group of persons engaged in enduring face-to-face reciprocal influence on each other's behaviour and experience. See Laing, R. D. and Esterson, A., *Sanity, Madness, and the Family*, Introduction.

socially intelligible occasion for what she was saying and doing. Indeed, they explicitly described their family as essentially harmonious. Their group definition may, therefore, be said to be: 'We are a family with a harmonious praxis, apart from a daughter, whose behaviour and experience is mad and socially senseless.'

Unless an observer is operating with a prior assumption about the nature of the problem, a group presenting and defining itself in this way invites certain questions. Namely: 'What is the pattern of this family's praxis? Is the daughter mad? Even if she is by some criterion, can her behaviour and experience be possibly a socially intelligible response to her family's pattern of interaction? In other words, despite their assertions to the contrary, are they unwittingly driving her mad, or driving her frantic as if she were mad?' It would have to be unwittingly, for there was no reason to disbelieve them when they said they saw the problem as primarily something gone wrong inside Sarah.

It was to these questions that the first study of the Danzigs was addressed. It was carried out in a movement that was regressive-progressive in form.

The evidence the parents adduced in support of their view of themselves was first examined. With the Danzigs, the evidence comprised various assertions and attributions, which were embodied in the clinical view. For instance: that Sarah was lazy; that she began lying in bed all day when she was seventeen (she was now twenty-three); that she flew into unaccountable rages; that she persisted in making various mistaken accusations, such as that her parents were intercepting her letters, that people in her father's office were talking about her – they too were intercepting her letters, and tearing them up to boot – that there was a mistake in her father's books, and so on.

Each family member's view of the senior members' definition, and of the alleged evidence they adduced, was ascertained. Each person's view of the relationships of the members to one another, and to the group as a whole, was elucidated. In every case, the member's view of each issue of alleged evidence, and of each relationship, was studied historically, starting with the earliest moment relevant to providing the context necessary to evaluate it. That is, each person's remembrance of when and how the events in question started was ascertained.

Conflicts, inconsistencies, paradoxes, and contradictions[1] were noted, particularly over issues relevant to the questions posed.

The observed pattern of family interaction was analysed with particular reference to their description of themselves, and to the historico-analytic findings. Inconsistencies, contradictions, and so on were noted.

For instance, in the matter of the parents' assertion that Sarah was persistently and wrongly accusing them of intercepting her letters, Sarah's view was elucidated. She confirmed her parents' statement that she accused them in this way, but she insisted she was not mistaken.

Her description of the situation, and of the events that led up to the alleged interceptions, was then obtained. Her story was found to be relevant, coherent, consistent, possible, and credible in the context of her account of the relationship between herself and her parents and brother up to and including the moment in question.

This contrasted with the descriptions of the situation given by the others. These accounts failed to meet one or more of the criteria.[2] On balance, therefore, Sarah's view was judged more probably true than those of the others, which were presented as shared, but which contradicted one another on certain crucial points. This assessment was confirmed when the parents eventually revealed they did open her letters.

The examination of the evidence adduced in support of the group definition comprised the analytic-regressive moment of the totalization.

There followed the synthetic-progressive movement. A possible

---

[1] Contradictions may be positive or negative. *Negative contradiction* is the paradoxical absence of affirmation or negation where, on phenomenological grounds, affirmation or negation could reasonably be expected to be present. The grounds for the expectation must be stated.

[2] Namely: relevance, coherence, consistency, possibility, and credibility in context.

principal contradiction was formulated,[1] and the viewpoints of the different members, and the contradictions observed, were related to the historical findings and to the observed pattern of interaction in a totalizing synthesis. The formulation was regarded as provisionally validated when it enabled the contradictions in the praxis relevant to the questions posed to be reconciled. The totalizing synthesis was embodied in the account[2] in *Sanity, Madness, and the Family*.

Thus, in this method the group's self-definition is identified. The implications of the definition are then examined, and specific questions formulated to be answered through a study of the pattern of interaction. Then follows an examination of what the members said and did in respect of the issues raised. And, lastly, the situation is totalized, and the data organized to discover how the family concert their actions to bring about a situation that makes intelligible their definition of themselves as a group. With the Danzigs, it revealed how they acted together in a way that drove Sarah frantic without their seeing what they were doing.

THE BASIC GROUP PRAXIS

The next task was to make this revealed pattern of interaction intelligible. This required it to be set in the wider context of the group's basic praxis. For this, a totalization had to be made, based on a formulation of a possible central principle.

How was this formulation to be reached? The method I used involved stating and examining certain paradoxes in the praxis of the group, revealed in and through the first totalization.

To understand fully the praxis of any person or group we must know, among other things: (1) why they do this; (2) in this way; (3) at this time. Reason, manner, and timing are all functions of the central principle of the person's or group's praxis.

In the case of the Danzigs I did not yet know the reason, nor understand the timing, but I did know the manner.

If I could find another pattern of praxis that appeared to

---

[1] Namely, the attribution of 'mad and bad' to Sarah's praxis.
[2] See Introduction.

contradict the pattern discovered, and I had valid reason for seeing the new pattern to be a function of the central principle, then in and through resolving the contradiction in a wider synthesis I should be able to discover a common theme that could be used to formulate a possible central principle. Out of the opposition a common law is found.

Where was I to seek the necessary contradiction? Precisely in the group's definition of itself.

It was a doubt about this definition that led me to study the pattern of interaction in the first place. And the pattern of inter-action the study revealed confirmed my doubt. This meant my view of the members' praxis contradicted theirs. But it also meant their view of their praxis contradicted mine.

If my view was validly established empirically, and yet there was no reason to suppose the members were lying about how they saw themselves, and they persisted in their shared view of them-selves, then they must either have been seeing something about themselves I did not see, or they were collectively misperceiving. In either case they were seeing what I did not see, and not seeing what I did see.

If their perception of themselves did not reflect, or barely reflected, what they were doing together as a group, then they were collectively experiencing their shared praxis as simply a relationship between objects of phantasy, without realizing it. A group misperceiving in this way could not be ongoing. They could not constitute and maintain themselves together in relation to the rest of their society. They could not be a family. Therefore, the members of a family whose shared perception of themselves as a group conflicted with an empirical viewpoint must have been seeing themselves sufficiently accurately for them to have been ongoing as the group they were. Therefore, I, as a pheno-menological observer, must examine their contradicting view to discover the truth it contained.

For instance, a man and woman in presenting themselves may describe themselves as a happily married couple whose greatest happiness is in being with one another. Study of their pattern of interaction reveals they each describe themselves as feeling happiest when she is gossiping with her women friends, and he is drinking with his cronies, and there is no reason to disbelieve them when they say this. We are then confronted with a contradiction: namely, that in the context of their relationship, they are happiest, not when they are with each other as they said, but when they are away from each other. And yet they insist they are happiest in being with each other.

To resolve the contradiction, we must examine what this couple understand by happiness, marriage, and being with one another. That is, having established their view of themselves as inaccurate, empirically speaking, the phenomenological method requires us to continue the study by establishing in what way their view is correct. This is dialectically valid praxis. It is an application of the principle of the negation of the negation referred to earlier. The observer, having negated for himself the group members' (in this case the pair's) view of themselves, negates his own negation, and affirms for himself the group's perception by discovering the truth it contains.

The affirmation is not made as the first, but as the last, stage of the dialectical cycle, since the truth the view is, can only be fully known against the ground of the truth it is not. Its validity is affirmed in and through discovering and formulating a principle that allows it to be reconciled in a more comprehensive synthesis with the contradicting empirical view.

Thus, in the case of the pair, their perception of their relationship is affirmed in and through the discovery of a theme that allows the observer to resolve the contradiction in their praxis, and reconcile their view of themselves as being happiest with each other, with his discovery that they are each happiest away from each other.

And because both views of the pair's praxis are established valid, each pattern perceived may be taken to be a function of the central principle. And their common theme may also be taken to be a similar function. It may, therefore, be used to formulate that principle.

Similarly with the Danzigs, using the disjunction between their view of their pattern of interaction, and my own, a possible central principle[1] was formulated, and used to totalize their basic group praxis. This totalization provided a context that facilitated clarifying why, and why at this time, they did what they did.

The formulation of the principle was validated by the test of reconciliation, specifically by reconciling all persistent contradictions in basic group praxis, particularly those that appeared to threaten the continued existence of the group.

The totalization was again carried out by a regressive-progressive movement.

The development of the family was studied historically, the earlier moments of praxis examined, starting with the earliest relevant moment.

Using the formulated principle, a progressive totalizing movement was then carried out showing the logic of development of the group praxis from past to present. The formulation was validated in the way described. The totalization was then continued into the immediate present, using the now validated principle, and showed how the group's perception of themselves was the necessary consequence of their central principle in the particular circumstances.[2]

INTEREXPERIENCE

This brings us to the nature of the group's experience.

To be fully understood, behaviour must be related to the experience it expresses. How is the experience to be elucidated?

Experience, phenomenologically speaking, occurs in a number of modalities of types[3] – perception, imagination, memory, dream, phantasy, transcendental experience – which appear to

---

[1] See Chapter 1.
[2] See Chapter 4.
[3] For other discussions on types of experience, see Sartre, J.-P., *The Psychology of Imagination*, and Laing, R. D., *The Self and Others*.

operate together in any particular moment of experience.[1] But, though an experiential moment involves more than one modality, one mode may appear to dominate in any particular instance. We implicitly recognize the simultaneous operation of these modalities, and the fact that one may tend to predominate in any given moment, when, for instance, we say of someone that he is experiencing primarily in phantasy, or that he is mainly imagining something.

Since we experience in more than one mode at a time, the object as experienced is always in a sense composite, deriving its characteristics as experienced from the particular modalities operating. Thus, John as an object of James's experience may comprise features derived from phantasy, imagination, and memory, when James thinks of him. While, as a present object of James's experience, John may comprise features derived from perception, memory, and phantasy, when James looks at him. The object experienced in this composite way is, therefore, present as a symbol, in the sense that it links the various modalities, unifying synthetically the different patterns of experience derived from these modes.[2]

However, though the object as experienced is modally composite, it is also possible to analyse the experience into its components, paying attention to the object as an object of one modality, while holding in parenthesis, so to speak, its appearance derived from the others.[3] The reflective recognition of this possibility is necessary for a phenomenological analysis of experience. A valid analysis requires us to distinguish between the different modalities, and to discern the modal differences in the experience of the object, for instance to discriminate between the phantasy and the perceptual component.

[1] How the different modalities operate together and influence one another has yet to be discovered.
[2] Objects constructed deliberately as symbols are designed to strike resonances in more than one modality. A truly symbolic object, event, or act resonates all modalities. Complete enlightenment may be defined as experiencing the world in all significations derived from all modalities.
[3] Psychoanalysis, which is concerned to help the person discover the phantasy component to his experience, makes use of this possibility.

But in trying to elucidate the experience of another, we immediately come up against a difficulty. Experience, unlike action, cannot be directly observed. It can only be inferred from our experience of the other, and our datum of experience is what the other says and does. If we are dealing primarily with the perceptual component this is no great problem. The other can be invited to confirm or disconfirm our inference. In the case of the phantasy component, however, we cannot rely on the other's assent to validate our constructions, since we must expect he is either unaware of the content or, if he is aware of it, he is unaware of the extent to which he is experiencing in phantasy. And, since we are approaching the problem phenomenologically, we cannot refer what he says and does to a pre-existing system of references whereby we would say a particular pattern of behaviour and experience expresses a particular experience in phantasy; for example, a spire in a daydream means a penis. This does not mean, of course, that cases may not resemble one another in their constellations of phantasy experience, but it does mean that each case must be approached afresh without presuppositions about the meaning in phantasy of the 'manifest' content.

How, then, are we to construe the other's experience, and test our inferences? In and through a dialectical logic of inference, a logic in three moments.

In its first moment the behaviour of the other is assumed to be a response to an object or event in the shared world of perceptual experience. The second moment is the negation of this assumption. The negation is made when contradictions appear between the other's experience of the event, and empirical experience. The other's experience is either not shared empirically or, if shared, it fails to account for contradictions in the other's praxis. In the third moment the object or event of the other's experience is referred to another experiential modality or context, and the other's praxis referred to the inferred experience. A totalization is then made, transcending and reconciling in a wider experiential synthesis the contradictions of experience and behaviour. The reconciliation in detail of all contradictions of praxis is the test of the validity of the inference.

The following example demonstrates the principles of this logic.

We may reasonably assume that John's behaviour is a simple congruent response to James if John says it is; for instance if he says he is very frightened, and this is because James is hostile towards him. We negate our assumption if a phenomenological study of their relationship fails to validate John's perception empirically (i.e. if James neither experiences nor manifests hostility) or, if his perception is validated, James's behaviour fails to account for contradictions in John's; for instance, if James is indeed hostile, and openly so, but John alternates between appearing frightened and appearing smilingly indifferent when he says he is afraid.

If we have no reason to suppose John is lying when he says he is frightened, or lying when he refers this fear to James, we may infer that his experience of James is to a significant extent an experience in a modality other than perceptual experience; for example, significantly an experience in phantasy. The inference is validated if, by its use, all contradictions in John's behaviour in respect of James are reconciled in detail; for instance, why sometimes he appears to feel what he says he feels, while at other he appears to feel one thing when saying he is feeling another.

Such a logic of inference is applicable to the praxis of groups.

Common praxis is a function of shared experience. A group's contradictory praxis becomes fully intelligible in and through elucidating the experience this praxis expresses. The experience the common praxis expresses may be termed the central shared experience of the group. How may it be discovered?

First, we identify what may be termed the common object of the problematic pattern of praxis. This object is that familial feature, characteristic, or event, present at the time of study, to which the members refer, explicitly or implicitly, when making intelligible the contradictions of the praxis under study. With the Danzigs it was Sarah. They justified what, from a dialectical viewpoint, were contradictions in their behaviour, as simple, congruent responses to her.

Next, the significant mode or modes in which the group experiences the object must be identified. This is done in the way I have just described; namely, by comparing what the group says and does in respect of the object with a view of the object empirically established. If, then, they are judged to be experiencing significantly in phantasy, for instance, the nature of the phantasy must be inferred. This may be done in and through examining the attributions made by the group members, severally and collectively, about the object. This inference is the possible central shared experience.[1] The formulation is tested in and through a new totalization, relating in detail interexperience with interaction. It is judged true if all contradictions of the relevant praxis are resolved through its use.

It may be asked: Why choose the Danzigs for this study? Apart from the pattern of mystification and radical invalidation which they have in common with the other families described in *Sanity, Madness, and the Family*, I have at this time insufficient scientifically respectable evidence to say whether or not the central principle of their group praxis or their pattern of interexperience is typical of the rest, though they are certainly typical of some families of 'schizophrenics'. Then why write of them?

The question is really twofold. Why write of one family, and why of this one in particular?

I am writing of one family because at this stage of development of a phenomenologically valid methodology, it is necessary to establish adequate social and existential paradigms[2] for other observers and subsequent studies.

Such paradigms are studies of experience and action, which go to the heart of the matter in question, catching and conveying the spirit of the events described, while illustrating and illumining the principles and theory of the method used.

[1] See Chapter 5.

[2] For a study of the place of the paradigm in natural science, and its relationship to revolutions in that science, see Kuhn, Thomas S., *The Structure of Scientific Revolutions*.

But why the Danzigs as the particular paradigmatic family?

Simply because I was moved to do so. The dialectic is a movement in the observer and the system observed, and is fully realized when so experienced. And the scientist who allows himself to be moved, and later discovers the why and wherefore, is acting correctly dialectically. A dialectical enterprise always requires a degree of personal commitment by the investigator, who is always to some extent feeling his way in the dark. And when working in the dark, one choice is as good as another. This involves a risk, but risk is integral to the enterprise. Though, in the event, a crucial aspect of the praxis of this family was found to be the way it functioned to destroy the possibility of dialectical reasoning in Sarah, while maintaining the parents in their radical alienation from it.

Valid dialectical reasoning always involves a double clarification: personal and societal. Personal relates to self-knowledge, societal to the system. Personal clarification, though significant to me, does not in itself validate this study as a paradigm, though such clarification must always be present. Societal clarification should simultaneously clarify the system, the method of clarifying, and the principle of the method. Dialectical knowledge is knowledge of the dialectic, and as such it is reflective knowledge in, through, and for social and historical action. A dialectical paradigm is validated if it helps others to reason and act dialectically. Subsequent students will judge.

APPENDIX A

Reversion

Reversion may be seen as a form of regression carried past what seems to be the individual's personal historical starting-point. While regression is an emotional and experiential going-back in personal time, reversion involves entering a world without time. There appears to be a varying period after biological birth during which there is no continuing experience of personal continuity in space and time.[1] In reversion the person may experience himself carried back both to this period and to the period spent in the womb before biological birth.

Thus, while regression allows one to re-experience the earliest moments of personal development, reversion appears to take one into a world that is pre-personal and even non-personal. The experience may last a few seconds or many weeks. It may recur over months or years. This experience has been termed 'transcendental'. It is different from phantasy experience, which I include in what may be termed 'the world of the personal'. By this, I mean the world of one's experience of one's personal being-for-self in respect of oneself and others. It includes how one relates to oneself and others, and to aspects of oneself and others, including the body and its parts.

The personal world may be seen to include, too, the experience of one's animal self. Though perhaps this should be seen more as a transitional region between the personal and the pre-personal. For it may be experienced as the area where the pre-personal and

[1] For a discussion of this experience within the psychoanalytic tradition, see, for instance, Winnicott, D. W., *Collected Papers*, in particular the chapter 'Primitive Emotional Development'.

257

cosmic becomes transmuted and transformed into the personal and mundane, i.e. as the region where the possibility of reflective experience becomes incarnate. It appears to correspond to the lowest of the three levels of awareness in the Kabbalistic tradition.[1] This level, in which no distinction is experienced between what is felt and the experience of what is felt – for example, between the emotion and the awareness of it – is called in Kabbalah *animal* or *natural* soul, and is present in all men. The other levels are not naturally present, and must be striven for to be reached.

The Christian tradition of Jesus as symbol of the incarnation of the Divine, and as sacrificial lamb – the animal to be made whole[2] – may be seen, too, to refer to an original experience of the instinctual as the region of the incarnation of the possibility of reflection. The paschal lamb in the Jewish tradition is a memorial of Israel's redemption from Egypt, which traditionally symbolizes those imprisoned in darkness and non-reflection. Becoming wholly human thus involves integrating into a new personal unity that region of oneself wherein the possibility of reflective experience becomes incarnate, in and through bringing it into the light of living awareness.

The experience of one's personal being-for-self may be seen, too, to comprise three moments. The first is that described above, the level of simple non-reflective impulsion to act in respect of what is feared or desired. If the person is asked why he did what he did, he is liable to reply that he just felt like it, or just wanted to, or he felt frightened, and so on. He is only non-reflectively aware of his impulsion.

The second is a moment of reflective discrimination and reciprocal unity of what is to be experienced, and the experiencing of what is to be experienced; for example, of feelings *and* experiencing them. It is, for instance, becoming aware of emotions hitherto not experienced reflectively, or lost to such experience.

---

[1] In that tradition awareness is variously equated with soul, light, spirit, depending on the level. The highest level may be seen as equivalent to what we call 'experience'.

[2] Sacrifice from the Latin *sacer* (holy) and *facere* (to make).

The third is a trinity in unity comprising what is to be experienced, experiencing what is to be experienced, and the experience of experiencing. In this moment, with the experiencing of them and the experience of experiencing, the emotions become integrated into a new personal unity.

Regression, by putting one in touch with the early moments of personal development, functions to undo repression and may bring into reflective awareness one's animal self. Reversion functions to bring into awareness experience as such.

Reversion may occur in the course of a project of self-discovery, as in yogic exercises, or during psychoanalysis, where the logic of the enterprise requires the person to allow himself to enter the pre-personal and non-personal regions. Or it may be the outcome of personal fragmentation in a social situation that is experienced as unlivable due to mystifying interpersonal pressures. Or it may result, for instance, from the action of chemical agents such as mescaline, LSD, and the like. Such agents may, of course, be used as part of an enterprise of self-discovery. They should not be used without proper preparation and discipline. Much of what is currently termed 'transcendental experience' seems to be a mixture of experience derived from regression and reversion.

In the timeless world of reversion there is no experience of self and not-self, no distinction between here and not-here, no perceptual discrimination. The person is, therefore, helpless and socially dependent. The experience is non-egoic and pre-egoic. By *egoic* experience, I mean 'I' experience, and phenomenologically this refers to the pattern of *personal* experience and being, the pattern of experience and being of a discrete self experiencing discretely in respect of others. By *self*, I mean an experiencer experiencing himself experiencing. A personal or egoic self thus distinguishes constantly between self and other, and in distinguishing discriminates between different aspects of himself, while perceiving differences between others who are otherwise experienced as similar. During reversion the capacity to discriminate perceptually is lost in varying degrees.

For instance, in complete reversion, the 'I' becomes lost without trace in what may be termed the 'primary matrix of experience'. The person experiences total dissolution of himself, i.e. of personal self and personal identity. In such dissolution the experiencer no longer says 'I', for 'I' indicates personal experience. While in the moment of total dissolution the experiencer no longer experiences personally. Or rather the experiencer *does* not experience personally. For in that moment, if endured, the moment changes from one of time to one of experience, and the person passing through the eye of the needle disappears into a world without linear time or durance, where all is experienced ecstatically present. This moment of total dissolution is a moment of transcendental truth in which all is revealed as one. It is not pre-personal. It is in a sense non-personal, because it is also in a sense all-personal. In my view, the term 'transcendental experience' should be confined to this moment.

As the person emerges linear time is re-established, and with it remembering. For in the world without time there is not even the remembering of dissolution. Only in retrospect as he emerges may the experiencer 'realize' he has been dissolved, if he remembers the moment of dissolution. For persons emerging frequently forget selectively many aspects of the experience, including the experience of having been there.

Emergence is the forming of the personal experiencer from the primary matrix of experience, or rather from the primary matrix of experiencing. For the matrix is the non-presence of distinction between experiencer, experiencing, and experienced. This forming may be experienced as re-forming if the dissolution is remembered.

Remembering is extremely important. Re-membering is the gathering together and reconciling in a comprehensive unity, of the changing aspects of experience, up to and including the moment of remembering. Remembering can go on for an indefinite period after the person has emerged.

Though the experiencer is reconstituted by forces that are not himself personally, in reconciling the various aspects of the experience, the experiencer in a sense reconstitutes himself. In so doing, however, he must avoid imposing his own schema. For his own schema is liable to be derived from his personal conditioning, and so liable to perpetuate his pattern of alienation and his existential shortcomings. Much of the symbolism of the experience refers to these. The experience should be examined dialectically over an indefinite period if its truth is to be fully discovered and integrated. This may help undo the imposition of a false schema. The recommendation to refrain from imposing one's own schema is, of course, a counsel of perfection in the strictest sense.

Reversion, in dissolving the person's existing ego pattern, may facilitate a shift from a centring of consciousness on the 'I' – ego-centring of personal consciousness – to a centring at what may be termed the interface of experience.[1] This is the experience of being centred between the personal known and the Unknown, between male and female, between reflection and instinct, between positional awareness and non-positional. The centre cannot be grasped or known positionally. It is experienced only implicitly, i.e. non-positionally, as immediate awareness of experiencing centred as at an interface. A person centred in this way is aware of the presence of the Unknown as such, though not, of course, of specific content. He is open, however, to experience emerging to consciousness from this region.

There appear to be degrees of ego-centring of personal consciousness. Some persons appear to be more ego-centred, or more egoic than others. By *ego-centred*, I mean a centring of personal consciousness on its personal self. A highly ego-centred person, I term *egotistic*. An egotistic person is one whose primary existential project is to maintain his feeling of being constantly, in and through maintaining without interruption his experience of personal continuity. This does not mean that egoism in this sense

---

[1] Cf. the tradition of the veil before the Holy of Holies in the Temple at Jerusalem. The tradition may be seen to symbolize this experience. Worship takes place before the veil. Only the High Priest, symbolizing the person who has undergone adequate self-preparation, may pass through the veil, and only on the Day of Atonement. The Holy of Holies was completely empty. For a statement on atonement, see pp. 168-9.

is not present with other persons, but it is a question of the nature of the primary existential project.

The consciousness of an egotistic person tends to be exclusively immanent, i.e. positivist, analytic, and estranged from its non-thetic awareness of itself. The person tends not to be reflectively aware of the non-positional. If such a person tries to examine his consciousness he persists in seeking it as if it was an object, i.e. positionally, tending to confuse consciousness with what he discovers on introspection. Seeking positionally, he fails to realize that the consciousness he seeks is the consciousness seeking it.

Of course, this is liable to happen with any person, even to the least egoic. The experience of centring at the interface has to be discovered and rediscovered repeatedly.

Ego-centrism seems invariably associated with alteration of identity. Alteration functions implicitly to obviate the experience of the anxiety of non-being. However, the altered identities of certain persons whom I am calling 'egotistic' are explicitly adapted to this end. The other they invite the other to see them to be, is an other who is effectively maintaining without interruption his personal continuity. Such a person is proud of not breaking down. The pride is an intensified feeling of being. The person sees himself, and requires the other to see him variously as tough, strong-willed, self-controlled, stable, and so on, and despises those who undergo regression or reversion as soft, weak-willed, emotional, unstable. The despised ones are serial objects that embody for the strong one denied, split-off, and exteriorized phantasy aspects of himself. In reversion the altered component of an identity may be undermined.

Successful reversion may be likened to a regressive-progressive movement. From the state of unintegration the consciousness comes forward, so to speak, to the starting-point of personal integration. The complete movement may facilitate a new personal emergence, and a new experience of the possibility of a non-ego-centred self. It may facilitate consciousness of authentic personal possibilities, and awareness of the possibility of actualizing these.

However, reversion carries certain dangers. It may be used unconsciously as a defence against the experience of regression. When this happens the other dangers are increased.

For instance, manifestations may be experienced which have been variously termed 'archetypal', 'mystical', 'spiritual', 'transcendental', 'mythological', 'cosmogonic', and so on. These phenomena must be evaluated dialectically if the experience is to be assimilated by the person. Otherwise he may become assimilated by the experience.

Risks include failure to reintegrate and/or becoming identified with mythic presences. Failure to reintegrate is often, though not necessarily, the result of interference by others. Reintegration seems part of a natural process, but a tranquil social setting is required, one where there is no mystifying or disruptively impinging interaction. Persons seen in a state of unintegration by those who do not understand what is happening, or persons who fail to reintegrate, or who become archetypally identified, are usually seen as mad and in our society are liable to be diagnosed 'schizophrenic', though not all persons labelled schizophrenic are in a state of unintegration or explicitly identified with archetypal presences.

Even the occurrence of reintegration does not necessarily mean that all is well. Shift of centre of consciousness may not occur, or the person may egoically absorb and become possessed by the mythic mood, though without becoming or experiencing himself identified with any specific mythic manifestation. He may feel himself special and charismatic, though he may not act in a way that is usually seen as psychotic. But the mythic possession may express itself in arrogance, or in subtle omnipotence or omniscience, whereby he tends to make utterances, for instance, rather than speak with others. This is particularly dangerous for himself and others when the person does have qualities of leadership, because the qualities tend to mask the omnipotence from himself while blinding others to it in him.

In its grossest form this type of ego-centredness may express itself in religious fanaticism or in fanatical religious and political movements. In the recent history of Europe it expressed itself in Nazism.

It is not yet generally realized that the Nazis were mystics, inducing in themselves transcendental experiences in which they experienced themselves in touch with the Absolute.[1] At the 1936 Nuremberg Rally, Hitler announced in the course of his speech that he received his instructions from God. He was not speaking metaphorically. The Nazis seemed to have been involved with a corrupt form of Buddhism, which no doubt made it easier to designate the Japanese honorary Aryans. The swastika is, of course, a common Buddhist symbol.

Reversion, therefore, may reinforce ego-centredness. And this may happen in a way that leaves the person with the experience that it has been diminished or even abolished. Such persons may implicitly advertise themselves by proclaiming themselves saved, or better persons, or as having seen the light, or as persons who know the way and can show it to others if the others would let them, and so on. It may show itself in a self-advertising humility in which the person proclaims, 'We are all sinners', or 'We are all existentially crippled and spiritually corrupt' – the equivalent of the holy beggar displaying his sores.

Thus, reversion involves considerable risk, and if undergone by a person who is not sufficiently already truly centred it is liable to lead to personal catastrophe. It is often experienced as a rebirth, but a rebirth is a birth, a new beginning – an infancy, not manhood or womanhood. In my view, the ecstasy of reversion should not be regarded as a position that can be reached by repeatedly repeating the experience. It is perhaps better seen as a promise, as

---

[1] The Nazis had secret societies engaged in initiating members into transcendental regions. These societies were not apparently touched by denazification, because the Allied leadership was divorced from these regions in themselves, and so could not realize the importance of the societies. Nor apparently did they receive any guidance from their Church leaders, who seemed to have been just as alienated from the transcendental.

It is worth considering whether similar societies are currently operating in respect of the West German neo-Nazis. In Britain some of the fascist groups appear to be engaging currently in mystical initiations using psychedelic drugs.

the revelation of the possibility of personal unity and healing which may be attained in and through committing oneself to the life-long task of systematically clarifying one's relation to oneself and others.[1]

True centring, shift of centre of consciousness from 'I' experience to interface, does not mean that the person with a non-ego-centred consciousness has no longer any experience of 'I'. It means that he lives with a reformed ego experience, an experience of self in which the ego is simply himself as instrument attempting to actualize in openness with others his authentic personal possibilities in the light of his experience of the pattern of personal destruction and reformation, and his relationship to the source of this experience.

[1] Developing the analogy of the Temple veil (see footnote p. 261), we may say that there are two forms of danger, both the result of a rent, so to speak in the veil's fabric. The forms may be characterized by their extremes.

On the one hand, there is the person so afraid of what may emerge through the rent that he is engaged in a defence that results in his being radically alienated (i.e. alienated without knowing there is something from which he is alienated) from the possibility of experiencing the worlds of phantasy and the transcendental. At the other extreme is the person so totally immersed in emerging phantasy and transcendental experience that he is radically divorced from the shared world of social reality.

To be healed, each must discover that from which he is divorced, and he must do so in a way that allows the integrity of the veil to be reconstituted. This requires each to discover the reality of the veil itself – the interface. The healed man worships – lives and serves – before the veil, open to what filters through in a way that lets this happen in its own manner, in its own time.

There may thus be described two forms of desecration of the Temple, i.e. of personal desecration: one that results in oneself, and the others to whom one relates, becoming radically divorced from that aspect of the world experienced as inner; and one that attempts to take the inner by storm, ravaging its silence, seeking to wrest from it the secret of its stillness. This may be attempted with drugs, exercises that alter one's biochemistry, and so on. In the biblical tradition this has been called 'making strange fire' (Leviticus x. 1-2).

APPENDIX B

The Azazel

Azazel does not simply mean 'scapegoat', in the sense that it is currently understood. The ceremony is a truly symbolic act, in that it strikes multiple resonances, carrying and fulfilling multiple meanings and functions, according to the level of understanding and sensibility of the congregants.

At the simplest level the ceremony has a cathartic and pro- phylactic value. It vicariously relieves the unsophisticated of the burden of guilt and hatred through the sacrificial exile of a living creature, while at the same time it obviates guilt over participating in the sacrificial ceremony, through the selection of an animal, and not a human being. The action of the Danzigs in sending away their daughter thus carries overtones of a reversion to a non-Mosaic, pagan, social practice of human sacrifice. At this level the Azazel ceremony might be described as a function of the repression of the instinctual in the group. While the Danzigs' action might be described as a shared return of the repressed instinct in a non-instinctual form.

However, the ceremony has further significations. For instance, Azazel is also traditionally the name of an angel who, when tempted, fell into the same sin as that of which he had been accus- ing mankind. He was tempted by a beautiful woman and fell victim. Traditionally he is also the angel who persisted in leading men astray into sensuality by teaching women how to allure them; that is, he seduced the human race into trying to control and possess the things and persons embodying their projected feared and desired phantasy objects. In one tradition he is identified with Satan (the Hinderer or Adversary, or Opposer, or Contradictor) and with the serpent who, in Eden, seduced Adam and Eve into introjecting the fruit of the Tree of Knowledge of Good and Evil (the tree of dialectical knowledge of contradiction) when they should have arrived at the result (the fruit) for themselves, through progressive totalizations – the fruit being the visible expression of wisdom, not information to be serially imparted and acquired. The wisdom is the wisdom of progressive inner change, culminating in complete change of heart. Accordingly, Azazel is also said to have taught mankind techniques of mastery over nature before the race had the wisdom to use them properly. This nature includes man's personal nature.

The Good and Evil of the Tree of Knowledge refer among other things to the Good and Evil impulses, which in the Jewish tradition are fundamental to human nature. Impulse in Hebrew is *yetser*, and has the connotation of 'forming'. Thus, Man is formed of Good and Evil. The Tree of Knowledge of Good and Evil may thus be seen to refer to the necessity for men continually to experience and reconcile dialectically the potentially creative contradictory Good and Evil primal impulses of their nature. Freud, who sprang from the Jewish mystical tradition,[1] attempted to express a similar doctrine in his theory of life and death instincts, Eros and Thanatos, self-creation and self-destruction. The serpent-Azazel is thus responsible for teaching immature men techniques of manipulation of their consciousnesses and nature. He is the Contradictor who seduces men away from the dialectical experience of conflict as both intra- and interpersonal towards the non-dialectical experience of conflict as exclusively interpersonal.[2] But since, in the Jewish tradition, the Contradictor is the servant of God, this seduction may be seen as functioning to sharpen the experience of conflict to a point where men begin to repent, which in its first stages requires them to reflect on their acts and the structure of their experience.

The function of this repentance is to bring forth the same fruit as that of the Tree of Knowledge; namely, the redeemed man.

[1] See Bakan, D., *Sigmund Freud and the Jewish Mystical Tradition.*
[2] Or intergroup.

The sin of Adam and Eve may be seen to result in an alterated identity based on each interiorizing the other's view of himself. Hence their shame before each other. The Hebrew for 'ashamed', in Genesis ii. 25, is a reflexive verb, *yitboshashu*, meaning 'ashamed before each other'. Since a reflexive verb carries the connotation of a relationship to oneself, *yitboshashu* implies an experience by each in relation to himself and to the other experiencing each; that is, each experienced himself in and through the experience of the other experiencing him.

References

BAKAN, D. (1959). *Sigmund Freud and the Jewish Mystical Tradition.* Princeton: Van Nostrand.

BATESON, G., JACKSON, D. D., HALEY, J., and WEAKLAND, J. (1956). 'Towards a Theory of Schizophrenia'. *Behavioural Science,* I.

DJILAS, M. (1957). *The New Class.* London: Thames and Hudson.

FOUCAULT, M. (1967). *Madness and Civilization.* London: Tavistock Publications; New York: Pantheon (1965).

GARFINKEL, H. (1956). 'Conditions of Successful Degradation Ceremonies'. *American Journal of Sociology,* LXI.

GOFFMAN, E. (1961). *Asylums: Essays on the Social Situation of Mental Patients and Other Inmates.* New York: Doubleday and Anchor Books; Harmondsworth: Penguin.

KUHN, THOMAS S. (1962). *The Structure of Scientific Revolutions.* Chicago: University of Chicago Press.

LAING, R. D. (1960). *The Divided Self.* London: Tavistock Publications; New York: Pantheon (1970).

LAING, R. D. (1961). *The Self and Others* (second edition, 1969). London: Tavistock Publications; New York: Pantheon (1970).

LAING, R. D. (1967). *The Politics of Experience and the Bird of Paradise.* Harmondsworth: Penguin Books; New York: Pantheon.

LAING, R. D. and COOPER, D. (1964). *Reason and Violence: A Decade of Sartre's Philosophy 1950-1960.* London: Tavistock Publications.

LAING, R. D. and ESTERSON, A. (1964). *Sanity, Madness, and the Family: Families of Schizophrenics.* London: Tavistock Publications; New York: Basic Books.

LAING, R. D., PHILLIPSON, H., and LEE, A. R. (1966). *Interpersonal Perception.* London: Tavistock Publications; New York: Springer.

MACMURRAY, J. (1957). *The Form of the Personal*, Vol. I, *The Self as Agent*. London: Faber and Faber.

MACMURRAY, J. (1961). *The Form of the Personal*, Vol, II, *Persons in Relation*. London: Faber and Faber.

SARTRE, J.-P. (1950). *The Psychology of Imagination*. London: Rider.

SARTRE, J.-P. (1957). *Being and Nothingness*. London: Methuen.

SARTRE, J.-P. (1960). *Critique de la Raison Dialectique*. Paris: Librairie Gallimard.

SARTRE, J.-P. (1963). *The Problem of Method*. London: Methuen.

SCHEFF, T. (1966). *Being Mentally Ill*. London: Weidenfeld and Nicolson.

TARSIS, VALERIY (1965). *Ward 7*. London: Collins and Harvill Press.

WATZLAWICK, P., BEAVIN, J. H., and JACKSON, D. D. (1967). *Pragmatics of Human Communication*. New York: W. W. Norton.

WINNICOTT, D. W. (1958). *Collected Papers*. London: Tavistock Publications.

Index

sexual experience/feelings, 113-15,
    118-19, 127-8, 132, 145
sexual gratification, vicarious, 146ff,
    154, 158
sexual maturity, 126, 165
sexual phantasy
    anal, 124, 130, 138, 147
    bowel, 115, 118, 122-4, 147, 153,
        158-9
    Oedipal, 131
sexual relations of parents, 116-19,
    143, 145
sexual union, 175
shared object of phantasy experience,
    12
sick and scandalous behaviour, 6, 46
    see also scandal
social intelligibility, see intelligibility
socialist economic praxis, 225
socialization, 44
spiral of reciprocal mistrust, 155
splitting, 50, 233
success as appearance, 9-10, 24, 32, 34,
    83-4
    see also reputation; public opin-
        ion
Sullivan tradition, the, xi
supersession of the principal contradic-
    tion, 199n, 213-16
symbols, 251, 261
synthesis, xi, 50, 199, 206, 208, 247
    see also experiential synthesis

Temple veil, the, 261n, 265n
test of dialectical truth, 202, 204-5, 211
    practical, 202, 204
    of reconciliation, 205, 211
    theoretical, 202, 205
    see also validation
'them', see public opinion

θεορία, 205
'Thought of Chairman Mao', 217
tidiness, see cleanliness/tidiness
Torah, the, 71n, 104, 175, 176n, 177
totality, 45, 212
totalization, 10, 13, 45, 49, 198-203,
    211-12, 216-17, 241, 243, 247,
    250, 252
    see also synthesis; negation
transcendental experience, 257, 259-60,
    264-5
transference/counter-transference, 207
transference enactment, 213
transpersonal defence, 73
    see also embodiment of pro-
        jected bowels
t'shuvah, 176n

unconscious conflict, 207
    phantasy, 129, 207
    see also phantasy experience;
        unrecognized phantasy
unexpected, the, 198, 200, 227
Unknown, the, 261
unrecognized conflict, 159, 207n
    phantasy, 48, 54-5, 63, 83, 90, 99,
        122, 159, 172, 194, 207n
    see also phantasy experience;
        unconscious phantasy

validation, 52, 161, 212, 216, 251, 253
    see also confirmation
value judgements, 50

Western Science, 190
witch-hunting and psychiatric praxis,
    235